The Global Economic Crisis and Migration

Offering an in-depth analysis of the impact of the economic crisis (2008–2012) on immigration movements and policies in the United States and Europe, this book is guided by two key questions: What is the scope of change and did the crisis motivate this change or did other factors do so?

The contributions to the book find that the crisis had immediate effects on migration patterns – migrants left crisis-stricken countries, naturalised in non-crisis countries where they had previously settled, or stopped migrating to formerly attractive countries which had been negatively affected by the crisis. Whereas prior to the crisis the majority of migrants were highly-skilled, during the crisis there was a shift to vulnerable groups such as low-skilled workers and women.

The book also finds that migration policies have indeed changed in times of crisis. However, these changes are neither exclusively restrictions nor liberalisations, but encompass changes in both directions. Despite the coincidence of many policy changes with the crisis, these changes are not primarily induced by the crisis. Instead, politicians rhetorically used the crisis to promote both liberal and restrictive policy changes which were already in the making before the crisis.

This book was originally published as a special issue of the *Journal of Ethnic and Migration Studies.*

Christof Roos is an Assistant Professor in European and Global Governance at University of Flensburg, Germany, and Associate Researcher at the Institute for European Studies, Vrije Unversiteit Brussel, Belgium. His work focuses on EU integration in Justice and Home Affairs, EU migration and asylum policy, and freedom of movement.

Natascha Zaun is an Assistant Professor in Migration Studies at the European Institute of the London School of Economics and Political Science, UK. Her research focuses on EU asylum and immigration policy as well as global refugee and visas policy.

Research in Ethnic and Migration Studies

Edited by
Paul Statham
Director, Sussex Centre for Migration Research (SCMR), University of Sussex, UK

The *Research in Ethnic and Migration Studies* series publishes the results of high-quality, cutting-edge research that addresses key questions relating to ethnic relations, diversity and migration. The series is open to a range of disciplines and brings together research collaborations on specific defined topics on all aspects of migration and its consequences, including migration processes, migrants and their experiences, ethnic relations, discrimination, integration, racism, transnationalism, citizenship, identity and cultural diversity. Contributions are especially welcome when they are the result of comparative research, either across countries, cities or groups. All articles have previously been published in the *Journal of Ethnic and Migration Studies* (*JEMS*), which has a rigorous peer review system. Collective volumes in this series are either the product of special issues published in the journal or published articles that the editor has selected from individual submissions.

Titles in the series:

International Organisations and the Politics of Migration
Edited by Martin Geiger and Antoine Pécoud

Regulation of Speech in Multicultural Societies
Edited by Marcel Maussen and Ralph Grillo

Deportation, Anxiety, Justice
New ethnographic perspectives
Edited by Heike Drotbohm and Ines Hasselberg

Migrants, Minorities, and the Media
Information, representations, and participation in the public sphere
Edited by Erik Bleich, Irene Bloemraad and Els de Graauw

The Global Economic Crisis and Migration
Edited by Christof Roos and Natascha Zaun

Muslims in Europe
Comparative perspectives on socio-cultural integration
Edited by Paul Statham and Jean Tillie

The Global Economic Crisis and Migration

Edited by
Christof Roos and Natascha Zaun

Routledge
Taylor & Francis Group
LONDON AND NEW YORK

First published 2018 by Routledge

2 Park Square, Milton Park, Abingdon, Oxfordshire OX14 4RN
52 Vanderbilt Avenue, New York, NY 10017

Routledge is an imprint of the Taylor & Francis Group, an informa business

First issued in paperback 2019

British Library Cataloguing in Publication Data
A catalogue record for this book is available from the British Library

ISBN 13: 978-1-138-50191-1 (hbk)
ISBN 13: 978-0-367-32192-5 (pbk)

Typeset in TimesNewRomanPSMT
by diacriTech, Chennai

Publisher's Note
The publisher accepts responsibility for any inconsistencies that may have arisen during the conversion of this book from journal articles to book chapters, namely the possible inclusion of journal terminology.

Contents

Citation Information

The chapters in this book were originally published in the *Journal of Ethnic and Migration Studies*, volume 42, issue 10 (September–October 2016). When citing this material, please use the original page numbering for each article, as follows:

Introduction
The global economic crisis as a critical juncture? The crisis's impact on migration movements and policies in Europe and the U.S.
Christof Roos and Natascha Zaun
Journal of Ethnic and Migration Studies, volume 42, issue 10
(September–October 2016) pp. 1579–1589

Chapter 1
Circumventing deadlock through venue-shopping: why there is more than just talk in US immigration politics in times of economic crisis
Natascha Zaun, Christof Roos and Fabian Gülzau
Journal of Ethnic and Migration Studies, volume 42, issue 10
(September–October 2016) pp. 1590–1609

Chapter 2
The crisis as an opportunity for change? High-skilled immigration policies across Europe
Lucie Cerna
Journal of Ethnic and Migration Studies, volume 42, issue 10
(September–October 2016) pp. 1610–1630

Chapter 3
Negotiating varieties of capitalism? Crisis and change in contemporary British and German labour migration policies
Regine Paul
Journal of Ethnic and Migration Studies, volume 42, issue 10
(September–October 2016) pp. 1631–1650

Chapter 4
Migration policy reforms in the context of economic and political crises: the case of Belgium
Sonia Gsir, Jean-Michel Lafleur and Mikolaj Stanek
Journal of Ethnic and Migration Studies, volume 42, issue 10 (September–October 2016) pp. 1651–1669

Chapter 5
Citizenship in the shadow of the Euro crisis: explaining changing patterns in naturalisation among intra-EU migrants
John Graeber
Journal of Ethnic and Migration Studies, volume 42, issue 10 (September–October 2016) pp. 1670–1692

Chapter 6
Mobilities in the crisis and post-crisis times: migration strategies of Poles on the EU labour market
Anna Janicka and Paweł Kaczmarczyk
Journal of Ethnic and Migration Studies, volume 42, issue 10 (September–October 2016) pp. 1693–1710

Chapter 7
The economic crisis as a driver of cross-border labour mobility? A multi-method perspective on the case of the Central European Region
Laura Wiesböck, Roland Verwiebe, Christoph Reinprecht and Raimund Haindorfer
Journal of Ethnic and Migration Studies, volume 42, issue 10 (September–October 2016) pp. 1711–1728

Notes on Contributors

Lucie Cerna is an Analyst in the Directorate for Education and Skills at the OECD, Paris, France, and a Research Associate at COMPAS, Oxford, UK.

John Graeber is an Assistant Professor at the Department of Political Science at High Point University, USA.

Sonia Gsir is a Researcher at the Centre for Ethnic and Migration Studies (CEDEM), University of Liège, Belgium.

Fabian Gülzau is a Research Assistant at the Department of Social Sciences, Humboldt-Universität zu Berlin, Germany.

Raimund Haindorfer is based at the Department of Sociology, University of Vienna, Austria.

Anna Janicka is Assistant Professor at the Faculty of Economic Sciences, University of Warsaw, Poland.

Paweł Kaczmarczyk is Director of the Centre of Migration Research at the University of Warsaw, Poland.

Jean-Michel Lafleur is Associate Director of the Centre for Ethnic and Migration Studies (CEDEM), University of Liège, Belgium.

Regine Paul is a Researcher at the Law and Society Unit, Faculty of Sociology, University of Bielefeld, Germany and John F. Kennedy Fellow 2017/18 at the Minda de Gunzburg Center for European Studies, Harvard University, USA.

Christoph Reinprecht is a Professor at the Department of Sociology, University of Vienna, Austria.

Christof Roos is an Assistant Professor in European and Global Governance at University of Flensburg, Germany and Associate Researcher at the Institute for European Studies, Vrije Unversiteit Brussel, Belgium.

Mikolaj Stanek is an Assistant Professor at the Department of Sociology and Communication, University of Salamanca, Spain.

Roland Verwiebe is Professor at the Department of Sociology, University of Vienna, Austria.

Laura Wiesböck is based at the Department of Sociology, University of Vienna, Austria.

Natascha Zaun is an Assistant Professor in Migration Studies at the European Institute of the London School of Economics and Political Science, UK.

INTRODUCTION

The global economic crisis as a critical juncture? The crisis's impact on migration movements and policies in Europe and the U.S.

Christof Roos and Natascha Zaun

Introduction

The current global economic crisis has resulted in the strongest recession in the Organisation for Economic Cooperation and Development (OECD) countries since the Great Depression in the early 1930s and the 1970s oil shocks. This special issue sets out to explore how the most recent economic crisis impacted immigration and immigration-related policy in the U.S. and in European countries that are part of the OECD. The crisis of the late 2000s was offset by the collapse of the subprime U.S. housing market, destabilising the financial system and leading to a sovereign debt crisis. The shock was marked by a 'sudden […] deterioration of most, or all, key macroeconomic indicators' such as the gross domestic product (GDP) growth, the unemployment rate, the level of inflation, and the public debt (Starke, Kaasch, and van Hooren 2013, 5). The GDP in OECD countries shrank by 3.49% in 2009, whereas it previously had grown by around 2–3% annually. Additionally, the unemployment rate in the OECD rose from 5.9% of the total labour force in 2008 to more than 8% in 2009 and subsequent years. During that time, the youth unemployment rate in the European Union (EU), the number of unemployed 15–24 year olds, increased steeply from 15 to more than 20%. In countries that were heavily affected by the crisis such as Greece and Spain youth unemployment rose from 20 to over 50% between 2008 and 2012 (OECD 2016). This resulted in a decline in demand for labour force. Common wisdom holds that economic recessions and high unemployment have an impact on the decisions of migrants to move, as well as on governments to consider restrictions in immigration policy. Yet, empirical findings on the crisis–migration nexus are sometimes contradictory and while some find a clear causal link between the crisis and changes in migration patterns and policies, others refute its existence.

Comparing the economic crises in the 1930s, 1970s, and the 2010s in Australia, Canada, and the U.S., Hatton suggests that these had a direct impact on immigration. According to his 10% rule 'every 100 jobs lost result in 10 fewer immigrants' (2014, 28). In Europe, studies found that immigration has decreased and countries that were countries of emigration prior to the crisis experienced a decline in emigration and a rise in numbers of migrants returning (Koehler et al. 2010, 3; Papademetriou et al. 2010, 13). Besides this impact on the movement of migrants, the crisis can also be assumed to have had an impact on immigration policies. According to Kuptsch (2012, 20–22), countries that had practiced an open door policy in the 2000s, such as the U.K., Spain, or the Czech Republic, used the crisis for instigating restrictive changes. Yet, these changes are suggested to be only modest in scope (Papademetriou et al. 2010, 16). Others identify a clear trend in terms of restrictions that are crisis induced. Accordingly, the crisis could be identified as a factor pushing for reductions in admission quotas and general recruitment in EU countries that were hit hardest by the economic downturn: foremost Italy, Portugal, Spain, and the U.K. (Koehler et al. 2010, 28–30; Pastore 2012, 146). At the supranational EU level no policy change in reaction to the economic crisis could be observed. Rather, the budget constraints of public administration impacted on some southern EU member states' capacity in fully implementing EU border and asylum policy. But also beyond the southern EU member states, crisis-related budget constraints can restrain expenditures related to a countries' asylum-seekers' reception system and hence impact on the quality of reception conditions in individual states (Trauner 2016). Researching discourse, Lindley's edited volume (2014) points to crisis effects in terms of a government practice that links immigration to insecurity. Hatton (2014) arrives at a completely different conclusion and hardly sees any policy change during the time that European states responded to the crisis. He explains this by public opinion being focused on fiscal policies rather than the labour market. In addition, he argues that restrictions in immigration policy can only be exercised within a narrow margin. For instance, in the EU, access of asylum seekers and family members of migrants is guaranteed by EU law. These are hence non-discretionary forms of migration on which states are not free to regulate in case they want to reduce immigrant admission (Roos and Zaun 2014).

Given these contradictive findings already concluded in 2009 and 2010, this special issue reflects on a broader time frame and data analysed in 2014 in the aftermath of the crisis. The contributions aim for a more up-to-date and in depth analysis of the crisis's actual impact on immigration movements and policies in the U.S. and Europe. When asking *What is the impact of the crisis on migration movements and policies in Europe and the U.S.?*, we also ask *What is the scope of change?* and *Did the crisis motivate this change or did other factors do so?* Thus, we intend to avoid spurious conclusions that find a coincidence between changes in policies and the crisis where the causal link is missing. In investigating these questions we cover a range of different topics and countries affected differently by the crisis. Within Europe, we specifically aim at investigating countries representing different geographical zones and economic traditions. In this regard we cover established economies such as Germany and the U.K. as well as 'emerging' economies in Eastern Europe. This allows for a multifaceted picture and an account of the complexity of the crisis and its effects. As to migratory movements, topics are investigated that include the crisis's impact on naturalisation of citizens from other EU Member States across the EU (Graeber), cross-border commuting in Central Europe (Wiesböck et al.), and the post-crisis migratory strategies of Polish migrant workers (Janicka and Kaczmarczyk). Concerning the crisis's impact on immigration policies, the special issue includes studies on its impact on immigration politics in the U.S. (Zaun, Roos and Gülzau), immigration and integration policies in Belgium (Gsir, Lafleur and Stanek), highly skilled policies across the EU (Cerna), and labour migration admissions more generally in the U.K. and Germany (Paul).

In investigating how the crisis affects migratory flows and immigration policies we contribute to the debate on what determines both migration and state responses to migration, placing a particular focus on the role of external shocks as the possible roots of critical junctures for policy change.

We find that the crisis had immediate effects on migration patterns. Migrants left crisis-stricken countries (Wiesböck et al.), naturalised in non-crisis countries where they had previously settled (Graeber), or stopped migrating to formerly attractive countries which were now negatively affected by the crisis (Janicka and Kaczmarczyk). Moreover, the crisis affected the type of migrants one can observe. Whereas prior to the crisis, highly skilled migrants represented the majority of migrants, during the crisis there has been a particular shift to vulnerable groups such as low-skilled workers and women (Janicka and Kaczmarczyk; Wiesböck et al.).

Moreover, we find that indeed migration policies have changed in times of crisis. Yet, these changes are neither exclusively restrictions nor liberalisations, but encompass changes in both directions. Despite the coincidence of many policy changes with the crisis, these changes are *not primarily* induced by the crisis. Instead they were based on policy programmes and ideas that were initiated long before the crisis even began. This temporal discrepancy provides evidence that the crisis *did not cause* the changes (cf. Paul; Zaun, Roos, Gülzau), but that these changes were due to long-term processes. While the crisis was not the root cause of policy changes, it served as an *ex post* justification for these changes (Czerna; Gsir, Lafleur, Stanek; Paul; Zaun, Roos, Gülzau). Similar to after the oil shocks in the 1970s, politicians rhetorically used the crisis to promote both liberal and restrictive policy changes which they had planned before the crisis.

In the following sections we will present our findings on both migration patterns and immigration policies in depth and demonstrate in how far these address existing gaps in the literature on the migration–crisis nexus.

The crisis's impact on movements: insights from the literature on push and pull factors

Scholars have suggested that migratory movements are influenced by so-called 'push and pull factors' (e.g. Ravenstein 1889; Lee 1966; Castles and Miller 1993). This literature asks what motivates people to undertake the risk of migration and provides an explanation based on classical economic rational actor models. *Push factors* are factors 'impelling people to leave the areas of origin' and imply 'demographic growth, low living standards, lack of economic opportunities and political repression' (Castles and Miller 1993, 19). Yet, migrants are usually not the poorest among the poor and, in fact, economic development has been shown to increase migratory pressures (Stalker 1994; Martin 2001; Cornelius 2002). *Pull factors* 'attract […] them [the migrants] to certain receiving countries' and comprise a 'demand for labo[u]r, availability of land, good economic opportunities and political freedoms' (Castles and Miller 1993, 19). While this model is often criticised for neglecting structural factors (Massey et al. 1998) and being ahistorical (Castles and Miller 1993) with its sole focus on the rational decisions of the individual migrants, there is broad evidence that migrants are indeed motivated by economic differentials when making the decision to migrate (Cornelius and Rosenblum 2005, 100). Hanson and Spilimbergo (1999), for instance, demonstrate that the wage gap between the U.S. and Mexico is a reliable predictor of migratory flows from Mexico to the U.S.

The global economic crisis can hence be expected to have significantly changed the configuration of a variety of push and pull factors in both the sending and the receiving countries. More specifically, the economic crisis would affect economic opportunities and the demand for labour force at both ends. Of course, the economic situation in the country of origin might still be worse than the one of the destination country which would result in little change in migratory patterns. However, if a destination country is hit particularly hard by the crisis, this could entail fewer movements to this country and change migratory movements. Given the increase in unemployment, demand for labour would decrease in crisis-stricken countries and hence an important pull factor for immigrants would disappear, motivating fewer immigrants to make the journey to reach the country in question (cf. McCormick 2012, 2). This dynamic applies specifically to sectors of the economy that offer low-status and temporary employment such as manufacturing, construction, hotel, and restaurant businesses. In these sectors migrant workers are overrepresented (Galgóczi, Leschke, and Watt 2012, 6–7). Moreover, countries which have previously attracted many immigrants can even be expected to have become countries of emigration during the crisis, as former immigrants would leave these countries to return to their countries of origin. Overall, the crisis could likely have presented a turning point for migratory movements to Europe and the U.S. While labour migration should be directly affected by the crisis, forced immigration and family migration may be expected to be influenced to a lesser extent by the crisis. Forced migration is heavily influenced by push factors such as wars and human rights violations in the migrant's country of origin. Family migration is based on migrants and migrant networks already being present in the destination country (cf. Waldinger 1997; Massey et al. 1998; Fussell and Massey 2004). Yet, if the path to labour migration was progressively closed in response to the crisis, migrants can also be expected to look for alternative entry points and to choose other forms of migration, applying for asylum or family reunification. This is because states face substantial constraints posed by international law in the areas of forced and family migration. While states can still try to limit these rights, they have less discretion in these policy areas than in labour migration. In addition, states member to the EU are constrained in limiting the access of EU nationals to their labour markets. Free movement of labour in the EU has substitution effects on recruitment of third-country nationals. As a consequence EU member states focus restriction on labour migration from third countries (Paul 2013, 125).

The special issue contributes to this discussion in two ways. Firstly, the authors in this issue confirm that the crisis had a direct impact on migratory movements (see Koehler et al. 2010, 3; Papademetriou et al. 2010, 13). Fewer migrants immigrate to or settle in countries hit hard by the crisis. Polish migrants for example, the most populous group of intra-European migrants since 2004 left their country of origin in fewer numbers during the crisis. At the same time, a wave of Poles returning to Poland could not be detected despite the favourable socio-economic development in Poland during the crisis (Janicka and Kaczmarczyk). Former migratory destinations that were not affected by the crisis maintain a steady level of immigration (Wiesböck et al.). Yet, as both the contributions of Janicka and Kaczmarczyk and Wiesböck et al. find for Central Europe, the composition of these migratory flows has changed. During the crisis they observe that particularly vulnerable groups affected by the crisis, such as women and the unskilled, migrate most specifically to the non-affected countries in their neighbourhood or the EU more broadly. Secondly, the contributions focusing on migration among EU member states show how the crisis and the structural conditions of free movement policy in the EU interact. As Graeber finds intra-EU migrants, particularly those from crisis-stricken countries, have often settled and naturalised in their destination country subsequent to the crisis, instead of leaving it due to the increased insecurity and uncertainty it has engendered. In addition, long-term immigrants stayed in their new home countries, while short-term immigrants returned when a demand in labour decreased as Janicka and Kaczmarczyk demonstrate for the case of Polish migrants. Thus, the initial rationale for free movement in the EU, that is, a labour supply that would flexibly adjust to changing economic conditions, at least partially finds some empirical confirmation.

The crisis's impact on policies: the crisis as a critical juncture?

Following historical institutionalism, policy-making is bound by institutional path dependence. Past decisions constrain and enable policy developments to a point where change becomes difficult or even impossible. The respective political system and its openness for veto players such as political parties or institutions (e.g. Parliament, President) can inhibit the scope of possible change further. This explains why policies remain stable rather than change radically (Hall and Taylor 1996, 938; Pierson 2000; Tsebelis, 2002). According to historical institutionalism, policies usually do not change, unless there is a 'critical juncture'. This is a moment of crisis or exogenous shock that weakens the path-dependent policy trajectory as well as participating actors' veto positions (Collier and Collier 1991).

Historically, the 1970s oil crisis is a prominent frame of reference for the hypothesis that external economic shocks can induce policy change. Following a steep increase in oil prices, Northwestern European economies experienced a severe crisis leading to high unemployment. Almost simultaneously, in 1973–1974, Western European states such as Belgium, France, Germany, and the Netherlands that had relied heavily on foreign labour fundamentally changed their recruitment policy. The post-war pattern of guest worker systems offering a flexible supply of labour for the economy came to a definite end in 1974 (Castles 1986, 771). Since then, the oil crisis has been referred to as the reason for policy change in labour migration policy. For Germany and France, however, it was shown that the government had planned to end recruitment before the crisis could take effect. Politically and economically, many had already doubted for some time whether guest worker schemes would be an effective labour market policy. More and more foreign workers had reunited with their families which increased the social costs of the recruitment scheme (Herbert and Hunn 2000, 308; Weil 2005). Thus, the crisis had reinforced the already existing intention to reform the recruitment of foreign labour. The crisis presented an ideal justification and a window of opportunity for this fundamental policy change. Admission policies for labour migration were suspended, at least temporarily. For movements, the effects of this policy change were equally drastic. Former guest workers finally settled and multi-ethnic societies would emerge in Northwestern Europe (Castles 1986, 775). Considering these changes, it is fair to assert that the oil crisis fundamentally impacted most European countries, albeit it could not entirely explain policy change in countries such as Germany and France. Whether a crisis is co-occurring or the reason for policy change that would have happened in its absence needs empirical testing (Pastore 2012, 142). The historical background of the 1970s crisis informs our assumption that the 2008–2012 economic crisis could also have offered a window of opportunity for actors looking for policy change.

The current literature on the latest economic crisis and its impact on migration policy is cautious in attributing effects similar to that in the aftermath of the 1970s crisis. With regard to policy, authors observed moderate rather than fundamental change (Koehler et al. 2010; Papademetriou et al. 2010; Kuptsch 2012). Different from the 1970s, the opening and closure of various immigration channels could concur and therefore only mitigate a trend towards restriction (Pastore 2012). Authors agree that policy responses to the crisis vary across countries and concentrate on forms of labour migration as a discretionary channel for admission (Green and Winters 2010, 1066; Pastore 2012, 142–143).

The contributions in this volume share the view that in most cases policy change can be observed to some extent during times of crisis. Yet, this does not imply that the crisis caused policy change. Defining the recent crisis as a critical juncture for policy would hence go too far. Neither have immigration policies in the U.S. and European countries changed dramatically nor can the crisis be singled out as the main driver for policy change.

Public policy theory defines the conditions for policy change as a change in government, national mood, or the occurrence of an urgent and pressing problem. The crisis is an opportunity that allows for advocates of policy change to attach their solutions to it (Kingdon 1995, 168–170). For policy change to happen, actors must be prepared to use pertinent opportunity structures. Additionally, they have to share the perception that the time for policy change has come (Kingdon 1995, 170–172). How a solution to a problem becomes the dominant alternative is related to the institutional resources of the actor proposing the policy. The absence of fundamental policy change during the crisis can thus be expected to be the result of actors having embarked on a policy path which they still consider to be valuable in times of crisis. Only in the few instances that actors reassess their policy ideas does change occur. Most of the changes we observe during the crisis, however, are based on pre-crisis decisions. Little is known about the conditions that link the current crisis and immigration policy. Therefore, the next section examines how actors such as political parties of the left and right, as well as unions and employers have an interest in using the crisis as a window for policy change.

Actors with vested interests in immigration policy are interest groups. The lens of partisan conflicts traditionally helps explain liberal or restrictive change in immigration policy. Respective actors influence on, or presence in, government is an important factor in predicting the immigration policy orientation of a country. Political parties usually position on a left-right scale regarding immigration issues with the left promoting human rights and social protectionist ideas (Helbling 2013, 26) and the right sharing nationalist as well as neo-liberal positions (Kitschelt 1995). Immigration is a divisive issue for both, the political left and right since claims for welfare protectionism or safeguarding national identity can lead to immigration restriction. Moderate parties from the centre-left and centre-right are not likely to take a strong position against immigration. Freeman associates an 'anti-populist norm' with social democrats, liberal conservatives, and Christian democrats (1995, 885). In fact, following an argument made by Starke,

Kaasch, and van Hooren (2013, 7) on crisis effects on the welfare state, one can also assume that the crisis would put aside partisan differences because a concern for the common good would substitute for partisan ideology.

In line with the general immigration and partisan politics literature, authors in this volume confirm party influence on policy change. For Belgium, Gsir, Lafleur, and Stanek show that a centre-right party put under pressure by a nationalist party in opposition pushed for restrictive change in immigration and integration policy. In this regard, the crisis served the parties' rhetoric as a facilitator in justifying policy change. Also, the U.S. case allows for insights into partisan conflicts during the crisis. Zaun, Roos, and Gülzau show how the crisis further aggravated parties' and other interest groups' conflicting positions on a comprehensive immigration reform. However, actors managed to promote policy change in alternative venues. Actors used the crisis as an additional justification for restrictive or expansive suggestions for reform they had already planned. For example, legalisation of the undocumented could be realised at the presidential level and the enforcement angle could be strengthened in certain states that, by majority, are governed by Republicans. For the U.K., Paul shows that the co-occurrence of government change and the perception of a migration control crisis explain the shift to induce radical restrictions. Public opinion against free mobility in the EU and liberal immigration policy enabled the newly elected conservatives to execute restrictions that were widely supported by the political mainstream at the time. Overall these findings detail how political parties influenced change. The crisis, however, is only one of many variables that intensified the need for some parties to push for change. Where parties felt no pressures for change, for example, because of a more favourable economic situation, policies remained stable. Policy paths that they had embarked on before the crisis were pursued further as the cases of Germany and Belgium (Paul; Gsir, Lafleur, Stanek) demonstrate.

An economic crisis also provides an opportunity for social partners to lobby the public and political parties on their behalf. In times of crisis, migrant workers are vulnerable to exploitation if employers try to maintain profit margins in spite of decreasing economic activity (Galgóczi, Leschke, and Watt 2012, 6–7). Labour unions have been found to put particular emphasis on migrant workers' equal rights (Freeman 1995, 885–888), they have criticised that labour migration could provoke a race-to-the-bottom in workers' rights and wage dumping. By organising and pushing for equal treatment and fair wages, unions can help avoid tensions with local workers (Heyes and Hyland 2012, 229). Along these lines, Cerna finds unions in the U.K. and Ireland to successfully lobby for restricting admission in order to avoid further pressure on the labour market. She argues that the cutback in recruitment of foreign workers by restricting the issuance of work permits is based on these lobbying efforts of unions which were due to the crisis. At the same time, the crisis not only opens a policy window for unions and their call for the enforcement of labour standards or restrictions in recruitment, but also for business to call for more liberalisation of labour markets. They can claim more flexibility with regard to wages and job security (Heyes and Hyland 2012). With regard to Sweden, Cerna confirms this assumption. As a result of earlier lobbying efforts, employers and the inauguration of a new centre-right and liberal government allowed the adoption of a completely demand-based labour migration system. Arguments for flexibility of labour were strong even during times of crisis. A similar long-term effect of lobbying efforts of employers and unions for policy liberalisation could be observed to take hold in Germany just as the crisis took effect in 2009. The good weathering of the crisis convinced the conservative-led government to push through previously planned liberalisation (Paul). Policy change can be assessed in all cases, however, in most cases policy change was traced back to decisions and actor preferences that were taken before the crisis.

The contributions in this volume show that the crisis could reinforce preferences of social partners or political parties. The crisis has pronounced actor preferences on both liberal and restrictive policies and emphasised the deficiencies of the national migration systems at the time. In fact, actors need to seize the window of opportunity which the crisis presents and frame it as a ground for policy change in order for actual change to happen (Kingdon 1995, 172–173). Yet, they will only be successful if the institutional setting allows them to do so. In the majority of countries investigated, the institutional setting as well as policies are characterised by path dependency. While partial policy change coincides with the crisis, our contributors find that change is mainly based on institutional dynamics, discourses, and actor preferences that were present before the crisis.

Conclusion

The question whether the most recent economic crisis should be considered a critical juncture for migration movements and migration policy in Europe and the U.S. cannot be definitively answered by the contributions to this volume. With regard to movements, the crisis indeed had direct effects, but by no means did it lead to similarly fundamental changes in movement patterns as the 1970s crisis when labour recruitment schemes were suspended. In terms of immigration policy, the authors examined the scope of change and the question of whether the crisis can be considered as the reason for change. Indeed, most of the case countries have changed certain elements of their immigration policies, mostly related to the recruitment of labour. However, these changes have often been prepared and envisaged by policy-makers for some time pre-dating the crisis. Thus, we could observe that the crisis was a reinforcing factor pushing for change. Similar findings have been made in comparative welfare state research. Starke et al. find, conditioned by the size of the welfare state, both retrenchment and expansion during the crisis. At the same time, the scope of welfare policy change is described as incremental rather than fundamental and policy response to external shocks as an exception rather than the norm (Starke, Kaasch, and van Hooren 2013, 182). By providing rigorous analysis on a so far under-researched topic, this special issue empirically clarified the actual scope of policy change as well as changes in movements. Methodologically, the variety of contributions in this special issue assess the crisis from different angles applying qualitative and quantitative methodologies. The qualitative contributions trace crisis effects on actors and show how institutional constraints open or close opportunities for policy change. The quantitative contributions enhance the external validity of the findings and shed light on interesting links between the crisis and movement as well as policies.

Theoretically, the special issue speaks to the debate on critical junctures (Collier and Collier 1991; Pierson 2000; Capoccia 2015) and opportunities for policy change. We provide further evidence for findings suggesting that the impact of external shocks should not be overrated, as they only translate into policy change when there are actors that actually use these crisis events to foster change. Hence external shocks do not induce a critical juncture per se. As such, one cannot look to external shocks as a predictor for policy change (Capoccia 2015). Partisan politics and who is in government at a specific time seem to moderate crisis effects. Overall, policy change is rather induced by new actors coming into power, or by existing actors gaining a more favourable opportunity structure to pursue their preferences when crises hit, than by an external shock. We therefore propose the study of partisan politics against the background of an institutional framework as crucial to the understanding of policy change in immigration policies. Overall, immigration policies are much more stable over time given institutional path dependencies and the stickiness of the political process in which today's policy programmes are the result of political processes that often pre-dated the crisis. However, we clearly see that the political rhetoric does change in relation to crisis and that policy-makers can use the crisis as a window of opportunity to push through change that they have already endorsed for reasons that have nothing to do with the crisis itself.

Whereas an external shock's impact on policy is limited, it does have a more direct effect on the phenomenon of migratory movements itself. While the crisis has not entailed a complete reconfiguration of migratory movements to the extent the oil shocks in the 1970s did, it did have some immediate effects on these movements. As this special issue shows, a change of the macro-economic situation of some countries directly affects the migration choices of individuals in both crisis-stricken and unaffected countries. The reason is that migrants can make their decisions rather independently and individually, whereas policy change relies on an institutionalised decision-making process which tends to be cumbersome. Thus, states do not automatically respond to a rise in unemployment with restriction in immigration policies. And, during the latest economic crisis the two processes of change in migration policies and migration patterns seem to be rather unconnected. This finding applies especially to movements internal to the EU. They could not be restricted by policy change at the national level.

Given these findings it would be interesting to investigate other external shocks that are expected to impact migration policies in receiving countries such as the Arab Spring or the current European 'refugee crisis' to see whether these do or do not have immediate effects.

Acknowledgements

We would like to thank Stephan Leibfried and Steffen Mau for the possibility to discuss the different papers presented in this Special Issue at the Collaborative Research Centre (CRC) 597 closing conference in April 2014.

Disclosure statement

No potential conflict of interest was reported by the authors.

Funding

Work on this editorial was funded through the FP 7 funded SOURCE project, the virtual centre of excellence for research support and coordination on societal security.

References

Capoccia, G. 2015. "Critical Junctures and Institutional Change." In *Advances in Comparative Historical Analysis*, edited by J. Mahoney and K. Thelen, 147–179. Cambridge: Cambridge University Press.

Castles, S. 1986. "The Guest Worker in Western Europe – An Obituary." *International Migration Review* 20 (4): 761–778. doi:10.2307/2545735.

Castles, S., and M. J. Miller. 1993. *The Age of Migration. International Population Movements in the Modern World*. Houndmills: Macmillan.

Collier, R. B., and C. David. 1991. *Shaping the Political Arena. Critical Junctures, the Labor Movement, and Regime Dynamics in Latin America*. Princeton, NJ: Princeton University Press.

Cornelius, W. A. 2002. "Impacts of NAFTA on Mexico-to-US Migration." In *NAFTA in the New Millennium*, edited by E. J. Chambers and P. H. Smith, 287–304. University of California, San Diego: Center for US-Mexican Studies.

Cornelius, W. A., and M. R. Rosenblum. 2005. "Immigration and Politics." *Annual Review of Political Science* 8: 99–119. doi:10.1146/annurev.polisci.8.082103.104854.

Freeman, G. 1995. "Modes of Immigration Politics in Liberal Democratic States." *International Migration Review* 29 (4): 881–902. doi:10.2307/2547729.

Fussell, E., and D. S. Massey. 2004. "The Limits to Cumulative Causation: International Migration from Mexican Urban Areas." *Demography* 41 (1): 51–7. doi:10.1353/dem.2004.0003.

Galgóczi, B., J. Leschke, and A. Watt. 2012. "EU Labour Migration and Labour Markcts in Troubled Times." In *EU Labour Migration in Troubled Times*, edited by B. Galgóczi, J. Leschke, and A. Watt, 1–44. Aldershot: Ashgate.

Green, T., and A. L. Winters. 2010. "Economic Crisis and Migration: Learning from the Past and the Present." *The World Economy* 33 (9): 1053–1072. doi:10.1111/j.1467-9701.2010.01313.x.

Hall, P. A., and R. C. R. Taylor. 1996. "Political Science and the Three New Institutionalisms." *Political Studies* 44 (5): 936–957. doi:10.1111/j.1467-9248.1996.tb00343.x.

Hanson, G. H., and A. Spilimbergo. 1999. "Illegal Immigration, Border Enforcement, and Relative Wages: Evidence from Apprehensions at the U.S.-Mexico Border." *The American Economic Review* 89 (5): 1337–1357.

Hatton, T. J. 2014. "The Slump and Immigration Policy in Europe." In *Crisis and Migration. Implications of the Eurozone Crisis for Perceptions, Politics, and Policies of Migration*, edited by P. Bevelander and B. Petersson, 25–47. Lund: Nordic Academic Press.

Helbling, M. 2013. "Framing Immigration in Western Europe." *Journal of Ethnic and Migration Studies* 40 (1): 21–41. doi:10.1080/1369183X.2013.830888.

Herbert, U., and K. Hunn. 2000. "Gastarbeiter und Gastarbeiterpolitik in der Bundesrepublik. Vom Beginn der offziellen Anwerbung bis zum Anwerbestopp (1958 bis 1973)." In *Dynamische Zeiten. Die 60er Jahre in beiden deutschen Gesellschaften*, edited by A. Schildt, D. Siegfried, and K. C. Lammers, 273–310. Hamburg: Hans Christians.

Heyes, J., and M. Hyland. 2012. "Supporting, Recruiting and Organising Migrant Workers in Ireland and the United Kingdom: A Review of Trade Union Practices." In *EU Labour Migration in Troubled Times*, edited by B. Galgóczi, J. Leschke, and A. Watt, 211–234. Aldershot: Ashgate.

Kingdon, J. W. 1995. *Agendas, Alternatives, and Public Policies*. New York: Longman.

Kitschelt, H. P. 1995. *The Radical Right in Western Europe: A Comparative Analysis*. Ann Arbor: University of Michigan Press.

Koehler, J., F. Laczko, C. Aghazarm, and J. Schad. 2010. *Migration and the Economic Crisis in the European Union: Implications for Policy*. Brussels: International Organization for Migration.

Kuptsch, C. 2012. "The Economic Crisis and Labour Migration Policy in European Countries." *Comparative Population Studies* 37 (1–2): 15–32. doi:10.4232/10.CPoS-2011-17en.

Lee, E. 1966. "A Theory of Migration." *Demography* 3 (1): 47–57.

Lindley, A. 2014. "Exploring crisis and migration: Concepts and Issues." In *Crisis and Migration: Critical Perspectives*, edited by A. Lindley, 1–23. Abingdon: Routledge.

Martin, P. L. 2001. "Trade and Migration: the Mexico-to-U.S. Case." In *International Migration: Trends, Policies, and Economic Impact*, edited by S. Djajic, 89–109. London: Routledge.
Massey, D., J. Arango, G. Hugo, A. Kouaouci, A. Pellegrino, and J. Edward Taylor. 1998. *Worlds in Motion: Understanding International Migration at the End of the Millenium*. Oxford: Clarendon.
McCormick, A. 2012. *A Statistical Note on Unemployment and Immigration in the 27 EU Member States, 2001–2012*. San Domenico di Fiesole: MPC Analytical and Synthetic Note 2012/06.
OECD. 2016. OECD Data. www.data.oecd.org.
Papademetriou, D., M. Sumption, A. Terrazas, C. Burkert, S. Loyal, and R. Ferrero-Terrión. 2010. *Migration and Immigrants two Years after the Financial Collapse: Where do we stand?* Washington, DC: Migration Policy Institute.
Pastore, F. 2012. "Europe." In *International Migration in Times of Crisis*, edited by H. Duncan, J. Nieuwenhuysen, and S. Neerup, 129–151. Kingston: School of Policy Studies, Queen's University at Kingston.
Paul, R. 2013. "Strategic Contextualisation: Free Movement, Labour Migration Policies and the Governance of Foreign Workers in Europe." *Policy Studies* 34 (2): 122–141.
Pierson, P. 2000. "Increasing Returns, Path Dependence, and the Study of Politics." *The American Political Science Review* 94 (2): 251–267. doi:10.2307/2586011.
Ravenstein, E. G. 1889. "The Laws of Migration." *Journal of the Royal Statistical Society* 52 (2): 241–305. doi:10.2307/2979333.
Roos, C., and N. Zaun. 2014. "Norms Matter! The Role of International Norms in EU Policies on Asylum and Immigration." *European Journal of Migration and Law* 16 (1): 45–68. doi:10.1163/15718166-00002048.
Stalker, P. 1994. *The Work of Strangers: A Survey of International Labour Migration*. Geneva: International Labour Office.
Starke, P., A. Kaasch, and F. van Hooren. 2013. *The Welfare State as a Crisis Manager. Explaining the Diversity of Policy Responses to Economic Crisis*. Basingstoke: Palgrave Macmillan.
Trauner, F. 2016. "Asylum Policy: the EU's 'Crises' and the Looming Policy Regime Failure." *Journal of European Integration* 1 (2): 2–4. doi:10.1080/07036337.2016.1140756.
Tsebelis, G. 2002. *Veto Players. How Political Institutions Work*. New York: Sage.
Waldinger, R. 1997. Social Capital or Social Closure? Immigrant Networks in the Labor Market. Working Paper 26. Los Angeles, CA: School of Public Policy and Social Research.
Weil, P. 2005. *La France et Ses Étrangers: Laventure Dune Politique de Limmigration de 1938 À Nos Jours*. Paris: Gallimard.

Circumventing deadlock through venue-shopping: why there is more than just talk in US immigration politics in times of economic crisis†

Natascha Zaun, Christof Roos and Fabian Gülzau

ABSTRACT

This article addresses the question of how the financial and economic crisis that hit the USA in the late 2000s impacted immigration policies. We find that the crisis has not significantly changed dynamics. Instead, it has highlighted and aggravated persisting trends. Drawing on Kingdon's multiple streams model and combining it with the notion of two-level games, we find that while the policy stream and the problem stream would call for both restrictive and liberalising changes, the political stream impedes change: the fact that Congress has been divided for a long time over comprehensive immigration reform (CIR) impedes any restrictive or liberalising changes. With problems resulting from current policies being intensified through the global economic crisis, however, actors favouring either restrictive or liberal policy change look for alternative venues to pursue their policy aims. Through legislative changes on the state level or via executive orders by the president, policies can be changed on a lower level without CIR.

1. Introduction

The global economic and financial crisis since 2008 has proved to be a major challenge for the Western world. It resulted in both a rise in unemployment rates and a decrease in public spending in many European countries and the United States (US).

External shocks such as the economic crises have been found to substantially impact immigration policies in the past. Given the rise in unemployment and the decreased demand on the labour force, crises can be expected to produce 'a climate conducive to a restrictive regime' (Beets and Willekens 2009, 6; Newton 2008, 60). Cases in point are the Depression of 1920/21 in the US and the economic downturn following the oil crisis in the 1970s, both of which led to the implementation of more restrictive immigration policies (Hatton and Williamson 2009). Yet at the same time, a crisis also makes more

†The interview data used was collected in 2012 as part of the research project 'From Containers to Open States? Border Regime Change and the Mobility of Persons' at the Collaborative Research Centre 597 'Transformations of the State' at University of Bremen.

pronounced the hardships of undocumented immigrants that have no access to social benefits and thus suffer significantly when losing their occupation. Increased restriction of labour migration, moreover, can lead to migrants seeking access via humanitarian channels for refugee protection or family reunification (Czaika and De Haas 2013).

The recent crisis has been described as the worst financial crisis since the Great Depression by the International Monetary Fund (*The Guardian*, 10 April, 2008) and can thus be expected to have significantly impacted immigration policies in the US, as the US were hit particularly hard by the crisis (*Huffington Post*, 21 June, 2012; *The Atlantic*, 20 March, 2013). For instance, the US faced a substantial rise in unemployment and a GDP decrease in the crisis years from 2008 to 2012. This article aims at answering the question of *how and to what extent the global economic crisis has impacted US immigration policies and politics*.

We find that while there is no policy change induced by Congress, substantive changes at the state levels and through presidential Executive Orders can be observed. While policy change is blocked through deadlock in Congress, pressures from their constituencies for either liberal or restrictive changes encourage politicians to search for alternative venues to realise their policy aims. Actors interviewed for this study substantiate the claim that the crisis had an accelerating impact on policy change at levels other than Congress. We argue that this situation can be explained based on a combination of both venue-shopping as introduced by Baumgartner and Jones (1993) and the multiple streams model suggested by Kingdon (1995). While both the policy stream (i.e. policy ideas that are present among politicians and experts) and the problem stream (i.e. the non-functionality of the current immigration system) would call for change, the political situation of deadlock in Congress impedes change. The reason for impeded change is that both actors with liberal preferences and actors with restrictive preferences present in the Congress rather have incentives for defection than cooperation on the issue matter, as defection results in more favourable policy outcomes for each of them. They are more willing to accept the absence of the policy change they desire than they are willing to adopt changes to the status quo based on the policy preferences of their adversaries. Thus, proponents of restrictive change, such as political actors from (mainly Republican governed) US states that are affected disproportionately by undocumented immigration, foster restrictive change on the local level and adopt policy aiming at immigration control enforcement that has so far been blocked in Congress (Jones and Chou 2014 ; Steil and Vasi 2014). In contrast, examples for liberal change are the executive orders launched by President Obama aiming at temporary relief from deportation as well as the right to apply for work permits for certain undocumented immigrants.

With this study we aim to contribute to the wider debate on whether external shocks entail either restrictive or liberalising policy change. Our core finding is that while external shocks create pressures for change, these pressures need to be taken up by political actors in order to be transformed into actual policy change. Where change does not happen, pressures for change look for alternative venues and entail a politicisation of the issue. This study is based on an analysis of literature as well as policy documents on a number of decisions that have been made in the immigration policy area in the US between 2008 and 2012. In addition, we conducted 15 interviews in Fall 2012, at the height of the economic crisis, in which collective actors, such as unions and employers, but also politicians and experts from think tanks, elaborated on what they considered viable policies in times of crisis.

2. Multiple streams and venue-shopping as a theoretical framework to study policy change in times of crisis

We aim at explaining the impact of the crisis on US immigration policies by drawing on Kingdon's multiple streams approach and combining it with the venue-shopping theory (Baumgartner and Jones 1993). According to Kingdon (1995), policy change can be explained by a convergence of the problem stream, the policy stream and the politics stream. Analogously, the lack of change is based on an absence of this convergence. In line with Kingdon, the problem stream means the issue or the policy problem to be addressed. The policy stream covers the policy ideas that aim at its solution. The politics stream is the institutional setting and the political actors involved. In this article, we argue that the absence of a political stream favourable to change can account for the policy deadlock that we observe in US immigration politics in Congress. Moreover, we argue that the absence of such a favourable political stream can be best explained by drawing on the deadlock game in game theory. Following this model, non-cooperation is most beneficial to all actors involved, both individually and collectively, which eventually leads to policy stasis. Yet, given the immense pressures for change by their constituencies, which were amplified through the economic crisis, we argue that proponents of change look for alternative venues to pursue their aims. Thus, we contribute to the empirically rich body of literature on policy stasis in the US (Mansbridge and Martin 2013; McCarthy 2007) by adding an as of yet missing theoretical explanation for this state of affairs.

According to the multiple streams model, the policy stream concerns policy ideas that are constantly around in what Kingdon calls the 'policy primeval soup' (Kingdon 1995, 116). These policy ideas are usually based on different preferences. While some actors might be more concerned about immigrants' effective access to rights, others might favour a limitation of immigration levels or aim at more selectivity in immigrant admission. Based on these preferences, actors build ideas of both causal relationships (i.e. about what *is*) and what could be policy responses to tackle problems. The policy ideas thus are solutions which they can sell to decision-makers. Yet, crucial events are needed for these policy ideas to get noticed and gain political weight (Kingdon 1995, 113). In fact, dissent about the number, nature and national origin of desirable immigration is a constant feature of the US debate (Zolberg 2008 [2006]). At the same time, immigrants are depicted as 'villainous invaders' and 'heroic founders' (Newton 2008, 1). Thus, a crisis entailing a rise in numbers of unemployment can arguably help promoters of restriction of immigration gain ground (Newton 2008, 60). These could use the event to argue for a cut in immigration to ensure a stronger protection of national workers. Simultaneously, a crisis highlights the hardship undergone by undocumented immigrants as their socio-structural position makes them especially vulnerable to economic slumps (Papademetriou and Terrazas 2010 ; Tilly 2011). Yet, to implement restrictive or liberalising policy changes, the political stream has to come in as well. The political stream comprises things such as 'the public mood, pressure group campaigns, election results, partisan or ideological distributions in Congress, and changes of administration' (Kingdon 1995, 145). For instance, it has been argued that the increasing number of Latino voters puts pressure on the Democrats to introduce liberalising changes for the legalisation of their as of yet 'irregularly staying' family and friends. In 2005, 84% of the Latino population supported the legalisation through the so-called 'path to citizenship' (Suro 2005, 10). We assert that it is particularly the political stream which impedes change in Congress through deadlock. According to game theory, actors involved in a deadlock game benefit rather from defection than from cooperation. In this sense the game is a zero sum game. Each actor would benefit most in case of their own defection and the cooperation of the other actor. Yet, the second best outcome for actors would be that both of them defect. The least beneficial outcome for either of them would be obviously their own cooperation and the defection of the other actor. Thus, an outcome where both of them defect is highly likely.

However, with the crisis, the problem stream that supports the preferences of proponents of both liberal and restrictive change swells and their policy ideas face a rising demand with the electorate, at least in some highly affected states (Fetzer 2006). Thus, with deadlock in Congress, politicians need to look for alternative political venues (Baumgartner and Jones 1993) to pursue their aims and satisfy their constituencies. Our time of observation (2008–2012) spans, at least partly, from the 110th (2007–2009) to the 112th Congress (2011–2013). During the 110th Congress under the Bush administration, the House of Representatives as well as the Senate had a Democrat majority.[1] In the 111th Congress, Obama was presiding over a Democrat majority in the House and Senate. Eventually, Republicans gained the majority in the House of Representatives in the 112th Congress, however, still under Obama administration. Generally, immigration politics in the US is divisive and politicians do not necessarily hold uniform positions that reflect a party platform (Ilias, Fennelly, and Federico 2008, 748). On specific issues, however, a partisan divide has become visible. Republicans more often prefer restrictive policies, particularly as regards border enforcement (Fetzer 2006; Milner and Tingley 2008). Democrats, on the other hand, have stronger preferences for the legalisation of undocumented immigrants (Boyer 2012, 2–3; Lopez and Minushkin 2008).

We argue that the situation of deadlock in Congress in combination with the crisis makes policy-makers particularly susceptible to the dynamics of venue-shopping. While US policy-makers have already passed immigration policies in alternative venues before the beginning of the crisis, we argue that dynamics of venue-shopping in this area have intensified with the crisis.

Republicans searched for venues where they did not encounter liberal veto players. The Democrats could circumvent restrictive veto players through presidential Executive Orders, which the president was able to pass without any interference of the opposing party in Congress. How the crisis promoted this search for alternative venues can be shown by applying the multiple stream model to US immigration politics.

3. The problem stream: an ineffective immigration system in times of economic crisis

The US immigration system in the 2010s is widely acknowledged as dysfunctional. Not only has President Obama characterised the system as 'broken', [2] but there is also consensus in scholarly debates that the current status quo is 'bad for migrants, employers and the national interest' (Martin 2011a, 24). This is especially due to high hurdles immigrants face. Unless someone has family-ties to US citizens, it is quite difficult to immigrate to the US. Visa streams for high- and low-skilled immigrants are criticised as they are overly complex and do not match business demands adequately (Hansen 2009, 11–13; Hanson 2009, 4). In addition, a large number of undocumented immigrants entered the country in the past two decades, of which some moved to states that did not previously have experiences with immigration (Jones-Correa 2012, 4). [3] The latest estimates from January 2012 suggest an overall number of 11.4 million undocumented immigrants residing in the US, with a share of 59% being of Mexican origin (Baker and Rytina 2013). It is estimated that 30–45% of the unauthorised population legally entered the country but then overstayed their visa (Hanson 2009, 3; Pew 2006).[4] The economic crisis hit legal and, in particular, undocumented immigrants most severely, as sectors in which many immigrants had previously found employment (i.e. construction, retail and food) were highly affected by the economic downturn (Green and Winters 2010, 1068; Papademetriou and Terrazas 2010, 44–46; Tilly 2011, 679). Scholars, moreover, found that the economic crisis led to stagnating numbers in the (estimated) population of undocumented immigrants or even decreasing undocumented immigration (Hoefer, Baker, and Rytina 2012, 1).

The last major legislative reforms addressing the shortcomings of the US immigration system were the Immigration Reform and Control Act (IRCA) in 1986, the Immigration Act of 1990 and the Illegal Immigration Reform and Immigrant Responsibility Act (IIRIRA) in 1996 (Migration Policy Institute 2013; Schain 2012, 210–215). While IRCA tried to tackle the situation of a growing population of undocumented immigrants with amnesty and employer sanctions, the Immigration Act of 1990 aimed especially to raise the numbers of skilled workers through the creation of the H-1B visa programme (Schain 2012, 210–215, 104 Stat. 4978, §205). In addition, the IIRIRA combined greater border enforcement with a cut in social security benefits for immigrants (i.e. Social Security Federal public benefits, 110, Stat. 3009; see also Newton 2008, 53–63). Moreover, the IIRIRA enabled 'local and state police […] to enforce federal immigration law' (Varsanyi 2010, 2) under provision 287(g). This is remarkable paradigm shift since immigration enforcement was an exclusive federal competence with states having 'virtually no role in the construction or enforcement of immigration law' (Wishnie 2002, 285). [5] Nevertheless, IRCA was unsuccessful in diminishing the inflow of undocumented migrants and the Immigration Act of 1990 played its part in increasing the complexity of the immigration system (Martin 2011b, 80; Schain 2012, 213). Not surprisingly, the widely acknowledged problems of the current US immigration policies also influence public opinion. The Pew Research Center (2013, 2) found that 75% of the respondents see the need for at least major changes in the US immigration system. More precisely, the same survey observed that while three-fourths of the respondents want a possibility for undocumented immigrants to stay legally (73%) and think that the government can do more to reduce undocumented immigration (a lot more: 53%; somewhat more: 30%), there is little consensus on whether to increase or reduce legal immigration (increase: 25%, decrease: 36%).

In summary, the 'problem stream' of US immigration policies is that the immigration system is considered dysfunctional by the majority of policy-makers involved. Both proponents of restriction (e.g. in the areas of border protection or family immigration) and liberalisation (e.g. concerning legalisation of immigrants already in the country or supporters of increased immigration by labour) do not benefit from the system as it is. In the following section we will show that while all actors agreed that the immigration system needed to be reformed, the policy ideas to fix the broken system varied significantly between the actors.

4. The policy stream: ideas for the reform of an ineffective immigration policy

This section demonstrates that the comprehensive immigration reform (CIR) comprises a set of major ideas for reinvigorating the effectiveness of US immigration policy. According to Kingdon, policy ideas need to be on the floor already for actors to take them up and translate them into policy change. We will show how actors' preferences either coincided or collided with the CIR in times of economic crisis. Against the background of the picture drawn in the previous section, CIR – including border enforcement, regularisation of the undocumented and a guest worker scheme – becomes a compelling solution to the problems of the US immigration system. Since the 2000s, various forms of CIR have been debated in the US (for a history of proposed CIRs cf. Rosenblum 2011). Moreover, two presidents supported a CIR, although until now with little effect (Hanson 2009, 3). 'CIR' not only entails the promise of fixing an ineffective immigration policy, but also insinuates that actors would be more willing to agree on a package deal rather than individual policy. Comprehensiveness means that every major stakeholder's primary interest would be achieved, while at the same time the adoption of all policies would entail compromises on actors' positions (Freeman 2009, 65–69; Rosenblum 2011, 10–13). Put differently, every stakeholder receives something, while having to give in on other issues. CIRs in the past entailed – in different compositions – 'increased enforcement, a guest worker scheme and a path to legalization' (Freeman 2009, 69; Rosenblum 2011, 1). These three elements of immigration reform are key areas of US immigration policy. A CIR would tackle all of these policy areas. First, the call for increased enforcement touches upon border control, primarily at the southern US border, and stepping up internal control measures by means of ID and status checks at the work place ('E-verify') as well as in public places. Second, the expansion of guest worker schemes is meant to broaden the legal channel for the temporal demand for low- and highly-skilled labour. Such measures accommodate the demands of industry and business for a steady supply of labour. Third, with legalisation the estimated 10–12 million undocumented migrants in the US would be getting the opportunity to legalise their status. Interestingly, points that are also debated, namely the significance of family reunification or the problem of visa overstaying, do not expand into proposals for a CIR. The rationale of a CIR is to get the approval of all stakeholders by implementing parts of their agenda and making 'package deals' (Marquez and Witte 2009, 3). Accordingly, actors worried by the level of undocumented immigration should be won for the reform by the plan to step up border control and internal enforcement. Amnesty on a broad scale could win the consent of unions and civil rights groups traditionally concerned with measures protecting people from exploitation. Employers' interest in labour supply is met by the offer of temporary labour migration programmes (Freeman 2009, 65–69; Rosenblum 2011, 10–13).

In 2012 the slim chance for an agreement on this package deal disappeared in light of the economic crisis.[6] The research on actors that promoted either legalisation of undocumented immigrants or temporary labour migration for skilled and unskilled workers felt that they had a harder time lobbying for their cause (Interview Chamber of Commerce,

National Council of la Raza (NCLR) 2012). All collective actors who we have interviewed, regardless of political affiliation, see the crisis as a reason for an increasing polarisation of opinions in the immigration policy area (Interviews US 2012). In particular, those parts of the CIR package were met with resistance that not only debated closure, but also legalisation of the undocumented and openness for select groups of migrant workers. Concerning the debate, representatives of think tanks leaning to both the left and right confirmed that immigration had become a highly politicised topic. A policy advisor from the left-leaning think tank, the National Immigration Forum (Interview National Immigration Forum 2012), confirmed, that '[i]t is controversial to talk about the idea of foreign born individuals coming to the US when there are people here who are struggling to survive, who are native born Americans'. Speaking more bluntly, a representative from the conservative Center for Immigration Studies (Interview Center for Immigration Studies 2012) held that 'people do not have jobs, and they see illegal aliens having jobs. And we, as Americans, do not have them. So, there are numbers of levels of outrage that have caused devastation'.

In a nutshell, there are a variety of policy ideas on how to reform the US immigration system. These address different aspects of the immigration system and are underpinned by different ideological positions. Some actors, for instance, consider border enforcement crucial to minimise the inflow of undocumented migrants from Mexico. Others, in contrast, hold that creating legal paths to immigration, for example , through guest worker schemes could help addressing this issue. Yet another group of stakeholders suggests that the hardship of those already staying in the country undocumented should be alleviated through regularisation. The presence of policy ideas for reform is an essential prerequisite in Kingdon's multiple streams model. However, these policy ideas need to be taken up by policy-makers in the political process.

In the next section, we will demonstrate that the politics stream was not favourable for substantive policy change on the federal level. While the crisis increased pressure for change, it further politicised the issue and clearly separated the policy streams from one another. The different stakeholders hence grew even more apart from each other's positions. Given the divisiveness of the topic of immigration, the candidates in the 2012 presidential election did not address this issue. A unionist observed: '[P]olitical campaigns avoid the topic like the plague. You will see very little about immigration, if anything at all, in the current presidential campaign. From the politicians' standpoint, immigration is just a divisive issue on all sides' (Interview AFL-CIO 2012).

5. The politics stream: why there is deadlock in Congress over immigration reform

Compromise among actors proved to be impossible since the crisis not only highlighted the divisiveness of the positions among actors but also because defection and maintenance of the status quo was more beneficial for actors than cooperation. This uncompromising stance in combination with institutional constraints in congressional politics reinforced deadlock over immigration reform. The US Congress is not only divided on content, but is also blocked institutionally. The US political system contains 'multiple veto points' (Hansen 2009, 13; Rosenblum 2011, 11): For instance, the presidential veto or the Senate filibuster (Fennelly, Pearson, and Hackett 2015, 1424; Martin 2013). US bicameralism makes it necessary that both chambers agree on a bill for it to become law. In the

US system, politicians' interest representation does not necessarily overlap with general party positions. Even though Democrats have a broader immigrant constituency than Republicans, leading to a more pro-immigration and pro-rights attitude (Schain 2006, 386), US politics leave room for very local and specific interests (Interview Republican Senator 2012). Positions of politicians in the House of Representatives or Senate6 are defined by the interest of their respective constituencies, as well as business, unions, and other groups in these constituencies (Facchini and Steinhardt 2011, 735). Thus, it cannot be assumed that Republicans would show a tough stance on undocumented migration and call for border enforcement while Democrats would all be in favour of immigration and the granting of rights to the undocumented. In fact, Republicans that are open to the interests of business in their constituency, for example, in the agriculture, hotel and tourism industries, can turn a blind eye on efforts for border enforcement against undocumented immigration. Similarly, the Democrats' assumed liberal stance on immigration into the US could be obstructed by organised labour, claiming the depression of wages due to immigration (Interview AILA 2012). The interests of the main stakeholders, capital and labour, can be decisive in US immigration politics. Their influence on political groups can further impede compromise. We interviewed representatives of two union umbrella organisations: the AFL-CIO (American Federation of Labor and Congress of Industrial Organizations) representing 13.5 million workers, and the smaller Change to Win Federation (4.2 million members) which speaks for many Latino workers. Both unions strongly support an immigration reform that focuses on the rights of both migrant and native workers. The unions' policies to improve access to rights as well as working conditions includes the legalisation of the undocumented, opposition to temporary guest worker programmes, and a focus on worksite enforcement instead of border enforcement. For a representative of the AFL-CIO, the essence of immigration reform boils down to 'employer accountability' (Interview AFL-CIO 2012). If migrant workers are able to claim rights with their employer and these rights are enforced at the worksite, exploitation of workers because of unfair working conditions can be reduced. Hence, an amnesty for the undocumented is an indispensable condition for claiming rights (Interview Change to Win 2012). From the interview data it can be deduced that for unions, border enforcement is less of an issue as long as illegal employment is contained. The representatives of labour claim that employment opportunities for the undocumented create an incentive for crossing the border unauthorised. Unions criticise employers for 'fabricating' labour shortages in order to claim for the expansion of temporary worker programmes (Interview AFL-CIO 2012). Those programmes are not only said to affect wages negatively (Borjas 2005), but are also said to put the migrant worker in a dependent relationship with the employer since the working contract and residence status are combined (Interview AFL-CIO 2012). The rights focus of unions, as well as an interest in gaining more members, explains their opposition to temporary labour migration schemes and their lobby for legalisation. Thus, they would rather keep the status quo than compromise their position on temporary labour migration.

On the employers' side, the US Chamber of Commerce, which represents the interests of 3 million American businesses, considers immigration to be a tool for securing the economy's supply of labour. The focus of employers' lobbying efforts is on expanding temporary worker programmes, for highly as well as lesser skilled migrant workers. In this regard, opposition towards the unions' position is strongest (Interview US Chamber of

Commerce 2012). The Chamber views measures that improve worksite enforcement of immigration and labour law critically, but is not opposed to them. Employers claim a system that only applies to new hires leaves room to maintain undocumented employees in their workforce. However, this would not mean opposition to legalisation of undocumented immigrants. Employers have an interest in a 'stable workforce'. The argument in favour of legalisation builds on immigrants' contribution to the economy and compliance with a set of 'strict criteria' that would allow undocumented migrants to earn citizenship.[7] A steady supply of workers in all sectors fuels production and keeps wages, also for the highly skilled, lower (Borjas 2005). Although US employers face strong opposition from unions with regard to temporary labour migration programmes, common ground on the issue of legalisation can be observed. Therefore, legalisation is the area in which policy output was most likely.

For the US Chamber of Commerce, immigration is part of the 'American Fabric' which, managed in an orderly way, has an overwhelmingly positive impact on the economy and society. Whether immigration is still 'vitally important to the success' (National Immigration Forum 2012) of the US is questioned by some actors. The position of two lobby groups, Numbers USA as well as FAIR (Federation for American Immigration Reform) show how a high level of immigration to the US and suggestions for regulatory reform have become a heavily contested issue. The positions of FAIR and Numbers USA would mean a radical change to the idea of immigration as being part of the American Fabric. They want to substantially lower immigration levels and push strongly for the enforcement angle of the CIR. As a consequence, their influence on policy-makers renders compromise on a comprehensive reform package cumbersome since expansion of admission for temporary workers and legalisation of undocumented workers are fundamentally opposed (Beirich 2009; Tichenor 2014, 43–45).[8]

Both groups argue that high levels of immigration impact negatively on social justice in the US as well as on the environment. The focus of restriction-minded groups on welfare systems and social justice can be observed since the 1990s. The framing of immigration as a welfare issue replaced a former discourse that racialised the immigration issue (Schain 2006, 384). They claim that population growth based on immigration has a negative impact on wages, the distribution of welfare benefits, as well as the environment in the US. The latter point of criticism is based on 'urban sprawl' related to population growth and needs for housing. Roy Beck, an environmentalist and founder of Numbers USA, sees the American worker with lower skills and lower education being harmed by immigration. Pressure on wages particularly in the low-skilled sector would contribute to massive social injustice. At the same time, immigrants are blamed for being 'net users of government services' (Interview Numbers USA 2012). The same relationship between immigration and local poverty is made by FAIR (2012): 'We cannot afford to support the impoverished ranks if we continue to keep bringing in more and more. We do have a responsibility to the people of the US who are poor or do not have health insurance.' Concerning the economic crisis, it is criticised that immigration policy does not respond to changes in supply and demand for workers on the labour market. 'We are admitting the same number of people now our unemployment is over 8 per cent, as we did when it was under 5 per cent. […] how do we fix the immigration system that addresses the needs we have in this country?' (Interview FAIR 2012). Both groups aim for 'population stability', that is , the end of population growth induced by immigration.

This would entail the reduction of immigration to one-quarter of its current size of one million admissions per year. In order to achieve this threshold, the green card and diversity lotteries would be abolished, family-based migration would be reduced to spouses and children only, and border and worksite enforcement would be increased. Immigration would not be stopped, because in terms of labour migration, a strict focus on immigration of the highly skilled is claimed. According to their own evaluation, FAIR and Numbers USA were successful in lobbying Congress against legalisation of the undocumented (Beirich 2009, 12, 18; Interview FAIR and Numbers USA 2012). Both lobby groups consider the status quo in US immigration regulation, which currently allows a million people each year to immigrate, to benefit the parties' and buisnesses' interests. Allegedly, immigration policy change should not be expected from Congress since immigrants are likely to increase the Democrats' electorate and Republicans please their 'backbone', the industry and business with a steady supply of labour (Interview Numbers USA 2012).

Figure 1 provides information on interest groups and their objectives in a CIR. Points at the outer side of the triangle indicate support of stricter enforcement measures, while points in the centre show interest group position against this part of CIR. As explained above, stakeholders' and interest groups' positions are extremely divisive on the issue. On the one hand, the Latino civil rights organisation NCLR and the labour union AFL-CIO support an amnesty for unauthorised immigrants already residing in the US, while being opposed to extended enforcement. Their liberal position is partly supported by the US Chamber of Commerce. They, however, strongly favour temporary labour migration programmes that are not supported by the unions. On the other side of the 'ideological (…) divide' (Marquez and Witte 2009, 20), the nativist organisations FAIR and Numbers USA are opposed to any part of CIR except extended enforcement. Following the deadlock game in game theory, defection is indeed more beneficial than

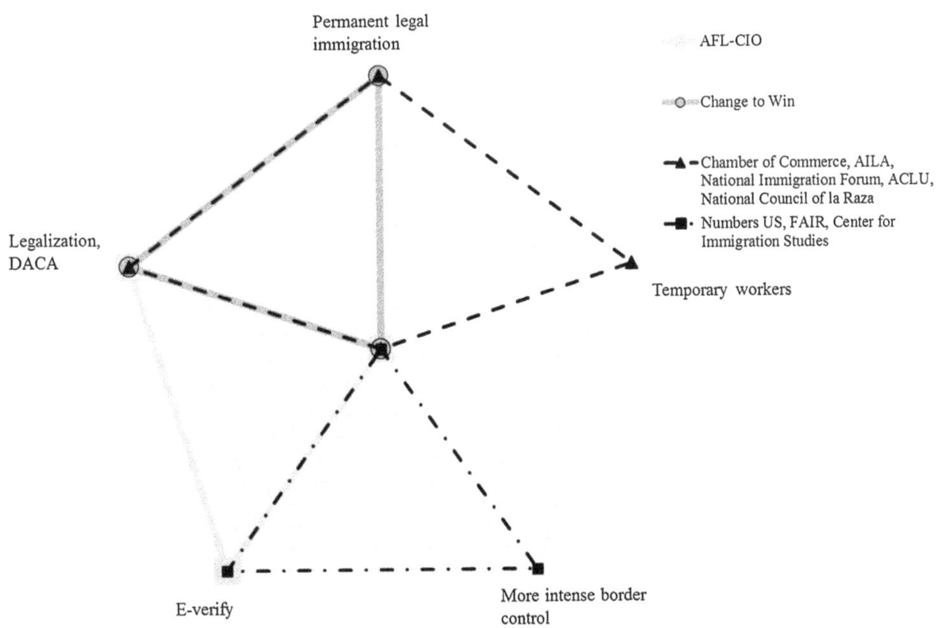

Figure 1. Interest group positions on immigration reform.

cooperation, as currently none of the actors want to compromise their position on: the increase in labour force (employers), no temporary labour migration policy (unions) and stepping up in enforcement (nativists).

Studying actors' divisiveness over a CIR, Martin (2011a, 25) holds that the status quo 'is the second-best option for those who cannot achieve their first-choice solution' as 'most unauthorised migrants get the higher wage jobs they seek and most employers get work done cheaper with such migrants' (Martin 2011a, 17). [9] Therefore, he observes 'talk but no action' (Martin 2011a, 32) in times of crisis. We contest this argument and show in the next sections how actors searched for alternative venues to bring about change in immigration policy.

6. In search of new venues: immigration control at the state level and executive orders by the president

The politics stream impeded change on the federal level due to the institutional setting and the divisiveness of actor positions which were emphasised by the crisis. Yet the problem stream became more prominent in recent years, especially but not only through the crisis and highlighted the need for policy change. This pressure hence led stakeholders to look for other venues to pursue their policy aims in which they would face fewer veto players.

Therefore, we find the claim that US politics were completely unable to produce legislative change to be slightly inaccurate. Change can be observed, albeit not on the federal level. Immigration policy-making shifts to the US states as well as to the president (Varsanyi 2010). [10] Against the procedural rules that are laid down in the Constitution, the 'states take immigration into their own hands' (Interview Immigration Policy Center 2012). Such policy devolution can be observed in southern US states most affected by undocumented border crossers. Recent anti-immigrant legislation in Arizona and Alabama that aims against undocumented immigrants' access to government services, such as education or infrastructure, have caused concern among policy observers (Boyer 2012, 1). Not only are states overstepping their competencies in this field, state legislation is overwhelmingly targeted at undocumented immigrants, of whom many happen to be Latinos, causing fear of a backlash against workers from Mexico or Central America (Interview National Immigration Forum 2012). In addition, anti-immigrant ordinances issued by municipalities (local level) are constantly on the rise since the failures of CIR (Gilbert 2009; Steil and Vasi 2014, 1110; Varsanyi 2010, 11).

Since the late nineteenth century, immigration policy-making has laid in the hands of the federal government. Only recently 'state and local immigration policy activism has exploded' (Varsanyi 2010, 9). This devolution was made possible by the 104th Congress under Republican majority through three aforementioned legislative acts that passed Congress in 1996: the Personal Responsibility and Work Opportunity Reconciliation Act (PRWORA), the Antiterrorism and Effective Death Penalty Act and the Illegal Immigration Reform Immigrant Responsibility Act (IIRIRA) (Varsanyi 2010, 2).[11] However, state and local actors did not use these newly created channels immediately at the time of establishment (Varsanyi 2010). Varsanyi (2010, 11) argues that politicians became more active on the state and local levels to 'earn political capital on the issue of immigration reform'. Only the repeated failures to reform the immigration system 'opened a veritable Pandora's Box of state and local immigration control initiatives seeking to fill the policy void'

(Cornelius 2010, vii). Cases in point are the 287(g) agreements between the U.S. Immigration and Customs Enforcement agencies (ICE) and local enforcement partners (police), which are by now in place in 17 states (Coleman 2012 ; ICE 2014), municipalities and city ordinances (Steil and Vasi 2014; Varsanyi 2008). In terms of party politics, scholars showed that Republicans are critical of the effectiveness of federal measures for immigration enforcement and push for devolution to the state level. In contrast, Democrats are opposed to state government attempts to take on immigration enforcement (Fennelly, Pearson, and Hackett 2015, 1423; Jones and Chou 2014).

Another example for a shift in venues are executive orders adopted by the president. These orders supersede majorities in the Congress and again highlight the inability of Congress to legislate. The DREAM Act, which would have legalised the status of young deserving undocumented migrants who had come as children, did not gain a majority in the Senate. Republican Senators blocked the bill in 2010. By executive order, President Obama bypassed approval of the Congress allowing for deferred action, abolishing execution of deportation for this specific group in August 2012. Among others, requirements for qualification are that undocumented youth must have no criminal record and pursue either military service or higher education. Legalisation was conditioned upon their 'deservingness'. The justification for the original bill was not only based on moral grounds such as fairness; the group in question was brought to the country by their parents and thus had not broken immigration law intentionally. Additionally, the White House referred to the economic crisis and the positive budgetary implications that legalisation of this group would entail: 'President Obama believes we need to do more than recover from the recession. […] An important part of rebuilding our economy with [these values] is making our immigration system functional, efficient, and accountable'. [12] Economic and security needs justified pressing for passage of CIR as well as the DREAM Act. It was calculated that passing the DREAM Act would bring $2.2 billion revenue over 10 years.[13] The executive order was not only the adoption of a first piece of the deadlocked CIR, but was also framed as a response to the crisis. In that sense, not only could venue-shopping be observed, but also the intersection of policy, problem and politics streams. The executive order offered a new political venue for decision-making. The unresolved problem of the undocumented immigrant population gained fiscal urgency during the crisis and met with a policy that had been debated for some time already. Some actors claimed their lobbying efforts of the Obama administration for this executive order (Change to Win, NCLR 2012). The unions, civil rights groups and organisations that represent Latino interests welcomed the president's initiative as a first step for large scale legalisation (ACLU, AFL-CIO, Change to Win, NCLR 2012). Others criticised that the executive order bypassed Congress in order to win the vote of the Latino community in the election year (Republican Senator, FAIR 2012). And restrictively minded groups feared that deferred action allowing for the DREAM Act to be executed would be the wedge for CIR (FAIR 2012).

State legislation on immigration, as well as executive orders, indicate a shift in venues for immigration policy-making. Enforcement is decided on the state level and legalisation of the undocumented is executed by bypassing a Congressional majority. Among the suggested policies that are part of a CIR, unions and employers would only agree on legalisation. Enforcement was not on their agenda and the temporary immigration of workers was heavily contested. Accordingly, the president maintained the status quo and opted for a piecemeal approach on legalisation. Observers from the left deemed this approach as the only way forward in a deadlocked Congress (Interview Change to Win, AFL-CIO, AILA, ACLU 2012).

In summary, the absence of policy change on the federal level intensified the problem stream, especially in times of economic crisis. Pressures for change therefore made their way to other venues. Republicans were able to enforce restrictive measures on border protection via the state and local levels, whereas Democrats could implement legalisation schemes through presidential decrees.

7. Conclusion

This paper set out to answer the question of what the impact of the economic and financial crisis is on immigration policies in the US, a country that has been hit hard by this crisis. We find that the crisis has highlighted policy problems that have been present before and has aggravated these problems. US immigration policies have been described as 'bad for migrants, employers and the national interest' (Martin 2011a, 24). Yet, a CIR is stuck in Congress given the absence of strong majorities and the divergent preferences between, but also among, Republicans and Democrats. Policy ideas for liberal and restrictive change have been present for a long time. Moreover, the problem stream is aggravating. In addition the increasing problems of unauthorised border crossings in combination with the hardship of people who have no access to any rights at all based on their undocumented status, motivate both policy proponents of liberalisation and restriction to look for alternative venues to pursue their policy aims. Republicans, who hold the majorities in most state legislatures, pass restrictive policies on the state level where they do not encounter liberal veto players. As far as the Democrats are concerned, the presidential decrees, for example , the deferred action on childhood arrivals from 2012 and others passed by President Barack Obama in 2014, can equally be considered as an attempt to shop for policy venues where no restrictive veto players can be found (Migration Policy Institute 2014).

The contribution of this article is twofold. On the one hand, we have theorised the current situations of deadlock on the CIR and policy change on the state levels, which have been widely discussed but so far not comprehensively explained. We demonstrate that combining the theoretical approaches of venue-shopping and multiple streams is particularly helpful to understand policy-making under deadlock, as the problem and policy streams would call for change but the politics stream impedes it and so actors search for other venues to pursue their policy aims. This also applies to other policy areas on which the US Congress is currently faced with deadlock. In the case of the EU others have argued that restrictively minded ministers of the interior have engaged in 'bottom-up' venue-shopping, that is , they have changed from the national to the EU level to pursue their policy aims (Guiraudon 2000; Maurer and Parkes 2007). Our study adds to this that venue-shopping is not a one-way process, but can also imply 'top-down' venue-shopping and a search for adequate venues on a lower, that is , subnational level. This seems to be part of a larger phenomenon. Examples for a trend towards devolution of immigration control and enforcement to subnational venues can be found in other federal political systems. More competences for local and regional entities are also claimed in Canada,

Spain, the UK and other countries (Thränhardt 2013). In which way the economic crisis intensified claims for devolution in other cases has yet to be researched.

On the other hand, we show that the crisis has rather aggravated or highlighted problems that have been present for a long time. Thus, the crisis cannot be considered to be the root of current policy change, but rather a moderating variable amplifying the problem pressure that entailed change. This leads us to conclude that external shocks like the global economic crisis never have an immediate impact and are never critical junctures *per se* but that these rather need to be translated into policy change by political actors.

Notes

1. The Senate was evenly split between Democrats and Republicans (49–49). However, two independent members voted with the Democrats.
2. Obama did so, for instance, in a speech at the American University on 1 July 2010, https://www.whitehouse.gov/the-press-office/remarks-president-comprehensive-immigration-reform (accessed 8 July 2015).
3. In fact, according to Jones-Correa (2012) the seven states with the largest growth in immigrant population (North Carolina, Georgia, Arkansas, Nevada, Tennessee, South Carolina and Nebraska) in the period from 1990 to 2009 'had attracted significant numbers of immigrants before 1990' (4). What is more, Steil and Vasi (2014, 1134) showed that the Latino population growth is a strong and significant predictor of the adoption of anti-immigrant ordinances at the local level in the period from 2006 to 2011.
4. However, those numbers vary dramatically, depending on the country of origin. For instance, while Mexicans rather cross the border uninspected, individuals from other Latin American countries rely on tourist visas to enter the USA and then become visa-overstayers (Massey and Riosmena 2010, 304).
5. In this regard, the IIRIRA can be seen as a prerequisite to devolution in the field of immigration policies. Additionally, the Personal Responsibility and Work Opportunity Reconciliation Act (PRWORA) and the Antiterrorism and Effective Death Penalty Act (both in 1996) were part of this development. While the PRWORA cut down legal immigrants' eligibility for social services (i.e. Food Stamps, Medicaid) and 'devolved authority over select social services to the states' (Varsanyi 2010, 2), the latter 'gave local police the authority to arrest previously deported noncitizen felons' (Varsanyi 2010; Wishnie 2002).
6. In 2006, a CIR was passed through a bipartisan initiative by Senators McCain (Republican) and Kennedy (Democrat) in the Senate. However, facing mid-term elections and increasing negative public opinion on the regularisation of undocumented migrants, the bill did not pass the House of Representatives. Instead, the rather sudden anti-immigrant backlash lead to the adoption of the Secure Fence Act, reinforcing border control at the US southern border (Rosenblum 2011, 7–8).
7. See US Chamber of Commerce 'Fixing our Broken Immigration System' http://immigration.uschamber.com/uploads/sites/400/Summary%20Immigration%20Priorities%20in%20the%20House%207-16-2013.pdf, accessed 10 October 2014.
8. The pro-immigrant Southern Poverty Law Center accuses FAIR and Numbers USA of pursuing a nativist agenda. The Center accounts for the lobby groups' influence on US immigration politics, in particular the failure of the DREAM Act as well as Comprehensive Immigration Reform. http://www.splcenter.org/get-informed/publications/the-nativist-lobby-three-faces-of-intolerance, accessed 15 June 2015.
9. A similar explanation for the inability reform is put forward by Hanson (2009).
10. A minor exemption is the American Recovery and Reinvestment Act (ARRA) of 2009 which entailed restrictions on the H-1B visa program for companies that received funds through the Troubled Asset Relief Program (TARP). However, the legislation only affected a small number of enterprises mainly in the banking sector and expired in 2011.

11. In fact, these restrictions can be seen as the results of earlier venue shopping. Judicially inhibited restrictions on access of the undocumented to public goods in California (Proposition 187) influenced immigration control legislation in the US Senate and the creation of legal options for devolution. In the early 1990s, economic crisis, recession and unemployment put pressure on state politicians to act against undocumented immigrants (Schain 2006, 383–384).
12. See the agenda of the White House for the Hispanic community from 2012: http://www.whitehouse.gov/sites/default/files/rss_viewer/hispanic_agenda_final.pdf, accessed 8 July 2015.
13. For the details of the programme, see the website of the Department of Homeland Security: http://www.dhs.gov/deferred-action-childhood-arrivals, accessed 8 July 2015.

Acknowledgements

The authors would like to thank Steffen Mau as head of the project and Heike Brabandt for conducting interviews with collective actors in the US as part of this project.

Disclosure statement

No potential conflict of interest was reported by the authors.

References

Baker, B., and N. Rytina. 2013. *Estimates of the Unauthorized Immigrant Population Residing in the United States: January 2012. Population Estimates.* Washington, DC: Department of Homeland Security, Office of Immigration Statistics. http://www.dhs.gov/sites/default/files/publications/ois_ill_pe_2012_2.pdf.

Baumgartner, F. R., and B. D. Jones. 1993. *Agendas and Instability in American Politics.* Chicago, IL: Chicago University Press.

Beets, G., and F. Willekens. 2009. *The Global Economic Crisis and International Migration: An Uncertain Outlook.* The Hague: Netherlands Interdisciplinary Demographic Institute.

Beirich, H. 2009. *The Nativist Lobby. Three Faces of Intolerance. A Report from the Southern Poverty Law Centre.* Montgomery: Southern Poverty Law Center. http://www.splcenter.org/sites/default/files/downloads/splc_nativistlobby.pdf.

Borjas, G. 2005. "The Economic Benefits from Immigration." *Journal of Economic Perspectives* 9 (2): 3–22.

Boyer, S. B. 2012. *Immigration and Integration in the 2012 U.S. Presidential Race, Perspective.* Washington, DC: Friedrich Ebert Stiftung. http://library.fes.de/pdf-files/id/09415.pdf.

Coleman, M. 2012. "The 'Local' Migration State: The Site-Specific Devolution of Immigration Enforcement in the U.S. South." *Law & Policy* 34 (2): 159–190.

Cornelius, W. A. 2010. "Preface." In *Taking Local Control. Immigration Policy Activism in U.S. Cities and States*, edited by M. W. Varsanyi, vii–viii. Stanford: Stanford University Press.

Czaika, M., and H. De Haas. 2013. "The Effectiveness of Immigration Policies." *Population and Development Review* 39 (3): 487–508.

Facchini, G., and M. F. Steinhardt. 2011. "What Drives U.S. Immigration Policy? Evidence from Congressional Roll Call Votes." *Journal of Public Economics* 95 (7): 734–743.

Fennelly, K., K. Pearson, and S. Hackett. 2015. "The US Congressional Immigration Agenda: Partisan Politics, Policy Stalemate and Political Posturing." *Journal of Ethnic and Migration Studies* 41 (9): 1412–1432.

Fetzer, J. S. 2006. "Why Did House Members Vote for H.R. 4437?" *International Migration Review* 40 (4): 698–706.

Freeman, G. P. 2009. "From Disordered Expansion to Disordered Stalemate: Immigration Politics in the United States." In *Nations of Immigrants. Australia and the US Compared*, edited by J. Higley and J. Nieuwenhuysen, 6–69. Cheltenham: Edward Elgar.

Gilbert, L. 2009. "Immigration as Local Politics: Re-Bordering Immigration and Multiculturalism Through Deterrence and Incapacitation." *International Journal of Urban and Regional Research* 33 (1): 26–42.

Green, T., and A. L. Winters. 2010. "Economic Crises and Migration: Learning from the Past and the Present." *The World Economy* 33 (9): 1053–1072.

Guiraudon, V. 2000. "European Integration and Migration Policy: Vertical Policy-Making as Venue Shopping." *Journal of Common Market Studies* 38 (2): 251–271.

Hansen, R. 2009. "Immigration & Immigration Reform in the United States: An Outsider's View." *The Forum* 7 (3): 1–13.

Hanson, G. H. 2009. *The Economics and Policy of Illegal Immigration in the United States.* Washington, DC: Migration Policy Institute.

Hatton, T. J., and J. G. Williamson. 2009. *Global Economic Slumps and Migration, VOX CEPR's Policy Portal.* http://www.voxeu.org/article/global-economic-slumps-and-migration.

Hoefer, M., B. Baker, and N. Rytina. 2012. *Estimates of the Unauthorized Immigrant Population Residing in the United States: January 2011. Population Estimates.* Washington, DC: Department of Homeland Security, Office of Immigration Statistics. http://www.dhs.gov/xlibrary/assets/statistics/publications/ois_ill_pe_2011.pdf.

ICE (U.S. Immigration and Customs Enforcement Agencies). 2014. "Delegation of Immigration Authority Section 287(g) Immigration and Nationality Act." http://www.ice.gov/factsheets/287g.

Ilias, S., K. Fennelly, and C. M. Federico. 2008. "American Attitudes Towards Guest Worker Policies." *International Migration Review* 42 (4): 741–766.

Jones, M. P., and B. Chou. 2014. "Immigration Policy and Partisan Politics in the State Legislatures: 2010–2012." In *Undecided Nation. Political Gridlock and the Immigration Crisis*, edited by T. Payan and E. de la Garza, 99–119. Cham: Springer.

Jones-Correa, M. 2012. *Contested Ground: Immigration in the United States.* Washington, DC: Migration Policy Institute. http://www.migrationpolicy.org/sites/default/files/publications/TCM-UScasestudy.pdf.

Kingdon, J. W. 1995. *Agendas, Alternatives, and Public Policies.* 2nd ed. New York: Longman.

Lopez, M. H., and S. Minushkin. 2008. *2008 National Survey of Latinos: Hispanic Voter Attitudes.* Washington, DC: Pew Research Center. http://www.pewhispanic.org/files/reports/90.pdf.

Mansbridge, J., and C. J. Martin, eds. 2013. *Negotiating Agreements in Politics. Report of the Task Force on Negotiating Agreement in Politics.* Washington, DC: American Political Science Association.

Marquez, B., and J. F. Witte. 2009. "Immigration Reform: Strategies for Legislative Action." *The Forum* 7 (3): 1–28.

Martin, P. 2011a. "Immigration, Labour Markets and Immigration Reform in the United States." In *Immigration and the Financial Crisis. The United States and Australia Compared*, edited by J. Higley, J. Nieuwenhuysen, and S. Neerup, 16–34. Cheltenham: Edward Elgar.

Martin, P. 2011b. "Mexico-US Migration, NAFTA and CAFTA, and US Immigration Policy." In *Migration, Nation States, and International Cooperation*, edited by R. Hansen, J. Koehler, and J. Money, 75–86. New York: Routledge.

Martin, C. J. 2013. "Negotiating Political Agreements." In *Negotiating Agreements in Politics. Report of the Task Force on Negotiating Agreement in Politics*, edited by J. Mansbridge and C. J. Martin, 1–18. Washington, DC: American Political Science Association.

Massey, D., and F. Riosmena. 2010. "Undocumented Migration from Latin America in an Era of Rising U.S. Enforcement." *The Annals of the American Academy of Political and Social Science* 630 (1): 294–321.

Maurer, A., and R. Parkes. 2007. "The Prospects for Policy Change in EU Asylum Policy: Venue and Image at the European Level." *European Journal of Migration and Law* 9 (2): 173–205.

McCarthy, N. 2007. "The Policy Effects of Political Polarization." In *The Transformation of American Politics. Activist Government and the Rise of Conservatism*, edited by P. Pierson and T. Skocpol, 223–255. Princeton, NJ: Princeton University Press.

Migration Policy Institute. 2013. *Key Immigration Laws and Policy Developments Since 1996*. Washington, DC: MPI Press Release. http://www.migrationpolicy.org/sites/default/files/publications/CIR-1986Timeline.pdf.

Migration Policy Institute. 2014. *MPI: As Many as 3.7 Million Unauthorized Immigrants Could Get Relief from Deportation Under Anticipated New Deferred Action Program*. Washington, DC: MPI Press Release. http://www.migrationpolicy.org.

Milner, H. V., and D. Tingley. 2008. "The Economic and Political Influences on Different Dimensions of United States Immigration Policy." Working paper prepared for the Midwest Political Science Association Meeting. http://www.princeton.edu/~hmilner/working%20papers/The%20Economic%20and%20Political%20Influences%20on%20Different%20Dimensions%20of%20United%20States%20Immigration%20Policy.pdf.

Newton, L. 2008. *Illegal, Alien, or Immigrant. The Politics of Immigration Reform*. New York: New York University Press.

Papademetriou, D. G., and A. Terrazas. 2010. "Immigrants and the US Economic Crisis: From Recession to Recovers." In *Migration and Immigrants Two Years After the Financial Collapse: Where Do We Stand?*, edited by D. G. Papademetriou, M. Sumption, A. Terrazas, C. Burkert, S. Loyal, and R. Ferrero-Turrión, 22–46. Washington, DC: Migration Policy Institute.

Pew Research Center. 2006. *Modes of Entry for the Undocumented Migrant Population*. Washington, DC: Pew Research Center. http://pewhispanic.org/files/factsheets/19.pdf.

Pew Research Center. 2013. *Most Say Immigration Policy Needs Big Changes. But Little Agreement on Specific Approaches*. Washington, DC: Pew Research Center. http://www.people-press.org/files/legacy-pdf/5-9-13%20Immigration%20Release.pdf.

Rosenblum, M. R. 2011. *US Immigration Policy Since 9/11: Understanding the Stalemate over Comprehensive Immigration Reform*. Washington, DC: Migration Policy Institute. http://www.migrationpolicy.org/sites/default/files/publications/RMSG-post-9-11policy.pdf.

Schain, M. A. 2006. "The Politics of Immigration in France, Britain and the United States. A Transatlantic Comparison." In *Immigration and the Transformation of Europe*, edited by C. A. Parsons and T. M. Smeeding, 362–392. Cambridge: Cambridge University Press.

Schain, M. A. 2012. *The Politics of Immigration in France, Britain, and the United States. A Comparative Study*. 2nd ed. New York: Palgrave Macmillan.

Steil, J. P., and I. B. Vasi. 2014. "The New Immigration Contestation: Social Movements and Local Immigration Policy Making in the United States, 2000–2011." *American Journal of Sociology* 119 (4): 1104–1155.

Suro, R. 2005. *Attitudes Toward Immigrants and Immigration Policy: Surveys among US Latinos and in Mexico*. Washington, DC: Pew Hispanic Center. http://www.pewhispanic.org/files/reports/52.pdf.

Thränhardt, D. 2013. "Immigration and Integration in European Federal Countries: A Comparative Evaluation." In *Immigration and Federalism in Europe. Federal, Stat and Local Regulatory Competencies in Austria, Belgium, Germany, Italy, Russia, Spain and Switzerland*, edited by D. Thränhardt, 7–20. Osnabrück: IMIS.

Tichenor, D. J. 2014. "The Congressional Dynamics of Immigration Reform." In *Undecided Nation. Political Gridlock and the Immigration Crisis*, edited by T. Payan and E. de la Garza, 23–48. Cham: Springer.

Tilly, C. 2011. "The Impact of the Economic Crisis on International Migration: A Review." *Work, Employment and Society* 25 (4): 675–692.

Varsanyi, M. W. 2008. "Immigration Policing Through the Backdoor: City Ordinances, the 'Right to the City,' and the Exclusion of Undocumented Day Laborers." *Urban Geography* 29 (1): 29–52.

Varsanyi, M. W. 2010. "Immigration Policy Activism in U.S. Cities and States: Interdisciplinary Perspectives." In *Taking Local Control. Immigration Policy Activism in U.S. Cities and States*, edited by M. W. Varsanyi, 1–27. Stanford: Stanford University Press.

Wishnie, M. J. 2002. "Introduction: Immigration and Federalism." *Annual Survey of American Law* 58 (3): 283–293.

Zolberg, A. R. 2008. *A Nation by Design. Immigration Policy in the Fashioning of America*. Cambridge, MA: Harvard University Press.

Appendix A

Table A1. Detailed interest group positions on immigration reform.

Interest group	Admission		Enforcement		Amnesty
	Permanent legal immigration = Family Economic migration	Temporary workers	More intense border control, apprehension and deportation, local enforcement by states	E-verify "employer verification"[a]	Legalisation, DREAM Act (DACA, deferred action for childhood arrivals)
AFL-CIO	Yes Labour immigration should strictly work on labour shortages	No	No	Yes	Yes
Change to Win	Yes = permanent legal immigration	No	No	No	Yes
Chamber of Commerce	Yes, but shift focus to employment Yes, reduce per country caps, first come first serve based on skills	Yes	No Borders need to be secure but not sealed	Yes and No More critical than supportive System should work in a manageable way	Yes
Numbers US	Yes, for spouses and minor children, no chain migration	Lower ceilings, open to skilled, cut the diversity and green card lottery	Yes	Yes	No
FAIR	Lower ceilings overall, focus on skills		Yes	Yes	No
AILA	Yes Family migration as well as economic migration is supported	Yes Facilitations for temporary worker programmes are demanded	No increase in control	No E-verify is flawed and puts a burden on businesses	Yes
National Immigration Forum	Yes on all issues		No Further enforcement, control intensity and costs are too high already	No Do not punish workers for an immigration system that does not work	Yes
Center for Immigration Studies	Lower ceilings Saturation point reached with immigration Get rid of family unity	Focus on people who can help the economy get going again	Yes	Yes Keep undocumented immigrants from being hired	No

(*Continued*)

Table A1. Continued.

Interest group		Admission		Enforcement		Amnesty
ACLU	Yes Family reunification is a human right	Not really their focus, but Yes	Not really their focus, but Yes For skilled and unskilled	No More intensification, against state level immigration control	No Concerns about privacy and accuracy of the system	Yes
National Council of la Raza	Yes In favour of family reunification	Not really their focus, but Yes Permanent labour migration better than temporary	Yes Particularly for seasonal workers	No Against states enforcing immigration law Against further intensification of control	No Will hurt Latino workers and Latino small businesses	Yes

[a]Employer verification systems are used to check workers' employment eligibility (now referred to as E-Verify) (see Rosenblum 2011, 6).

Appendix B

Table B1. Institutional affiliation of interviewees.

Institutional affiliations of US interviewees	Date of interview Washington, DC
American Immigration Lawyers Association (AILA)	11 September 2012
Immigration Policy Center	11 September 2012
American Federation of Labor and Congress of Industrial Organizations (AFL-CIO)	11 September 2012 15 October 2012
Federation for American Immigration Reform (FAIR)	12 September 2012
US Chamber of Commerce	13 September 2012
Numbers USA	13 September 2012
Change to Win	14 September 2012
Republican Senator	17 September 2012
National Immigration Forum	17 September 2012
Center for Immigration Studies	18 September 2012
American Civil Liberties Union (ACLU)	18 September 2012
National Council of La Raza (NCLR)	19 September 2012

The crisis as an opportunity for change? High-skilled immigration policies across Europe

Lucie Cerna

ABSTRACT

The recent economic crisis provided a shock to the system, and led governments to scramble for solutions to problems of falling economic growth, high unemployment and weak job creation. Many European governments responded to protectionist calls by restricting immigration policies, even towards the highly skilled. Yet countries have faced different challenges and thus the cross-national variation in the demand for policy closure or openness is remarkable. Some seized the opportunity to restrict their high-skilled immigration policies, while others took advantage of the crisis for further liberalisation. The article explores different reasons for this variation, ranging from socio-economic conditions, the inflow of labour migrants to the role of labour market institutions and political actors. Countries badly affected by the crisis and with a recent influx of labour migrants were more likely to respond to mobilised groups lobbying for restrictive policies than those countries weathering the crisis relatively better but suffering from continuing labour shortages. The article examines the changing conditions and the role of mobilised stakeholders to explain policy change in selected European countries. It also presents an updated index on states' openness to high-skilled immigrants to measure change over time. The findings are based on position statements of stakeholders, official documents and media coverage.

Introduction

The recent economic crisis provided a shock to the system, and led governments to scramble for solutions to problems of falling economic growth, high unemployment and weak job creation. Calls for the protection of native workers became louder and many European governments responded by restricting immigration policies, even towards the highly skilled. High-skilled immigrants are defined here as those with a university degree, working in occupations in relevant sectors (such as engineering, medical sciences, information communications and technology) and/or earning high incomes. European countries have faced different challenges and thus the cross-national variation in the demand for policy restrictions or openness is remarkable. Some countries used the crisis as an opportunity to restrict their high-skilled immigration (HSI thereafter) policies, while others took advantage of the crisis for further liberalisation. The article explores different reasons for this variation, ranging from socio-economic conditions, the inflow of labour migrants to the role of labour market institutions and political actors.[1] The global crisis response is important to study because the crisis has affected most parts of the world and, for the first time, national policies have also targeted highly skilled immigrants.

The argument is that countries badly affected by the crisis and with a recent influx of migrant workers were more likely to respond to mobilised groups lobbying for restrictive policies than those countries weathering the crisis relatively better but suffering from continuing labour shortages. This argument builds on existing literature on the crisis and migration policy responses (e.g. Awad 2009; Cerna, Hollifield, and Hynes 2015; Collett 2011; Ghosh 2011; Green and Winters 2010; Hatton 2014; Kuptsch 2012; Nieuwenhuysen, Duncan, and Neerup 2012), the power of stakeholders through business cycles, and voice and exit frameworks (e.g. Milner and Keohane 1996; Shughart, Tollison, and Kimenyi 1986), as well as the literature on the political mobilisation of actors (e.g. Birkland 1998; Kingdon 1995; Rowley and Moldoveanu 2003). The article provides two contributions to the literature. First, it offers an explanation of HSI policy changes in times of crisis by analysing different factors and how they have affected the mobilisation of stakeholders. Second, the article makes an empirical contribution by updating an existing index on states' openness to high-skilled immigrants to measure policy change over time.

The article proceeds as follows. First, it offers a literature review and develops the main argument and hypotheses. Next, the article measures HSI policy openness through a constructed index of openness to high-skilled immigrants, comparing 2007 and 2012. The subsequent section surveys selected European countries (Germany, Ireland, Sweden and the UK) and examines changing conditions as well as the actions of stakeholders to explain policy change. The article concludes with a discussion of the implications of the crisis on HSI policies for the study of public policy, and offers some ideas for further research. The findings are based on position statements of stakeholders, official documents and media coverage.

Literature and argument

How can we explain cross-national HSI policy change, promoted by an external shock such as the economic crisis? The article draws on three sets of literatures. First, scholars have analysed migration policy responses to the crisis and have identified different factors leading to policy change (see Awad 2009; Castles and Vezolli 2009; Cerna, Hollifield, and Hynes 2015; Collett 2011; Ghosh 2011; Kuptsch 2012; Nieuwenhuysen, Duncan, and Neerup 2012; Papademetriou and Terrazas 2009; Papademetriou et al. 2010). For instance, Kuptsch (2012) proposes that only countries with a recent high influx of migrants took drastic policy measures, while Collett (2011) suggests that policy responses (in migrant integration) varied due to factors such as the severity of the impact of the crisis, the nature of immigration and the length of time spent developing and implementing integration policies in each country. Others such as Hatton (2014) argue that the crisis has led to few restrictive changes. Hence it is necessary to analyse whether policy responses were an effect of the crisis or rather of long-term developments (see Green and Winters 2010).

A second set of literature considers the power of stakeholders linked with business cycles as well as voice and exit frameworks. Milner and Keohane (1996) have analysed the effects of internationalisation and argue that 'governments will have to be concerned about threats of exit and hence non-investment by mobile capital' since they benefit electorally from prosperity (Milner and Keohane 1996, 250). Owners of mobile factors of production (i.e. financial capital) and firms who are able to shift their production abroad gain bargaining power over immobile factors of production (e.g. mostly low-skilled labour) and firms relying on locally specific assets. These actors may be able to threaten an 'exit' in order to increase their influence (voice) in national politics (Hirschman 1970; Milner and Keohane 1996, 250). In times of economic prosperity, multinational companies (e. g. Microsoft) have threatened to relocate their operations outside the USA. Microsoft demonstrated credibility when it opened a subsidiary in Canada, a country with a more liberal HSI policy (Author's interview with Microsoft, October 2007). According to Shughart, Tollison, and Kimenyi (1986), as a country's economy goes through the business cycle, its policy-mix shifts. Capitalists/owners are more influential during economic growth because they have an incentive to lobby for more open immigration policies to relieve upward pressure on wages during tight labour markets (Shughart, Tollison, and Kimenyi 1986).

In economic downturns, however, demand for labour inputs decreases, pressuring wage levels downward. Workers receive greater leverage because unions have an incentive to lobby for more restrictive immigration policy to prevent an unfavourable expansion in the labour force. Employers are then burdened with increased wages due to smaller labour supply (Shughart, Tollison, and Kimenyi 1986, 85). Hence power asymmetries can change between actors depending on the conditions (Heyes and Hyland 2012).

A third group of scholars examines the political mobilisation of stakeholders to explain policy change. Birkland (1998) argues that focusing events (i.e. sudden relatively uncommon events such as a disaster or a crisis) can lead interest groups, government leaders, policy entrepreneurs or members of the public to identify new problems or pay greater attention to existing but dormant problems, searching for solutions in the wake of apparent policy failure. In a similar vein, Kingdon (1995) finds that the shared perception between actors that the time for a change has come is not sufficient, but requires a focusing event to become a political item on the agenda. Discontent (and organised) stakeholder groups also need to have (monetary or non-monetary) resources to be able to mobilise to pursue their common interests (Rowley and Moldoveanu 2003). The crisis can be further seen as a window of opportunity for policy change, but actors have to use the crisis in such a way to achieve their policy preferences (Kingdon 1995). While crises can trigger more restrictive immigration policies, this is more likely when public pressure for such changes had previously built up (Green and Winters 2010, 1063).

Framework

Drawing on these three sets of literatures, the preferences of actors regarding HSI policy responses to the crisis are expected to unfold in the following way. I assume there are three different actors in production, that is, native high-skilled labour, native low-skilled labour and capital. Economic theory suggests that high-skilled immigrants should be preferred by their complements in production (i.e. native low-skilled labour and capital). In contrast, they should be opposed by their substitutes, meaning native high-skilled labour, due to (at least perception of) labour market competition (e.g. Boeri et al. 2012; Chiswick 2005; Malhotra, Margalit, and Hyunjung Mo 2013; Mayda 2006).[2] With HSI, the supply of qualified workers increases, which then decreases the wages in the sector (Borjas 2003). Borjas's findings indicate that a 10% increase through immigration in the number of Ph.D. graduates in a given sector decreases the earnings by about 3–4% (Borjas 2006).

Native low-skilled labour is moderately pro-HSI as they are complements (Mayda 2006; O'Rourke and Sinnott 2006). These workers can benefit from HSI due to greater productivity and wages through increased demand for labour services (Chiswick 2005). Capital[3] is here the owners/employers in high-skilled sectors (e.g. engineering and high-technology) who will strongly favour HSI because they can benefit from lower wages. These employers will support HSI more in the case of sectoral labour market shortages where outsourcing is not possible, for instance in immobile sectors or occupations with personal contact (Farrell 2005).

In a few cases, one actor has enough power to achieve the desired policy output. This is also more likely in a crisis which may grant one group more power to lobby and achieve policy change. However, in most cases actors have to work together to reach their preferences such as through building coalitions, especially in countries where both labour and capital groups are part of policy-making (see Cerna 2014a). Winners are determined through the institutional set-up, including a privileged position in the political system through financial means or voters.

Policy change can take place when exogenous factors intensify preferences of actors who then lobby harder for their desired interests. These structural factors can be shifting economic and social conditions (e.g. higher unemployment, greater labour market shortages, worsening economic growth and greater influx of migrant workers) or change in government. Once preferences of actors intensify, they will seek to mobilise to achieve their desired policy output.

Actors' preferences are particularly strong when aggregated at the institutional level. As Bartram (2005, 25) notes, 'institutions distribute power unequally to different types of actors – power to set the agendas as well as to determine outcomes'. In order to aggregate preferences, the three actors can gain representation through interest groups (i.e. unions/professional associations and employers' associations) or the political system (i.e. political parties, links between interest groups and parties) (Cerna 2014a).[4]

Interest groups who represent particular actors (such as unions or professional associations) play an active role in influencing HSI policy (see Facchini, Mayda, and Mishra 2011; Freeman 1995, 2006).[5] Unions have often taken a protectionist position though some have been more open towards immigrants (for an overview of different union positions, see Penninx and Roosblad 2000). This has varied according to their organisation along skill lines, union density, union confederation centralisation/coordination and access to policy-making (Freeman and Kessler 2008, 671). Hence unions have not always been pro-immigration as some of the literature might suggest (see Penninx and Roosblad 2000). Professional associations and high-skilled unions representing native high-skilled workers have been active in some countries in pushing for more restrictions.

In times of economic crisis, the protection of native (high-skilled) workers has been even more important as political parties have sought to gain electoral votes and offered representation for more restrictive HSI preferences. In a 2009 survey, the majority of the population in five European Union (EU) countries (Italy, Spain, the UK, Germany and France) favoured further restrictions on (overall) immigration; for the first three of these countries, the percentage was higher than 75% (Pew Research Centre 2009). Governments have reacted quickly to changing economic conditions and citizen demands. It is surprising, Koser (2010, 18) argues, that 'within just six months of the onset of the global financial crisis ... a number of governments responded by placing restrictions either on the entry of migrant workers or on their terms of employment'. The changes did not take place on the basis of economic evidence, but rather in 'response to political and popular pressure' (Koser 2010).

While political parties play a role in proposing policy changes and reacting to voters' demands (Breunig and Luedtke 2008; Helbling 2013), it is more difficult to predict their position regarding HSI on the left-right spectrum. Since workers can be low- or high-skilled, it is not always clear which party will support their preferences. For instance, left parties have represented the interests of workers and called for protection in some countries (such as Sweden), while these parties have also pushed through more open HSI policies in Germany or the UK due to their 'new left' stance. Conversely, right (liberal) parties have sometimes called for more open policies to respond to their business constituency (e.g. Ireland, Sweden), but in other countries including the UK, conservative parties have proposed and implemented policy restrictions towards the highly skilled to respond to their more nativist constituency and high-income voters. In addition, parties on the far-right spectrum are more likely to call for restrictions of immigrants in general (Helbling 2013; Kitschelt 1995).

As we would expect from the literature, capital has lost power during the crisis due to decreased demand and political leverage, while (high-skilled) labour has gained influence in order to push for its restrictive preferences. In many countries, the crisis has led to a shift of power and influence from capital to (high-skilled) labour as regulators have redistributed labour's losses to companies (Shughart, Tollison, and Kimenyi 1986).[6] National institutions have often given advantage to organised groups (in this case high-skilled unions/professional associations), affording them access and voice and thus preventing capital from taking full advantage of its mobility (Milner and Keohane 1996, 250). High-skilled and low-skilled labour have sometimes united in efforts to support the protection of all workers by pushing for restrictions on (high-skilled) immigrants.

Drawing on the political mobilisation literature, the economic crisis can be classified as a focusing event which was harmful to a number of sectors. The mobilisation of stakeholders means that the crisis provided an opportunity for negatively affected groups to increase their efforts for a policy change and offered advantage in overcoming barriers of access (Birkland 1998; Kingdon 1995). For instance, organised high-skilled workers were able to demand more protection and lobby successfully for restrictions in HSI policy, despite not being in a politically advantaged position before the crisis. These pro-change groups could mobilise in several ways, ranging from membership drives and appeals to donations, to writing letters to political leaders and demonstrating (Birkland 1998). Based on this logic, we could expect countries badly affected by the crisis more likely to respond to mobilised groups lobbying for restrictive policies than those countries weathering the crisis relatively better but suffering from continuing labour shortages.

Evidence of changing policy openness to high-skilled immigrants

There are different ways of analysing policy change during the crisis. For instance, Kuptsch (2012, 23) categorises the level of change by (1) new rules (e.g. introducing new legislation or programmes), (2) adaptation of rules (e.g. reducing numeral limits) and (3) application of rules such as greater scrutiny of labour market tests). For simplicity reasons, policy responses are differentiated here only by restrictions or greater openness/liberalisation.

Based on the OECD (2009), restrictiveness is defined in the following way: when one of the following elements is altered to make the policy more restrictive, such as giving preferential treatment to native workers, omitting sectors from shortage occupation lists, reinforcing labour market tests, decreasing numbers of quotas/numerical limits, limiting non-discretionary flows (e.g. family reunification, work permits for spouses) and halting certain immigration programmes. Openness/liberalisation is the opposite but can also refer to no change in the status quo.

Measuring policy change over time

To demonstrate policy variation in HSI policies, it is important to measure policy openness and restrictiveness. Earlier work (e.g. Cerna 2014b) includes a 2007 index on states' openness to high-skilled immigrants, while this article presents an updated 2012 version. The index applies only to temporary (often demand-led) programmes, thus while some countries are depicted to have imposed restrictions, their permanent (supply-led) programmes might not have changed. Temporary policy is expected to be affected the most by the economic crisis because it responds more quickly to changing conditions and labour demands.

Twenty countries were chosen to represent different migration histories, and interest groups' involvement in policy-making. The index is disaggregated into admissions mechanism and work permit rights (made up of six indicators: numerical caps, labour market test, labour protection, employer portability, spouse's work rights and permanent residency rights). Scores are assigned to each of the six categories from 3 (=highly restrictive), 2 (=moderately restrictive), 1 (=minimally restrictive) to 0 (=highly open). All policies are ranked on the same criteria. The individual points for the six categories are then added and converted into an index, where the most restrictive country receives a value of 100 (Cerna 2014b).

Figure 1 indicates that considerable change has taken place within five years in the countries under consideration. 'Policy change' refers to a change in legislation, leading to shifts in one or more of the policy indicators of the index. Some countries became more HSI-restrictive while others liberalised their HSI policies. The economic crisis has played a key role in a number of countries who then restricted their policies to respond to the demands of their native workers or used the crisis as an opportunity to justify implementing restrictions.

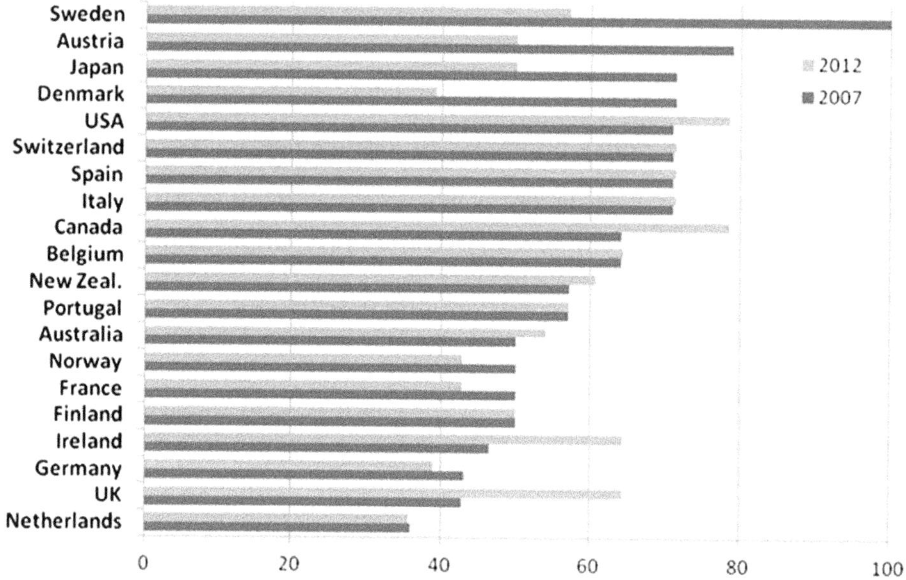

Figure 1. Change in HSI openness index (2007–2012). Source: Author's own data. Notes: The higher the overall score, the more HSI restrictive is the country. 100 = Sweden in 2007. All points relate to its base score.

The figure above suggests that Sweden underwent a significant liberalisation of HSI policy, as have Austria, Denmark and Japan. In contrast, the UK and Ireland became considerably more restrictive. Canada also restricted its HSI policy over the five year period, mostly due to the crisis and subsequent policy response in the temporary labour immigration policy.[7] Many countries experienced some change in policy (though mostly minor). However, few countries (e.g. France, Portugal, The Netherlands) did not have any major policy change. How can we explain the varying HSI policy responses?

Sources of change and hypotheses

According to the argument advanced earlier, countries are more likely to respond with policy restrictions when socio-economic conditions have deteriorated and/or a high influx of immigrants has taken place before the crisis, whereas policy liberalisation is more likely when labour shortages persist. This is linked with the previously discussed exogenous factors which can intensify the preferences of actors in the proposed framework. The mobilisation of stakeholders then acts as an intermediate variable. The following hypotheses are proposed.

> Hypothesis 1: If countries are badly affected by the crisis (in terms of economic output or unemployment rate), they are more likely to respond with restrictive policies. Mobilisation of (high-skilled) labour is expected in this instance. (This implies that if countries are not affected, restrictive policies are less likely.)

The extent of the impact of the crisis on countries (measured here by GDP growth and unemployment rate) is hypothesised to play an important role in influencing countries' policy responses (e.g. Collett 2011). The largest decreases in economic output in 2009 took place in Ireland (−7%), followed by Denmark and Italy (see Table 1).

The unemployment rate also indicates the extent of the economic crisis and is expected to be important for policy responses. Most countries below have experienced an increase in their rates especially in 2009. Ireland and Spain stand out with significant changes from 2008 to 2009. When differentiated by educational attainment (taken as proxy for skill level), the unemployment rate for the tertiary educated increased in many countries, particularly again, Ireland and Spain (Table 2).

> Hypothesis 2: If countries have had a high influx of labour immigrants before the crisis, they are more likely to adopt restrictive policies. Mobilisation of (high-skilled) labour is expected in this instance.

The extent of immigration inflows before the crisis is expected to play an important role in influencing countries' policy responses (see Kuptsch 2012). Figure 2 portrays the inflow of foreign workers into selected OECD countries. While some countries experienced growth in 2008 (such as Australia, Canada and New Zealand), this could be due to a backlog in applications. In 2009, inflows of labour migrants mostly decreased.

> Hypothesis 3: If more than one of these conditions (economic output, unemployment rate, and high influx of immigrants) occur simultaneously, countries are more likely to respond with severely more restrictive HSI policies. Mobilisation of (high-skilled) labour is expected in this instance.

I hypothesise that the likelihood of adopting a more restrictive policy will be even greater when these conditions occur simultaneously.

Table 1. World economic output in selected countries.

	2007	2008	2009	2010
Australia	4.7	2.5	1.4	2.5
Austria	3.7	1.4	−3.8	2.3
Canada	2.2	0.7	−2.8	3.2
Czech Republic	5.7	3.1	−4.7	2.7
Denmark	1.6	−0.8	−5.8	1.3
Finland	5.3	0.3	−8.4	3.7
France	2.2	−0.2	−2.6	1.4
Germany	3.4	0.8	−5.1	3.6
Ireland	5.2	−3.0	−7.0	−0.4
Italy	1.7	−1.2	−5.5	1.8
Japan	2.2	−1.0	−5.5	4.4
Korea	5.1	2.3	0.3	6.3
Netherlands	3.9	1.8	−3.6	1.6
New Zealand	2.8	−0.1	−2.1	1.2
Portugal	2.4	0.0	−2.9	1.4
Spain	3.5	0.9	−3.7	−0.1
Sweden	3.4	−0.8	−4.8	5.8
Switzerland	3.6	2.1	−1.9	2.7
UK	3.5	−1.1	−4.1	2.1
USA	1.9	0.3	−3.5	3.0

Source: IMF, World Economic Outlook (2012, 191).
Note: Measured as annual per cent change in real GDP.

Table 2. Unemployment rates for 25–64 year olds in selected countries, total and by tertiary education.

	2007		2008		2009		2010	
	Total	T. ed.	Total	T. ed.	Total	T. ed.	Total	T. ed.
Australia	4.5	2.2	4.3	2.1	5.7	3.3	5.3	2.8
Austria	4.5	2.4	3.9	1.7	4.8	2.2	4.5	2.3
Canada	6.1	3.9	6.2	4.1	8.4	5.3	6.2	5.4
Czech Republic	5.4	1.5	4.4	1.5	6.8	2.2	7.4	2.5
Denmark	3.8	3.0	3.5	2.2	6.1	3.7	7.6	4.6
Finland	6.9	3.6	6.4	3.3	8.4	4.0	8.5	4.4
France	8.0	4.7	7.4	4.0	9.2	5.0	9.4	4.9
Germany	8.7	3.8	7.6	3.3	7.8	3.4	7.2	3.1
Ireland	4.9	2.3	5.8	3.0	12.2	6.1	13.9	6.8
Italy	6.2	4.2	6.8	4.3	7.9	5.1	8.5	5.6
Japan	4.1	2.9	4.2	3.1	5.3	3.6	5.3	3.8
Korea	3.4	2.9	3.3	2.6	3.8	3.2	3.8	3.3
Netherlands	3.6	1.8	3.0	1.6	3.7	2.0	4.5	2.3
New Zealand	3.8	2.2	4.3	2.4	6.3	3.3	6.7	3.8
Portugal	8.5	6.6	8.1	5.8	10.0	5.6	11.4	6.3
Spain	8.3	4.8	11.4	5.8	18.1	9.0	20.2	10.4
Sweden	6.2	3.4	6.1	3.3	8.5	4.3	8.5	4.3
Switzerland	3.7	2.1	3.4	1.8	4.2	2.7	4.6	3.0
UK	5.3	2.2	5.4	2.8	7.8	3.4	7.9	3.4
USA	4.7	2.1	5.8	2.4	9.4	4.9	9.8	5.3

Source: OECD statistics and OECD 2012a, 134–135.

Notes: Measured as percentage of labour force. T. ed. refers to tertiary education (both Type B and Type A and advanced research programmes in ISCED 1997 classification).

Hypothesis 4: If countries face continuing labour shortages, they are more likely to respond with liberal policies. Mobilisation of capital is expected in this instance.

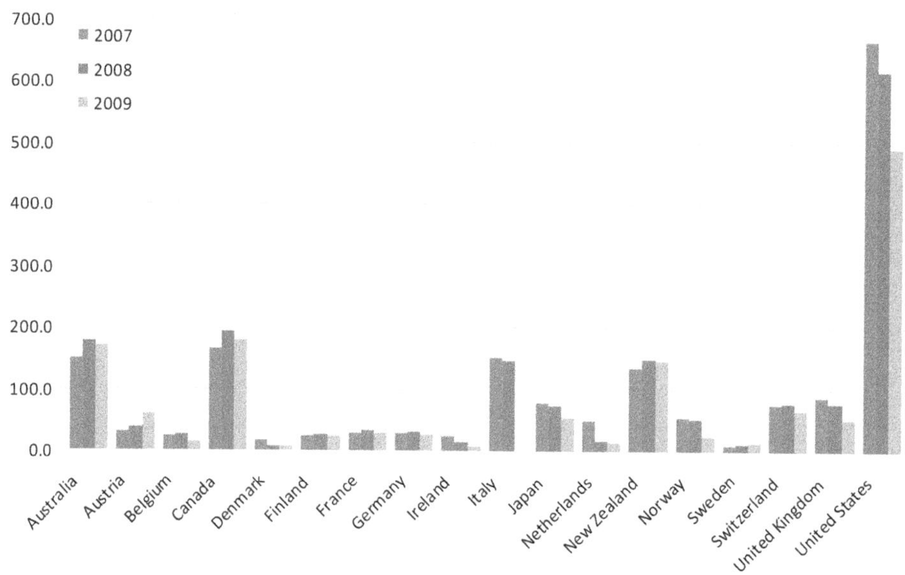

Figure 2. Inflows of foreign workers into selected OECD countries (permanent and temporary migration combined). Source: OECD statistics. Note: Portugal and Spain was excluded from the figure since only 2007 data is available (102,500 workers for Spain). Unfortunately the data does not differentiate between high- and low-skilled immigrants.

Policy liberalisation is expected when countries continue to suffer from labour shortages during the crisis. To examine the extent of labour shortages, Table 3 presents job vacancy rates in selected European countries, which differ cross-nationally. Overall, there was a peak in job vacancy rates in the EU area in 2007, though it decreased considerably in 2008 and had a historic low in 2009.

In all of these cases, the changing conditions can intensify the preferences of actors who then mobilise to push for their desired output. The extent of mobilisation is assessed here as the level of political activity displayed by the stakeholder group (labour or capital). Groups can mobilise in different ways, such as writing letters to political leaders, taking part in consultations or protests, lobbying and building alliances with other groups. They can affect outcomes by displaying legitimacy, urgency or power (Mitchell, Agle, and Wood 1997).

In order to explain policy variation during the economic crisis, Table 4 presents a typology of the presented factors (i.e. economic output, unemployment rate, influx of migrants, extent of labour shortages) and the policy response categories across four countries. Qualitative comparative analysis (QCA),[8] in particular fuzzy sets,[9] is used as a typology building tool which can be helpful for studying variation in policy responses. It allows to access qualitative and quantitative differentiation for the degree and type of HSI policy responses to the crisis (Kvist 2006, 171–175).

Immigration responses to the crisis

This section examines the proposed hypotheses and typology by presenting a qualitative look at recent policy responses in the HSI area, based on a review of secondary sources.[10] Many countries have responded to the crisis by tightening access to labour migration channels which also often targeted the highly skilled (OECD 2010). This included cutting quotas (e.g. Italy, Spain), changing the labour market test (e.g. the UK, Canada) and redrawing shortage lists (e.g. Australia, New Zealand, the UK) (OECD 2010, 79). Some countries (e.g. the UK and the USA) have made it harder for employers to hire migrant workers by imposing stricter conditions on job advertisements and work permit renewals (Migration News 2009a).

Table 3. Job vacancy rates in European countries.

	2007	2008	2009	2010
Austria	2.0	..	1.5	1.7
Czech Republic	2.8	3.2	1.2	1.0
Finland	2.5	2.3	1.6	1.7
Germany	3.6	3.1	2.2	2.2
Ireland	..	..	0.4	0.4
Netherlands	3.0	2.9	1.7	1.6
Portugal	0.6	0.6	0.4	0.4
Spain	0.8	0.7	0.7	0.9
Sweden	1.4	1.2	0.8	1.0
Switzerland	1.6	1.5	1.0	1.1
UK	2.4	2.2	1.6	1.6

Source: Eurostat.

Note: Measured as unmet labour demand. Some missing data for particular years or countries. Data do not distinguish between low- and high-skilled vacancies.

Table 4. Typology of factors and policy responses during the crisis.

	Economic output (change)	Unemployment rate (change)	Influx of labour migrants before crisis	Extent of labour shortages	Mobilisation of stakeholders	Policy change
Germany	−5.1 (medium)	0.1 (low)	Relatively low	High	Capital	Open (minor)
Ireland	−7.0 (high)	3.1 (high)	Relatively high	Low	Labour	Restrictive (major)
Sweden	−4.8 (medium)	1.0 (medium)	Relatively low	Medium-high	Capital	Open (major)
UK	−4.4 (medium)	0.6 (medium)	Relatively high	Medium	Labour	Restrictive (major)

Source: Data is based on Tables 1–3, and Figures 1 and 2.

Notes: Economic output (real GDP) is measured as annual percent change in 2009; unemployment rate is measured as percentage of labour force with tertiary education from 2008 to 2009.

Economic output (Table 1) ranges from −7.0 to 1.4. Low = change < 2.0, medium = 2.0≤change < 6.0, high = change ≥ 6.0

Unemployment rate change in tertiary education (Table 2) ranges from −0.2 to 3.2. Low = change < 0.5, medium = 0.5≤change < 1.5, high = change ≥ 1.5

Influx of labour migrants (Figure 2) considers numbers relative to the population/labour force.

Extent of labour shortages (Table 3) considers the job vacancy rate (or unmet labour demand) in 2009, and ranges from 0.4 to 2.2 for available data. Low = rate < 0.5, medium = 0.5≤rate < 2.0, high = ≥ 2.0.

Mobilisation of stakeholders is based on expectations from different factors.

Policy change (Figure 1): Minor = change < 20 points in index scores, major = change ≥ 20 points in index scores. It is possible that change occurred due to other reasons than the economic crisis. In this case, it is further explained in the qualitative part of the article.

However, there are differences in countries' responses. Some countries have not implemented new restrictions or even liberalised policy as they considered HSI as a stimulus during the economic crisis. There are several reasons for this. Labour shortages can persist due to geographic mismatches and occupations with specialised knowledge, such as health care and certain technical jobs (e.g. engineering, ICT and advanced sciences) (OECD 2009, 2012b). Native workers cannot easily and quickly retrain for these jobs (The Economist 2009a, 2009b). In addition, (unemployed) native or migrant workers might be unwilling to move to regions with jobs because they have family ties or might not want to take unattractive jobs (Papademetriou and Terrazas 2009). Education and experience remain important and high-skilled migrants are seen as a stimulus for ailing economies.

In contrast, adopting restrictive labour migration policies during the crisis is likely to be 'sticky and stay even when recovery is achieved for a variety of reasons' (Abella and Ducanes 2009, 10). The ILO stated that 'the global crisis will not be solved by protectionist solutions. Rather, such solutions would depress world trade and investment, further aggravating the recession' (ILO 2009, 59). Thomas Friedman, a *New York Times* op-ed columnist, argued that the main principle 'should be to stimulate everything that makes us smarter and attracts more smart people to our shores. That is the best way to create good jobs' (Friedman 2009). Overall, the impact of the crisis and its policy responses have varied, which the next sections highlight.

Selected European cases

This section discusses several European cases (namely Germany, Ireland, Sweden and the UK), which display a variation of key factors (such as the impact of the economic crisis, the inflow of immigrants and the extent of labour shortages) and policy responses (see Table 4). In particular, it analyses how certain stakeholders became mobilised and elaborates on reasons why HSI policy change occurred between 2007 and 2012 as provided by the constructed index above.

While many European countries responded to the crisis by changing their national HSI policies, developments in this domain were also visible at the EU level. In May 2009, the Council of the EU adopted the Directive on the Blue Card, which created some common conditions for high-skilled immigrants (Council 2009). All EU member states participated, except for Denmark, Ireland and the UK who used the opt-out mechanism in the case of EU immigration policies. The Blue Card was a result of long discussions among member states and the European Commission, and was formulated by the Commission already in the 2005 Policy Plan on Legal Migration. Thus it was not a direct result of the crisis. The Blue Card is not explored further in this article as it was only implemented in Germany in 2012 and Sweden in 2013, and the following case studies focus on national policy responses to the crisis.

UK

The UK used to be one of the most open countries to high-skilled immigrants, starting with its two-tier work permit system in the 1990s, followed by the 2002 Highly Skilled Migrant Programme, and the 2008 Points-Based System – where high-skilled immigrants could qualify for a work permit with sufficient points (in Tier 1). Capital actors, later joined by low-skilled labour (such as the Trade Union Congress – TUC), lobbied successfully for an open HSI policy.

Nevertheless, the former Labour government implemented some policy restrictions as a response to the economic crisis: admissions were decreased based on a reduction of certain skills on labour shortage lists and the entry for non-EU migrants to enter the UK was made more difficult (BBC 2009; IOM 2010; Migration News 2009b). More specifically, the minimum salary level and qualification level was raised for Tier 1 of the Points-Based System (IOM 2010). For Tier 2 (skilled workers with a job offer), more rules on the advertising on jobs was placed, required a four-week advertising period from autumn 2009. Additionally, the number of shortage occupations on the shortage list was reduced and arrangements for building a domestic skills base were strengthened (IOM 2010, 198).

The new Conservative-Liberal Democratic government then announced in the fall of 2010 that an immigration cap would be imposed from April 2011, applying especially to HSI. Tier 1 (General Route) was discontinued, and a new 'exceptional talent visa' for 1,000 scientists and engineers per year was introduced in late 2011 (Cerna 2014a). In addition, the UK decreased admissions based on reduction of certain skills on labour shortage lists and made it more difficult for non-EU migrants to enter the UK (IOM 2010). High-skilled immigrants could continue entering the UK under Tier 2 (general migrant) visa once they had a job offer and fulfilled other conditions.

The UK has experienced a significant policy shift over 20 years – from very open where capital pushed for HSI liberalisation to recently a more restrictive policy. High-skilled labour's preferences intensified with the economic crisis as the unemployment rate increased, economic output decreased and a relatively large influx of migrants had arrived before the crisis.

Hence groups of native workers became involved in lobbying for increased HSI restrictions. Unions/professional associations were supported in their push for policy restrictions by political representatives. For example, former Labour Prime Minister Gordon Brown called for 'British jobs for British workers' (Summers 2009). High-skilled labour achieved that more restrictive conditions were imposed on policies towards high-skilled immigrants. Hence the crisis served as a window of opportunity to implement these restrictions.

When the new Conservative coalition government came into power in 2010, a more restrictive policy was further implemented to send a clear signal to voters that it was protecting native workers. In addition, while not analysed in detail here, some non-economic factors played a role in the government's decision to implement restrictions. The government wanted to reduce the number of immigrants[11] to respond to general anti-immigration calls from the population and to rectify 'policy failures' by the previous Labour government (BBC 2012).

As the typology would predict, the UK implemented significant restrictions. The country had a relatively high influx of labour migrants (Hypothesis 2), and was affected by the crisis in terms of unemployment rate and economic output (Hypothesis 1). This prompted (high-skilled) labour representatives to mobilise even more and push for HSI restrictions (broadly confirming Hypothesis 3). Nevertheless, the implemented restrictions were more severe than we would expect from the typology since the unemployment rate of the highly educated (and labour shortages) changed only to some extent. The more severe policy response is likely due to a change in government with a generally restrictive stance on immigration for both economic and political reasons (see Paul, this volume). The considerable policy change is visible in the 2012 index.

Ireland

Ireland is another country which implemented considerable policy restrictions as the economy was badly affected during the crisis, especially in terms of unemployment rate and economic output and relatively high influx of migrants before the crisis. The extent of its labour shortages also decreased during the crisis, which reduced the need for immigrants (including high-skilled ones).

Ireland has had two ways of attracting high-skilled immigrants: (1) the work permit system and (2) since 2007, the Green Card programme. The work permit system was liberalised in 2001 and allowed a significant number of migrants to obtain a work permit. Under the Green Card programme, if a migrant worker earned more than €60,000/year, there were no restrictions (e.g. ICT occupations) (IOM 2010). If his/her yearly salary was between €30,000 and €60,000, the migrant worker could only apply for occupations in sectors with labour market shortages (Cerna 2010). Ireland's booming economy and the demand of employers for foreign labour encouraged the government to look favourably towards an open labour immigration policy (OECD 2007). This open policy is also visible in the 2007 index of openness to high-skilled immigrants.

However, the government tightened up its immigrant work permit system in response to growing unemployment and decreased economic output during the economic crisis. These restrictions were prompted since 'fear of job losses, increasing competition for resources and heightened feelings of insecurity have led to scapegoating and increased racism towards migrants for "taking Irish jobs"' (IOM 2010, 92). This echoed with representatives of native workers who lost out due to the crisis. Some politicians called for a clampdown on work permits and the creation of tougher permit rules. For instance, former Fianna Fail Member of Parliament Noel O'Flynn remarked: 'What in the name of God are we doing bringing workers in when we haven't work for our own people?' (Molony 2009).

Real policy change followed this rhetoric across the political spectrum. The stricter rules, involving a revision of the qualifying conditions for new permits, came into effect on 1 June 2009. Mary Coughlan, former Minister for Enterprise, Trade and Employment, said that a 'labour-market needs test for all future applications and renewals would allow "maximum opportunity" for any available job vacancies to be filled by Irish people and those from the European Economic Area' (AFP 2009). This was clearly a response to the economic crisis.

From 1 June 2009, employers who wanted to hire non-EU foreigners had to pay them at least EUR 30,000 a year. Some occupations were closed for them, and the spouses of non-EU migrant workers had to qualify separately for work permits. Instead of seeking local workers for four weeks, Irish employers had to recruit locally for eight weeks before they received permission to hire non-EU foreigners (Migration News 2009b).[12] These crisis-induced restrictions can be seen in the updated 2012 index, as Ireland moved in the ranking towards the more restrictive group of countries.

A survey carried out by *The Irish Times* in October 2009 found that over two thirds of Irish people (72%) wanted to see a reduction in the number of (overall labour) migrants, with almost 30% preferring most migrants to leave (O'Brien 2009). Poles and other nationals from the accession countries (i.e. A8) were EU citizens and could not be expelled. However, 'the 30,000 non-EU foreigners among Ireland's two million workers had no such protections' (Migration News 2009b). Ireland could restrict policies towards third-country nationals, which were not treated under EU directives (Cerna 2010).

As the typology would predict, representatives of labour (including the highly skilled) mobilised to lobby for restrictions in Ireland, as the country was badly affected by the crisis in terms of economic output and unemployment rate (Hypothesis 1), and had received a recent influx of labour migrants (Hypothesis 2). Policy-makers introduced policy restrictions to respond to calls of native workers for job protection. The Irish case largely confirms Hypothesis 3 as several conditions occurred simultaneously, intensifying the impact on HSI policy.

Sweden

While the two aforementioned countries implemented policy restrictions, Sweden is a different case. It was the most restrictive country in the 2007 ranking due to a coalition between high- and low-skilled labour. They were represented through the link between the union confederations (SACO, TCO and LO)[13] and the Social Democrats in government at that time, and opposed any lobbying by employers for policy liberalisation (Cerna 2014a). However, the country finally implemented a new immigration law (for both high- and low-skilled immigration) in December 2008, which made labour immigration employer-driven and reduced the role of unions. If an applicant had a salary offer from a Swedish employer that corresponded with existing collective agreements, s/he was eligible to obtain a work permit. This policy change took place after years of lobbying by employers' associations, and was facilitated by the new centre-right (liberal) government which came to power. While a coalition between high- and low-skilled labour was able to block any policy change for many years (and they were supported by the previous Social Democratic government), this link was broken with the new government in 2006 (Cerna 2014a).

The following policy liberalisation is evident in the 2012 index – Sweden has experienced a considerable policy shift from restrictive to relatively open (indicated by the large difference in the index). Even though not a direct response, the policy was implemented during the economic crisis, and the criteria were not adjusted because the system was said to be flexible and employer-led (OECD 2011). The challenge of labour shortages and ageing population continued even during the crisis. Åsa Carlander, Counsellor at the Swedish Representation to the EU, noted that Sweden had a 'demand-driven system for labour migration in place that is self-regulatory' (Carlander 2009a). It was important to have a flexible system in order to respond to labour market demands when the negative economic trend would turn. She further argued that 'efforts to stifle migration are both unwise and short-sighted' (Carlander 2009b).

Nonetheless, such position could be supported because Sweden had a relatively low influx of migrants before the crisis, and was not affected economically to the same extent as other countries including Ireland and the UK (see Quirico 2012). In addition, labour shortages continued and were expected to increase even more in the future. This pushed employers to mobilise for more policy openness. Thus the typology predicts fairly well the Swedish case and broadly confirms Hypothesis 4.

Germany

Germany, placed relatively close to the UK in the 2007 index, experimented with a Green Card for ICT specialists in 2000, which was then extended to other sectors in the reformed 2005 Immigration Law. Due to continuing difficulties of attracting high-skilled immigrants, the Labour Migration Control Act of 2009 was implemented, which lowered salary requirements for immigrants and introduced provisions for students and the self-employed (Cerna 2014a). This policy liberalisation took place in times of crisis since Germany recognised that as 'a knowledge society and world economy, the country is dependent on the exchange of knowledge and ideas especially through HSI'.[14] More open HSI policy was possible due to the coalition between employers' and industrial associations (such as BDA and BDI) and low-skilled union confederation (DGB),[15] which were involved in policy-making with the government (Cerna 2014a). They argued that Germany needed high-skilled immigrants to fill increasing labour shortages and a restrictive policy would only hurt the economy and society. The low inflow of high-skilled immigrants and continued labour shortages during the crisis led to further lobbying by mostly capital and can explain the more open 2009 Labour Migration Act (IOM 2010). The open HSI policy and further change is also visible in the 2012 index.

In Germany, the effects anticipated by the typology fit rather well with HSI politics. In addition to the relatively low influx of high-skilled immigrants, Germany was one of the few European countries which recovered fairly quickly from the crisis (Hypothesis 1). It also continued to suffer from considerable labour shortages despite high unemployment rate and thus needed (high-skilled) immigrants. This led employers to mobilise for more liberal HSI policy during the crisis. Overall, the German case largely confirms

Hypothesis 4. Nevertheless, the policy change in 2009 was smaller than expected since a major change had already taken place in 2005.

Conclusions

In the past decade, the importance of and interest in HSI has grown worldwide. While HSI has been for a long time a key element of immigration policies in countries such as Australia and Canada, New Zealand and the USA, European policies have developed more gradually and to varying extent of liberalisation. Especially employers in high-tech and engineering sectors have pressured governments for more open HSI policies, while the position of unions has been rather sector dependent.

The article has analysed the impact of the recent economic crisis on migration and examined how selected European countries have responded in terms of their HSI policies. The crisis served as a window of opportunity for policy change, but it was used differently by countries. Whereas some implemented policy restrictions, others remained open towards high-skilled immigrants or even further liberalised their policies. The article has argued that this variation in policy responses is due to differential impact the crisis has had on countries as well as the recent influx of migrants which has prompted different stakeholders to mobilise. This mobilisation was conditioned on existing national labour market and political institutions. The article has proposed several hypotheses and a typology on HSI policy responses, and has examined them through four case studies (Germany, Ireland, Sweden and the UK).

The case studies have demonstrated varying national policy responses to the crisis. Whereas Ireland and the UK implemented some restrictions due to the mobilisation of (high-skilled) labour, Germany and Sweden introduced more open policies as employers continued to strongly lobby for and support this output. Even though the context is important in immigration policy, the four countries can represent wider country groupings. Other countries would be expected to follow a similar policy response if the socio-economic conditions and mobilisation of stakeholders were comparable to the cases in this article. This should be examined in future research through QCA methods since the article did not go as far as testing the proposed typology and hypotheses due to the limited number of data points.

The recent economic crisis has highlighted some challenges and pressures on governments. With increasing unemployment rates, falling GDP, and worsening economic and social conditions, it has been difficult to sell to voters that different sectors required high-skilled immigrants to fill labour shortages. Native workers have demanded more protection from the government and employers so that they would receive preference over immigrants. In addition, far right parties also posed a risk and the national immigration context should be considered (Caviedes 2010, 48).

The article has provided an empirical investigation of HSI policy openness by presenting change in indices between 2007 and 2012. There is a growing trend among scholars in political science, public policy and economics to build indices on the openness of immigration policies (for recent examples, see Ruhs 2013). This article's contribution to the index of openness to high-skilled immigrants will be a useful tool for testing the impact of policy outputs on policy outcomes, and should be extended in future work.

Recent research indicates that changes in legislation which favour highly skilled immigrants relative to the less educated resulted in an increase by 12% (Boeri et al. 2012, 68 and 87). However, policy liberalisation does not necessarily translate into desired policy outcome (i.e. greater inflow of high-skilled immigrants). Existing literature suggests that immigrants do not only select locations based on policies, but on their expectation which ones will provide the highest returns to their skills (Borjas, Bronars, and Trejo 1992; Greenwood 1985). Other factors also play a role in the selection, including language, presence of networks and family issues. This is an important finding for policy-making and should be analysed further.

Overall, the continuing impact of the economic crisis on HSI policy will remain important and thus scholars should consider this topic in their theoretical and empirical research. The area of HSI is not without contradictions and poses various challenges for scholars and policy-makers alike. This article has only served as a stepping stone to a fruitful research area.

Notes

1. While efforts were made to focus on attitudes, policies and flows of high-skilled immigrants, data were not always available in a disaggregated form, so information may at times refer to general labour immigration.
2. There are many debates in the literature on this assumption. Some critics argue that high-skilled immigrants can be complementary to native high-skilled workers, for instance due to agglomeration effects in technological hubs and cities (e.g. Florida 2002; Glaeser and Saiz 2003) or the innovative effects of migrants (Venturini, Montobbio, and Fassio 2012; Venturini 2013), while others claim that high-skilled labour always prefers high-skilled to low-skilled immigration (e.g. Hainmüller and Hiscox 2010). But the position of native high-skilled workers can vary across countries, sectors and age groups (for a nuanced discussion, see Venturini, Montobbio, and Fassio 2012; Venturini 2013; Strom, Venturini, and Villosio 2013).
3. For simplicity reasons, capital is not further differentiated into low- and high-skilled sectors as both can be open to more high-skilled immigrants.
4. While other actors can become engaged in the debate (e.g. independent and governmental analysts, research centres, and NGOs), the concentration lies on unions and employers' associations.
5. For the US case, Facchini, Mayda, and Mishra (2011) show that sectors with active labour unions and professional unions tend to see a lower number of high-skilled immigrants (measured in number of H-1B visas). In contrast, when employers increase their lobbying on immigration, it leads to an increase of H-1B visas allocated to the particular sector.
6. However, some argue that immigration policy does not follow the business cycle (see Hollifield and Wilson 2010).
7. Nevertheless, its permanent (points system) programme has not been changed as high-skilled immigrants were considered stimulus for the economy.
8. Incorporating qualitative and quantitative approaches, QCA combines different independent variables, which may explain the outcome (Ragin 1987).
9. Fuzzy sets can identify ideal types based on theoretical concepts and also measure the set membership of a case in an ideal type (see Kvist 2006).
10. This section builds upon earlier work on the economic crisis and HSI (Cerna 2010; Cerna, Hollifield, and Hynes 2015).
11. From 2010, the UK government has tried to reduce net migration from the hundreds of thousands to the tens of thousands.

12. However, some of these work permit restrictions were dropped in September 2009 (IOM 2010).
13. These refer to LO (Landsorganisationen i Sverige), TCO (Tjänstemännens Centralorganisation) and SACO (Sveriges akademikers centralorganisation) – union confederations of low-skilled, skilled and high-skilled workers, respectively.
14. Schütz (2010).
15. BDA refers to Bundesvereinigung Deutscher Arbeitgeberverbände (confederation of German employers), BDI to Bundesvereinigung der Deutschen Industrie (confederation of German industries) and DGB to Deutscher Gewerkschaftsbund (German union confederation).

Acknowledgements

I would like to thank William Hynes for his advice in preparing this article, and Ibrahim Awad, Michael Dorsch, Christof Roos, Natascha Zaun and the anonymous reviewers for their valuable comments at different stages. Earlier versions were presented at the Collaborative Research Centre 597 'Transformations of the State' final conference at the University of Bremen (4–5 April 2014) and a lecture at the Central European University (14 April 2014), and I am grateful to the participants for their helpful feedback.

Disclosure statement

No potential conflict of interest was reported by the author.

References

Abella, M., and G. Ducanes. 2009. "The Effect of the Global Economic Crisis on Asian Migrant Workers and Governments' Responses." *ILO Regional Office Paper*.

AFP (Agence France Press). 2009. "Ireland to Curb Immigrant Work Permit System." *Agence France Press*, April 17.

Awad, I. 2009. "The Global Economic Crisis and Migrant Workers: Impact and Response." *International Migration Programme*. Geneva: ILO.

Bartram, D. 2005. *International Labour Migration: Foreign Workers and Public Policy*. New York: Palgrave Macmillan.

BBC. 2009. "Migrants face tighter work rules." *BBC News*, February 22.

BBC. 2012. "Miliband Shifts Immigration Policy, Saying Labour 'Got it Wrong'." *BBC*, June 22.

Birkland, T. 1998. "Focusing Events, Mobilisation and Agenda-Setting." *Journal of Public Policy* 18 (1): 53–74.

Boeri, T. et al. 2012. *Brain Drain and Brain Gain: The Global Competition to Attract High-Skilled Migrants*. Oxford: Oxford University Press.

Borjas, G. 2003. "The Labour Demand Curve is Downward Sloping: Re-examining the Impact of Immigration on the Labour Market." *Quarterly Journal of Economics* 118 (4): 1335–1374.

Borjas, G. 2006. "Immigration in High-skill Labour Markets: The Impact of Foreign Students on the Earnings of Doctorates." *NBER Working Paper* 12085.

Borjas, G. J., S. G. Bronars, and S. J. Trejo. 1992. "Self-Selection and Internal Migration in the United States." *Journal of Urban Economics* 32 (2): 159–185.

Breunig, C., and A. Luedtke. 2008. "What Motivates the Gatekeepers? Explaining Governing Party Preferences on Immigration." *Governance* 21 (1): 123–146.

Carlander, A. 2009a. "Labour Migration and Circular Migration." *Statement*, Prague, June 5–6.

Carlander, A. 2009b. "Migration and the Economic Crisis." *Statement*, Brussels, December 10.

Castles, S., and S. Vezolli. 2009. "The Global Economic Crisis and Migration: Temporary Interruption or Structural Change?" *Paradigmes* 2: 68–75.

Caviedes, A. 2010. *Prying open Fortress Europe: The Turn to Sectoral Labour Migration*. Lanham: Lexington Books.

Cerna, L. 2010. "Policies and Practices of Highly Skilled Migration in Times of Economic Crisis." *International Migration Papers* 99. Geneva: International Labour Organisation.

Cerna, L. 2014a. "Attracting High-Skilled Immigrants: Policies in Comparative Perspective." *International Migration* 52 (3): 69–84.

Cerna, L. 2014b. "The EU Blue Card: Preferences, Policies and Negotiations between Member States." *Migration Studies* 2 (1): 73–96.

Cerna, L., J. Hollifield, and W. Hynes. 2015. "Trade, Migration and the Crisis of Globalisation." In *Palgrave Handbook of the Law and Policy of International Labour Migration*, edited by M. Panizzon, G. Zürcher, and E. Fornalé, 17–40. Basingstoke: Palgrave.

Chiswick, B. 2005. "High-skilled Immigration in the International Arena." *IZA Discussion Paper 1782.*

Collett, E. 2011. *Immigrant Integration in Europe in a Time of Austerity.* Washington, DC: Migration Policy Institute.

Council. 2009. *Council Directive 2009/50/EC of 25 May 2009 on the Conditions of Entry and Residence of Third-country Nationals for the Purposes of Highly Qualified Employment.* Brussels: Council of Ministers.

Facchini, G., A. M. Mayda, and P. Mishra. 2011. "Do Interest Groups Affect US Immigration Policy?" *Journal of International Economics* 85: 114–128.

Farrell, D. et al. 2005. *The Emerging Global Labour Market: Part 1- the Demand for Offshore Talent in Services.* San Francisco, CA: McKinsey Global Institute.

Florida, R. 2002. "The Economic Geography of Talent." *Annals of the Association of American Geographers* 92 (4): 743–755.

Freeman, G. 1995. "Modes of Immigration Politics in Liberal Democratic States." *International Migration Review* 29 (4): 881–902.

Freeman, G. 2006. "National Models, Policy Types and the Politics of Immigration in Liberal Democracies." *West European Politics* 29 (2): 227–247.

Freeman, G., and A. Kessler. 2008. "Political Economy and Migration Policy." *Journal of Ethnic and Migration Studies* 34 (4): 655–678.

Friedman, T. 2009. "The Open-door Bailout." *New York Times*, Op-Ed, February 11.

Ghosh, B. 2011. *The Global Economic Crisis and Migration: Where Do We Go From Here?* Geneva: International Organisation for Migration.

Glaeser, E., and A. Saiz. 2003. "The Rise of the Skilled City." *NBER Working Paper* 1091. Boston: NBER.

Green, T., and A. Winters. 2010. "Economic Crisis and Migration: Learning from the Past and the Present." *World Economy* 33 (9): 1053–1072.

Greenwood, M. J. 1985. "Human Migration: Theory, Models, and Empirical Studies." *Journal of Regional Science* 25 (4): 521–544.

Hainmüller, J., and M. Hiscox. 2010. "Attitudes Towards Highly Skilled and Low Skilled Immigration: Evidence from a Survey Experiment." *American Political Science Review* 104 (1): 61–84.

Hatton, T. 2014. "The Slump and Immigration Policy in Europe." *IZA Discussion Paper* 7985.

Helbling, M. 2013. "Framing Immigration in Western Europe." *Journal of Ethnic and Migration Studies* 40 (1): 21–41.

Heyes, J., and M. Hyland. 2012. "Supporting, Recruiting and Organizing Migrant Workers in Ireland the United Kingdom: A Review of Trade Unions Practices." In *EU Labour Migration and Labour Markets in Troubled Times. Skills Mismatch, Return and Policy Responses*, edited by B. Galgoczi, J. Leschke, and A. Watt, 211–234. Farnham: Ashgate.

Hirschman, A. 1970. *Exit, Voice and Loyalty: Responses to Decline in Firms, Organisations, and States.* Cambridge: Harvard University Press.

Hollifield, J., and C. Wilson. 2010. "Rights-Based Politics, Immigration and the Business Cycle, 1890–2008." In *High-Skilled Immigration in a Global Labour Market*, edited by B. R. Chiswick, 50–80. Washington, DC: AEI Press.

ILO. 2009. *The Financial Crisis: A Decent Work Response.* Geneva: ILO.

IMF. 2012. *World Economic Outlook: Growth Resuming, Dangers Remain.* Washington: IMF, April 2012.

IOM. 2010. *Migration and the Economic Crisis in the European Union: Implications for Policy.* Brussels: IOM.

Kingdon, J. 1995. *Agendas, Alternatives and Public Policies.* New York: Longman.

Kitschelt, H. 1995. *The Radical Right in Western Europe: A Comparative Analysis.* Ann Arbor: University of Michigan Press.

Koser, K. 2010. "The Impact of the Global Financial Crisis on International Migration." *The Whitehead Journal of Diplomacy and International Relations* 11 (1): 13–20.

Kuptsch, C. 2012. "The Economic Crisis and Labour Migration Policy in European Countries." *Comparative Population Studies* 37: 15–32.

Kvist, J. 2006. "Diversity, Ideal Types and Fuzzy Sets in Comparative Welfare State Research." In *Innovative Comparative Methods for Policy Analysis beyond the Quantitative-Qualitative Divide*, edited by B. Rihoux and H. Grimm, 167–184. New York: Springer.

Malhotra, N., Y. Margalit, and C. Hyunjung Mo. 2013. "Economic Explanations for Opposition to Immigration: Distinguishing between Prevalence and Conditional Impact." *American Journal of Political Science* 57 (2): 391–410.

Mayda, A. M. 2006. "Who is Against Immigration? A Cross-country Investigation of Individual Attitudes Towards Immigrants." *The Review of Economics and Statistics* 88: 510–530.

Migration News. 2009a. UC Davis, April 2009 16(2). Accessed July 24, 2015. http://migration.ucdavis.edu/mn/more_entireissue.php?idate=2009_04

Migration News. 2009b. "Obama, Congress." July 16(3). http://migration.ucdavis.edu.

Milner, H., and R. Keohane. 1996. *Internationalisation and Domestic Politics.* Cambridge, MA: Cambridge University Press.

Mitchell, R., V. Agle, and D. Wood. 1997. "Toward a Theory of Stakeholder Identification and Salience: Defining the Principle of Who and What Really Counts." *Academy of Management Review* 22: 853–886.

Molony, S. 2009. "Outspoken TC Calls for Work Permit Clampdown." *Irish Independent*, February 7.

Nieuwenhuysen, J., H. Duncan, and S. Neerup, eds. 2012. *International Migration in Uncertain Times.* Montreal: McGill-Queen's University Press.

O'Brien, C. 2009. "Lack of Jobs Brings Change in Attitudes to Migration." *The Irish Times*, November 24.

OECD. 2007. *International Migration Outlook 2007.* Paris: OECD.

OECD. 2009. *International Migration and the Financial Crisis: Understanding the Links and Shaping Policy Responses.* Paris: OECD.

OECD. 2010. *International Migration Outlook (SOPEMI 2010).* Paris: OECD.

OECD. 2011. *Recruiting Immigrant Workers: Sweden.* Paris: OECD.

OECD. 2012a. *Education at a Glance.* Paris: OECD.

OECD. 2012b. *International Migration Outlook (SOPEMI 2012).* Paris: OECD.

O'Rourke, K., and R. Sinnott. 2006. "The Determinants of Attitudes Towards Immigration." *European Journal of Political Economy* 22: 838–861.

Papademetriou, D., M. Sumption, A. Terrazas, with C. Burkert, S. Loyal, and R. Ferrero-Turión. 2010. *Migration and Immigrants: Two Years after the Financial Collapse: Where do we stand?* Washington, DC: Migration Policy Institute.

Papademetriou, D., and A. Terrazas. 2009. *Immigrants and the Current Economic Crisis: Research Evidence, Policy Challenges and Implications.* Washington, DC: Migration Policy Institute.

Penninx, R., and J. Roosblad, eds. 2000. *Trade Unions, Immigration and Immigrants in Europe 1960–1993.* New York: Berghahn Books.

Pew Research Centre. 2009. *The Pulse of Europe 2009: 20 Years After the Fall of the Berlin Wall – End of Communism Cheered but Now with More Reservations.* Pew Global Attitudes Survey Report, Washington, DC: Pew Research Centre.

Quirico, M. 2012. Labour Migration Governance in Contemporary Europe. The case of Sweden. FIERI – Forum Internazionale ed Europeo Di Richereche sull'Immigrazione, Working Papers, April.

Ragin, C. 1987. *The Comparative Method: Moving Beyond Qualitative and Quantitative Strategies.* Berkeley, CA: University of California Press.

Rowley, T., and Moldoveanu, M. 2003. "When Will Stakeholder Groups Act? An Interest- and Identity-Based Model of Stakeholder Group Mobilisation." *Academy of Management Review* 28 (2): 204–219.

Ruhs, M. 2013. *The Price of Rights: Regulating International Labour Migration*. Princeton, NJ: Princeton University Press.

Schütz, H.-P. 2010. "Bundesregierung befürchtet Notstand." *Stern*, November 17.

Shughart, W., R. Tollison, and M. Kimenyi. 1986. "The Political Economy of Immigration Restrictions." *Yale Journal on Regulation* 51: 79–97.

Strom, S., A. Venturini, and C. Villosio. 2013. "Wage Assimilation: Migrants Versus Natives, Internal Migrants Versus Foreign Migrants." MPC-RSCAS 2013–20.

Summers, D. 2009. "Brown Stands by British Jobs for British Workers Remark." *The Guardian*, January 30.

The Economist. 2009a. "The People Crunch." *The Economist*, January 15.

The Economist. 2009b. "People Protectionism." *The Economist* online, July 1.

Venturini, A. 2013. "Innovation and Human Capital: The Role of Migration." MPC-RSCAS Policy Brief, October.

Venturini, A., F. Montobbio, and C. Fassio. 2012. "Are Migrants Spurring Innovation?" MPC Research Report, November.

Negotiating varieties of capitalism? Crisis and change in contemporary British and German labour migration policies

Regine Paul

ABSTRACT

Just a decade ago, the liberal British and cautious German approaches to labour migration policy (LMP) counted as institutional spillovers of two opposed varieties of capitalism. Since 2014, however, Germany has offered one of the most liberal labour migration legislations across the rich world, while the Coalition government in London has severely curbed the rules of admission. Is the explanatory power of capitalist variation already exhausted for comparative labour migration policies? To what extent has the economic crisis disrupted policy paths? By adopting a cultural political economy perspective, this paper examines the interaction of crisis discourses and capitalist varieties in explaining LMP changes. A comparison shows that Britain treats the liberal market economy's openness to foreign workers as a root cause for a deeply felt migration control crisis and seeks to tame firms' profitability strategies with restrictive policies. By contrast, German decision-makers have come to view the skill provision mechanisms of the coordinated market economy as key cure to the perceived demographic crisis, liberalising migration routes alongside this economic coordination model. Overall, the paper dethrones capitalist varieties as seemingly deterministic informants of labour migration policies. Instead, policies have both the aim and capacity to negotiate national capitalisms according to shifting notions of crisis.

1. Introduction

Less than a decade ago, Britain and Germany counted as two diametrically opposed labour migration policy (LMP) regimes. The New Labour government in the UK had comprehensively liberalised admission policies for non-EU workers since the late 1990s and enabled full free movement for Eastern Europeans in 2004. German policies evolved rather cautiously and upheld restrictions for EU-8 mobility for as long as possible. In comparative political economy scholarship, this variation was interpreted as an institutional spillover of firms' skills provision strategies in two very diverse varieties of capitalism (VoC). Policies seemed to cater relatively neatly to the needs of well-established economic coordination models (Devitt 2011; Menz 2009, 2010). A decade later, in 2014, Britain and Germany have seemingly exchanged their positions as 'liberal' and 'restrictive' labour migration regimes: the OECD (2013) evaluates recent reforms in Berlin as steps towards one of the most liberal entry regimes across the rich world. Moving in the opposite direction, the Coalition government in London has reversed the openness of the early 2000s by curbing admission rules in its promise to limit annual net migration to 'the tens of thousands'.

The empirics of policy change challenges VoC accounts in LMP studies. If neat complementarity with firm's competitiveness strategies is no longer explanatory of policy directions, how else can we depict and explain the relationship between economic coordination and LMP change? This paper reconstructs this relationship from a cultural political economy perspective (Sum and Jessop 2013). I examine how crisis discourses shape policy-makers' (re-)interpretations of economic labour migration needs, trigger policy change, and, eventually, inform a negotiation of national capitalisms through LMPs.

From a cultural political economy perspective, 'crisis' is a central analytical category for the examination of policy shifts: the perception of crisis can disrupt dominant policy discourses and may favour new ideational and institutional arrangements (Sum and Jessop 2013). Such an impact of 'crisis' has proven as empirically valid: Ruhs (2013) argues that economic downturns such as the one experienced recently in Europe can dislocate the dominance of economic efficiency arguments in LMPs. The editorial of this special issue equally highlights the role of the economic crisis as a welcome frame, allowing policy-makers to induce otherwise desired migration policy change. 'Crisis' thus forms the empirical entry point to my *constitutive* comparative explanations of policy change (cf. Héritier 2008).

Adopting an ideographic comparative research design, I analyse the interaction of (a) policy-makers' specific crisis notions, [1] (b) the perceived need for LMP changes, and (c) the role ascribed to economic coordination models in justifying LMP as jointly constitutive for policy change. In order to do so, the approach takes on an interpretive policy analysis (IPA) (Wagenaar 2011; Yanow 2000) of key legislation, policy documents, official statements, and semi-structured expert interviews with 22 policy-makers. Interviews were conducted between 2009 and 2011 and then repeated to discuss policy changes and their relation to crisis[2] with several of the same experts in 2013 and 2014.

To develop my argument, the paper firstly outlines previous accounts that have analysed LMPs as compatible with the VoC. Based on key legislation and policy-makers' justification patterns for the initial revival of LMPs from the late 1990s to the mid-2000s, I reconstruct the ability of such studies to explain Britain and Germany's initial reactivation of labour admissions (Section 2). The neat alignment between LMPs and capitalist coordination models is unsettled empirically in Section 3. More recent legislation indicates considerable departure from VoC paths. A cultural political economy understanding of 'crisis frames' is proposed for a more suitable account of LMP change. In Section 4, policy-makers' justifications for LMP changes are reconstructed from the empirical material. The discussion reconsiders the interaction of capitalist varieties, LMPs and societal notions of crisis in light of our findings, also reflecting on the current refugee crisis in Europe which intensified after research for this article was conducted.

2. Labour migration policies as institutional complementarity in capitalisms

This section appraises the explanatory power initially ascribed to capitalist varieties in LMP research. This sets the ground for a subsequent problematisation of such explanations vis-à-vis more recent policy reforms. The active policy promotion of labour migration since the late 1990s in Europe – after decades of an official recruitment stop – has triggered large academic attention. Scholarship widely agrees that Western European countries shared the rediscovery of migrant workers as 'potentially useful human resources' (Menz 2009, 31), but that varieties of economic growth models have mitigated the meaning of utility in different countries (also see Caviedes 2010; Devitt 2011; Menz 2010). In his pilot study of LMPs in six EU countries, Menz (2009, 261) shows that 'different models of political economy shape distinct strategies for labour recruitment from abroad'. From early on in this emergent research field, divergence in LMPs was hence interpreted as an institutional spillover of different VoC and their skills provision rationalities.

In its original form, the VoC approach distinguishes between two modes of capitalist coordination on a firm level (Hall and Soskice 2001). Both types of capitalisms feature specific 'comparative advantages': liberal market economy (LME) firms tend to rely on radical innovation and short-term profitability while those in coordinated market economies (CMEs) tend to follow incremental innovation strategies. The key contribution of scholars, such as Georg Menz, Alex Caviedes, or Camilla Devitt, was to interrogate the extent to which labour migration could be analysed as yet another institutional complementarity in firms', sectors', and whole national economies' economic coordination strategies. As Menz (2009, 261) notes:

> CME production patterns ... require mainly highly skilled well-trained labour migrants that can easily be integrated into a high value-added production pattern ... LME production patterns necessitate a steady supply of labour migration into both low-wage low-skill service sector positions where poor working conditions and wages are combined with structural flexibility requirements lead to low staff retention. (Also see Menz 2010)

Devitt (2011, 579) adds that 'education and training institutions shape the domestic supply of labour in diverse ways across Western Europe, which has consequences for the quantity and skill-sets of economic migrants required'. These assumptions are partially confirmed in Martin Ruhs' recent analysis of LMPs across 46 receiving countries (2013, 38): 'in the short run we can expect the prevailing production regimes ... to constitute relatively strong and binding constraints on the policy space' and that 'effective policies need to be "incentive compatible" – namely, they need to be in line with and complement the mode of coordination inherent to the prevailing institutional structures'.

In these accounts, by and large, LMEs such as Britain's are associated with the need for generic and easily transferable skills paired with flexible recruitment and redundancy strategies, which allow firms to ensure short-term profitability. Migrant labour also finds its institutional fit as an abundant and flexible labour supply in lower skilled job markets. By contrast, in CMEs such as Germany, firms tend to opt for long-term productivity and stable reputation. They invest more in specialist and firm-specific skills, provide demand-oriented skills through vocational training, retain staff during minor economic downturns, and provide relatively secure and well-paid jobs when compared to LMEs. Here, labour migration would mainly serve as response to specific skills shortages in a cautious demand-oriented manner, but would tend to exclude lower skilled admissions in order to avoid unwanted competition for jobs and excess migration. The following reconstruction of LMPs and their justifications in Britain and Germany (before the recent policy changes) evidences the explanatory power of VoC in the mid-2000s.

2.1. Britain before crisis: flexible skills supply for the LME

Britain has liberalised entry conditions for foreign workers considerably since the late 1990s, earlier and more than elsewhere in Western Europe. While the entry of highly skilled individuals had already been facilitated in the early 1990s under a Conservative government, New Labour added a work permit system for skilled workers in professions experiencing recruitment problems (shortage jobs), a highly skilled migration programme (HSMP) and a sector-based scheme (SBS) for lower skilled migration. It is important to acknowledge that, apart from the SBS, lower skilled migration, though highly relevant as cheap and flexible labour supply according to the LME rationale, remained more strictly controlled in legislation. In practice, however, low-skills recruitment was largely enabled via other routes including family reunion, students, au pairs, working holidaymakers, and high levels of EU mobility as well as via mechanisms of 'semi-compliance' (Ruhs and Anderson 2010), precarious forms of employment and residence (Anderson 2013), and 'wilful negligence' (Wilkinson and Craig 2011) of informal labour markets.

These limitations apart, the liberalising policy changes lead to substantial increases in work permits issued per year with figures rocketing from under 40,000 in 1995 to around 90,000 in 2000, stabilising between 120,000 and 140,000 from 2002 to 2008 (Salt 2009, 92, Table 5.1). In 2008, the government consolidated all existent work routes into a point-based system (PBS). Prime Minister Tony Blair called labour migration 'essential for our continued prosperity' (Home Office 2005, 5). British employers had lobbied actively for permissive labour migration, stressing the advantages of flexible and pragmatic labour supply both in skilled and low-skilled echelons of the job market (Menz 2009, 156ff).

In retrospect, interviewees confirm that the introduction of the PBS was driven by 'the recognition that migrant workers add to the economy. They increase the supply of skills, our access to skills in the UK' (UK Border Agency official, November 2010). Economic openness was the name of the game, it seems, and a widely accepted one, too: 'When the PBS came in in 2008 it's seen as that great model which will help business, there was a very positive rhetoric and public opinion supported it' (former UK Border Agency official, February 2014). And indeed, in its original form, the PBS offered relatively liberal access: by virtue of their graduate level qualifications, earning potentials and professional experience, migrant workers could enter in tier 1 without a specific job offer, without a resident labour market test which would prioritise the employment of Brits, and without any numerical ceiling. Beneficial treatment also applied to domestic graduates who could stay on to look for a job for two years. Tier 2 was more limited as it required a resident labour market test or a job offer in a predefined shortage profession of a certain skill level. Yet, the qualifications threshold was no true barrier with the equivalent to a professional diploma or two A-levels sufficing. Furthermore, employers' mere statement of recruitment difficulty was enough to pass the resident labour market test (more detailed analysis in Paul 2015).

In short, the spirit of the PBS was initially rather welcoming towards newcomers, operating with a supply-driven logic for skilled and high-skilled migrant workers. This openness hinged on endogenous growth assumptions and human capital theory within New Labour's open economy philosophy (Düvell 2007; Layton-Henry 2004; Schain 2008; Somerville 2007) and was seen as 'a paradigmatic example of business-driven labour recruitment schemes' in the liberal market economy' (Menz 2009, 164). Numerical effects of liberalisations were remarkable, especially when compared to Germany. From 1999 to 2008, almost 800,000 incoming non-EU migrants received a work permit, making work and study (38% and 32%, respectively) the two single most important motives for migration to Britain in 2008 (Office for National Statistics 2009).

In addition, the relative openness to EU mobility after the Eastern enlargement constituted a second pillar of the permissive labour migration approach. As one of only three EU-15 countries (with Ireland and Sweden), Britain granted EU-8 nationals immediate labour mobility in 2004. Even though predictions of mobility figures largely underestimated the subsequent movements, policy-makers at the time predominantly regarded the mobility of Eastern Europeans as economically beneficial, especially so in the lower echelons of the labour market:

> What you tend to find is that A8 workers ... are quite flexible and will find their own place in the labour market for the gaps as they arise ... they find their way in, and they're quite resourceful, and quite useful at that lower skilled end of the labour market. (UK Border Agency official, November 2010)

The assumption that EU mobility can serve as a flexible buffer in lower skilled (and frequently not well-paid) labour markets was a core justification of the British liberal approach to free movement – very much in line with LME thinking. The Worker Registration Scheme counted almost 950,000 entries from the EU-8 between May 2004 and March 2009, with most newcomers being Polish (Office for National Statistics 2009). Policy-makers' economic drive aligned well with the paradigmatic needs of LME firms and found its reflection in entry statistics.

2.2. Germany before crisis: satisfying skills demands of the CME

In the late 1990s, when Britain was already actively opening its labour market for migrant workers, Germany was still considered a 'reluctant country of immigration' (e.g. Green 2004). A serious debate about the economic virtues of labour migration only started to gain ground since 2000. This was catalysed by the planned introduction of a German 'Green Card' for IT-specialists. When labour shortages in the IT sector with vacancies of up to 150,000 staff were reported, the verdict was that the national economy 'had to attract highly skilled immigrants to remain economically competitive' gained credibility (Green 2004, 112). Certainly underpinned by a governmental shift towards a Social Democrat-Green majority, this view gradually but significantly changed the policy debate (also see Menz 2009). However, a generally permissive migration policy remained deeply contested, especially by the conservative political opposition at the time. A compromised version of the first organic German Migration Law came into force in January 2005 (Bundesrepublik Deutschland 2004) and introduced rather cautious liberalisations of admission rules (Green 2007; Triadafilopoulos and Schönwälder 2006). Unsurprisingly then, when compared to the large-scale 'guest worker' recruitments in the 1950s and 1960s, entry numbers remained manageable: around 29,000 non-EU employees came to Germany in 2007 and slightly more than 26,000 in 2009 (Parusel and Schneider 2010, 60f).

The Migration Act introduced a permanent residence permit for high-skilled individuals (*Niederlassungserlaubnis*), allowing highly qualified foreigners to settle immediately without further integration requirements. However, the earnings threshold of initially over 80,000 Euros provided a genuine obstacle to high-skilled admissions and de facto jeopardised any supply-driven argumentation – roughly only 800 permits were issued between 2006 and 2010 (Bundesamt für Migration und Flüchtlinge 2011). Most workers came in via the standard temporary residence permit – between approximately 25,000 and 29,500 in the same period (Bundesamt für Migration und Flüchtlinge 2011). The *Aufenthaltserlaubnis* required a job contract, was fixed term, and – unlike for the high-skilled permit – did not offer free labour market access before a migrant worker proved a record of three years of social insurance contributions by means of regular employment. All new migrant workers needed a valid job offer and, with that in hand, to pass the residence labour market test from the responsible Employment Agencies. This demanding check also concerned the most high-skilled routes and thus contrasts the initial supply-driven British system.

The Federal Employment Agency could also block admissions if unemployment was particularly high either in general or in a specific sector or region. This further institutionalised demand-led recruitment, very much in line with what VoC analyses suggest (also see Ruhs 2013). Exceptions from the Agency's involvement include predefined shortages, bilateral agreements with sending countries, high-skilled migrant workers, scientists, IT specialists, and domestic graduates. In skilled shortage occupations, individual admission was facilitated by the 2005 Act. If the applicant's qualifications match a listed shortage, the resident labour market test is waived. The skilled specialist routes were well-used in the late 2000s and, together with domestic graduates, they accounted for almost 40% of all temporary residence permits issued in 2009 (Bundesamt für Migration und Flüchtlinge 2010). Additional labour market protection tools managed low-skilled jobs with the aim of avoiding negative consequences on German unemployment (again, more details in Paul 2015). Unemployment arguments also surfaced when Germany decided to apply transitional free movement restrictions to all but the highly skilled workers from the post 2004 EU accession member states (Labour Ministry official, December 2009).

As a result, much in contrast to the supply-driven thinking behind the British approach, the revival of German LMP has been chiefly demand-led and tightly controlled by labour market coordination institutions. Not even a decade ago then, both countries' LMPs neatly aligned with the institutions and logics of their respective capitalisms and formed an 'incentive-compatible' adjacent of firms' competition strategies (e.g. Ruhs 2013). Alas, recent policy changes challenge the assumption of institutional complementarity profoundly.

3. Policy changes: beyond institutional complementarity explanations

This section reconstructs the directions of labour migration policies in Britain and Germany after their initial reactivation, including policy reforms up to 2013. This demonstrates that both cases no longer follow the neat LME or CME labour migration coordination strategies that were apprehended to explain policy variation in the early 2000s. This section problematises these accounts and proposes an alternative, cultural political economy reading of the relationship between LMP, 'crisis', and capitalist coordination.

3.2. Britain: from laissez-faire to limiting net migration 'by hook or by crook'

Recent policy developments in Britain have fundamentally overhauled the liberal migration approach. After the 2010 inauguration of a Conservative-led government, with the Tories having campaigned on a restrictive migration policy ticket, the pledge for tough entry restrictions dominated the political agenda. Conservative Home Secretary Theresa May announced a reduction of net migration to the 'tens of thousands' until the end of the last parliamentary term (2015), arguing that numbers have been getting out of control (UK Border Agency 2010). Given the state's inability to restrict family reunion and asylum rights, work and student migration became key targets (Migration Advisory Committee 2010). LMP changes brought tougher interpretations of skills requirements, higher wage conditions, and multiplied controls of migrant residents (OECD 2012, 2013).

The supply drive has been diluted significantly, mainly by restrictions within existing policy instruments. The points-base required for entry clearance was raised in 2010, making higher qualifications and/or earnings a precondition. Tier 1 admissions have been limited to 1000 persons and tier 2 entries to 20,700 people annually since April 2011 (Home Office 2011). The abolition of the post-study work route came in 2012. An earnings requirement for tier 2 skilled workers (currently £20,300) as well as a so-called cooling-off period for the renewal of work visas followed. In April 2011, further tier 1 restrictions limited the pool of potentially successful applicants to investors, entrepreneurs, and persons 'with exceptional talent', comprising 'world-leading' scientists and artists with a renowned reputation (Salt 2010). More recently, tier 1 general was closed all together for applicants from overseas, meaning that applications are presently only accepted from persons who already have a permission to enter or stay in Britain (Home Office 2014).

A re-definition of 'skills' has further curtailed the scope for legal labour migration. While New Labour had defined 'skilled' workers in tier 2 as those with NQF level 3 qualifications and included 192 occupations on the shortage list in 2008, David Cameron's administration raised the skill requirements to professional diploma level in 2011 (NQF level 4 – 121 occupations) and to graduate level in 2013 (NQF 6 – 89 occupations) (Migration Advisory Committee 2013, 33).[3] At the same time, tier 3 for lower skilled professions remained inactive and the SBS was phased out alongside the EU's Eastern enlargement (only Bulgarians and Romanians were recruited from 2005 onwards). The coalition government made it clear in 2010 that the suspension of low-skilled recruitment from third countries would be maintained.

All restrictions apart, more beneficial admission and residence rights are still open to well-paid migrants who earn more than 150,000 annually, and to intra-corporate transferees (even though this route has seen some restrictions, too). Currently, no non-EU workers can enter the British labour market without a higher education degree or extensive high-skilled professional experience, and above-average earnings or substantial monetary investment capital. Overall, British policy changes since 2010 mark a turn-around from New Labour's laissez-faire approach, driven by the goal of bringing overall net migration down 'by hook or by crook' (Government advisor, April 2011). Had the relative laissez-faire approach under New Labour furnished the LME with a flexible supply of skills, partly even in the lower skilled echelons of the labour market, such institutional complementarities are severely challenged by the recent restrictive turn.

3.3. Germany: from cautious admissions to one of 'the most liberal admissions regimes'

Since the 2005 Migration Act, Germany has developed its LMP in almost the opposite direction when compared to Britain. Legal amendments introduced several exceptions to the cautious demand-led approach. This chiefly regards graduates of German universities, German schools abroad as well as those who were trained in the domestic vocational education system or acquired equivalent work experience within the country. In 2009, the resident labour market test was abolished all together for graduates of German universities (Bundesministerium für Arbeit und Soziales 2008). Since then, a post-study work permit enables them to seek employment in their academic specialty for up to a year. If successful, graduates can begin a job without subordination to available German and EU workers and receive a temporary residence permit for that purpose. In addition, the shortage list initiated for IT specialists was extended in 2009 to encompass other graduate professions such as medical doctors.

Usage of the settlement permit for high-skilled workers can be expected to increase as the second Merkel government has lowered the earnings threshold considerably in 2012, from initially 88,000 to currently 48,000 Euros. The earnings requirements for immediate settlement in Germany no longer constitute a real barrier for high-skilled applicants. This deliberately strengthens the supply of migrant workers (two Labour Ministry officials, September and October 2013). There have also been facilitations for skilled and unskilled newcomers. A 2013 law targets migrant workers with a vocational training who can fulfil jobs on a newly established 'white list' (*Positivliste*) of structural workforce shortages (Bundesministerium für Wirtschaft und Arbeit 2013). While the Federal Employment Agency still has to confirm admissions in this realm, the obligatory resident labour market test for skilled workers is waived. The same logic applies, for the first time in this form, to access to vocational training itself. Non-European adolescents can now compete on job training contracts openly with national and EU applicants. As the Federal Employment Agency can limit entries numerically, also by country of origin, on the grounds of regional labour market dynamics and integration potential, origin-based recruitment logics might of course survive in the subtext of the policy (on ethnic recruitment patterns see Paul 2013, 2015).

German policy reforms equal a rather large-scale expansion of the specialist demand logic typical of CME. Initially triggered by shortages in the isolated case of IT graduates, permissive LMPs have leaped into non-academic realms of recruitment, too, and have even trickled down to vocational training itself. While skilled foreign labour admissions still pursue demand-oriented logics – a job offer or a vocational training contract is required – the subordination to resident and EU workers is gone and supply-oriented arguments have gained relevance. As the OECD notes in its 2013 Migration Outlook: 'In an attempt to create a reservoir of highly qualified manpower with domestic qualifications, Germany is developing a comprehensive strategy to recruit foreign students to German vocational and university-level programmes and encourage them to stay after graduation' (2013, 152). Policymakers pride themselves for having created 'the most liberal admissions regime for work in the OECD world' (Labour Ministry official, September 2013).

While CME logics of demand-led and specific skills recruitment still play a role in policies, they no longer solely act as breaks to labour migration. They are also used to expand the realm of demand-led admissions into lower-skilled echelons of the labour market and to mainstream economic rationales for a more liberal LMP approach. An atmosphere of 'encouragement' in German LMP replaces the cautious approach initiated in the 2000s, and it most severely contrasts the contemporary British approach of discouraging entries for the sake of reduced net migration.

3.4. Beyond VoC? A cultural political economy lens on policy change

The LMP changes between the early 2000s and 2013 – from very liberal to increasingly restrictive in Britain and from extremely cautious to rather far-reaching liberalisation in Germany – problematise the assumption of neat institutional complementarity of LMPs with firms' paramount capitalist coordination strategies in different capitalisms (Section 2). It is flawed because it underestimates the ability of public policies to withdraw their full support for a dominant economic coordination model based on competing aims. With which alternative approaches can the relationship between economic coordination and LMP change be explained then?

Drawing on the cultural political economy framework of Sum and Jessop (2013), I understand policies as structurally bound but not determined by institutions such as a capitalist production model. From a cultural political economy perspective, any actual policy formation is seen as just one selection – presently dominant and discursively fortified – among many other potential options. The approach

> emphasises the role of semiosis and its material supports in securing social reproduction through the selection and retention of mutually supportive discourses. Conversely, the absence or relative weakness of one or more of these semiotic and/or extra-semiotic conditions may undermine previously dominant discourses … (Sum and Jessop 2013, 214)

By tracing the co-evolution of 'semiotic' (or discursive) and 'extra-semiotic' (or structural) elements of policy-making in a historical logic of scientific discovery (Sum and Jessop 2013), we can expose how LMPs ascribe changing relevance to capitalist coordination structures and how such discursive shifts relate to notions of 'crisis'. Cultural political economy enables us to treat VoC not as a determining structure for LMPs, but as one that is being negotiated with its mutable contextualisation in discourse. This perspective resonates with an IPA design (e.g. Wagenaar 2011; Yanow 2000). IPA acknowledges that policies do not pursue objective or 'given' rationalities, for instance, the economic efficiency logics of a capitalist variety. Rather, 'reason proceeds from choices to notice some things but not others, to include some things and exclude others, and to view the world in a particular way when other visions are possible' (Stone 2012, 380). Overall, LMPs thus represent inevitably *selective* representations of the wider social world which may or may not align with the institutional dynamics of a capitalist variety as a 'category of thought' (Stone 2012) in the pursuit of shifting discursive and political orders (more on selectivity in LMPs in Paul 2015).

4. The interaction of 'crises' frames and capitalist coordination in policy change

In order to capture the shifting norms vested in policies and to explain the restrictions of LMPs in the UK and their liberalisation in Germany against VoC assumptions, this section reconstructs crisis frames from policy-makers' justification of recent LMP changes and examines how and why these frames challenge dominant capitalist coordination models. The comparative analysis indicates that, while the different economic coordination models typically associated with Britain and Germany play an important explanatory role, they do not do so in a functionalist manner. Rather, LMPs reconstruct and negotiate the relationship between migrant labour, economic needs, and other societal concerns in the context of powerful crisis scenarios.

4.1. 'At the moment, economic arguments don't work'[4]: taming the LME in response to the British migration control 'crisis'

The (unexpectedly high) number of newcomers have put the first nails in the coffin of the comparatively liberal LMP approach in Britain (cf. Anderson 2013). The policy change is justified within two main crisis frames:

(1) High net migration[5] and its perceived adverse effects inform the notion of a profound *migration control crisis*. This serves to justify restrictions and dethrones economic efficiency as the dominant policy aim.
(2) With the liberal profitability strategies of employers persisting, the perception of a wider *skills provision crisis* triggers (half-hearted) political attempts to tame firms' recruitment logics in the LME.

Despite the positive fiscal effects of EU free movement (Dustmann, Frattini, and Halls 2010), which interviewees mention appreciatively, the laissez-faire approach to Eastern European mobility attracted increasing criticism. Discussions of 'adverse side effects' in social terms (UK Border Agency official, November 2010) gained ground over economic efficiency rationales:

> [W]e almost certainly made a mistake by opening up when … [others] didn't open up their borders to the A8. And that caused very large numbers to come in. I mean, the largest immigration proportionally that we've ever had in our history! So that was therefore in a sense fairly difficult to accommodate … you suddenly get some towns, which were never used to having any immigrants, and then suddenly they've got 10,000 people from Poland or Lithuania living there. Well that's bound to cause some tension, it can't not do. (Government advisor, November 2010)

The notion of a migration control crisis might have been sparked off by unexpectedly high EU mobility figures, but the Government's inability to restrict free movement directed repercussions mostly to non-EU foreign workers (cf. Ford, Jennings, and Somerville 2015). Indeed, the assumed abundant supply of lower skills within Europe continues to justify the non-admission of lower skilled workers from outside the EU (Paul 2013).

Public concern over migration control increased alongside EU-8 entries: 'net inflows became a large concern' (former UK Border Agency official, February 2014) and 'people thought that work was out of control' (Government advisor, November 2010). As high numbers were considered the cause of crisis, the promise of numerical admission limits became a trump card in the Tories' 2010 electoral campaign. The new Government's 'numbers' game' (Anderson and Ryan 2011) arguably came with a major ideational shift:

> The Labour government very strongly believed in the economic benefits of labour immigration […] Now of course, with the numbers going up drastically, and with public opinion really being very strongly in favour of reducing immigration, to the end of the Labour government they really had to do something. […]. So the concern now is all about numbers. […] it's really about bringing overall net migration down, by hook or by crook […]. (Government advisor, April 2011)
>
> The country just doesn't have confidence that we're running the system in the way that they expect it to be run. So we also need to control numbers, in this case by limiting numbers. (UK Border Agency official, November 2010)

At the same time, policy experts did not conceive of the concurring financial crisis as a driver of restrictive policy changes: 'The restrictions that we were involved in developing have not so much to do with the recession but have followed a trend that was there already' (Government advisor, February 2014). Another expert argues that 'you cannot really plot economic cycles against concerns over migration but you can perhaps plot higher numbers of migrants against public opinion' (former UK Border Agency official, February 2014). Only the reduction of the shortage list for tier 2 admissions and the abolition of the post-study work route in 2012 were justified by referring to increasing British unemployment (Government advisor, February 2014).

Clearly, the notion of a *migration control crisis*, caused by high entry figures and their felt adverse effects rather than by the financial crisis itself, has muted the LME firms' demand for openness for migrant workers. With the government change, [6] New Labour's economic efficiency rationale was marginalised in LMP: 'government decisions about migration since 2010 have not been economy-driven but fully political' (former UK Border Agency official, February 2014).

Considerations of macro-economic coordination also take on significance from another angle. The perceived migration control crisis has unearthed political discontent with businesses' recruitment and profitability strategies in relation to migrant labour. One advisor explains the 'large relevance of the intra-company transfer route in Britain' with a typical LME argument:

> It is well accepted in the UK economy that you can save money by offshoring parts of your business, and intra-corporate transfers then represent a key cog that links offshore parts of big firms back to the UK market and headquarters. (Former UK Border Agency official, February 2014)

On the flipside of this otherwise politically supported business model, interviewees depict a *skills provision crisis* in the LME as a second key justification for LMP restrictions. Prime Minister Cameron himself acknowledges, in an interview with *The Guardian* (2013), that 'Eastern European immigrants should not be blamed for seeking jobs in UK factories when not enough young people in Britain are fully capable of doing the same jobs'. British firms' flexible skilling strategies have increasingly been criticised for creating 'reliance' on migrant labour and not offering enough job opportunities for Brits: 'industries rely too much on low skilled migrant workers. … [they] need to pay people properly, train up Brits to do the jobs, and do not deserve to be supported by the migration system' (UK Border Agency official, February 2014). The same policy-maker, four years earlier, complained about the 'priorities of employers, considering the short term ahead of the long term' and 'not investing enough in skilling people within the country'. Alas, this priority should not surprise. The LME's voluntarist and ad hoc skills provision model with the state's role 'largely relegated to the realm of managing the supply side' has been considered an essential part of British capitalism (Durrant 2014, 1). When challenging firms' reliance on migrant labour government policies do no less than challenge the LME-typical staffing strategy of British firms. Indeed, some comments of policy-makers suggest that, by the help of increased selectivity, Britain tries to focus more on high end and specific skills otherwise associated with a CME:

> The Minister for Immigration was quite struck in India, where he saw applications for [a pizza chain's] store managers going through tier two ICT ... which isn't what the route should be for. So, we see it [the restrictive points recalibration] as a long snake, if you like, and it's like cutting the tail off and keeping the important part. (UK Border Agency official, November 2010)

In this context, the Home Office declared intentions to link the allocation of migrant sponsorship licences to employers' training efforts at home and to even prohibit migrant recruitment in 'priority areas of up-skilling' (UK Border Agency 2010). No specification of these aims has followed as yet: 'we all pay lip service to up-skilling, but it is not really happening or being formalised' (Government advisor, February 2014). The Labour Party has proposed to link firms' establishment of apprenticeship programmes closely to their right to bring in migrant workers (i.e. one apprentice per every migrant sponsored). Yet, this attempt to coordinate British employers' skills strategies in a CME manner is considered 'hard to push through' in an otherwise liberal economy (former UK Border Agency official, February 2014). Indeed, it would ask firms to depart from LME institutions and coordinate training like a CME. If we take VoC serious, such an adoption is impossible without the change of an overall profitability strategy to more trust-based and incremental innovation processes.

The British government seems trapped between the flexible skills demands of the LME and the restriction impulses during a perceived migration control crisis. While not setting out to change the underlying economic coordination model, LMPs currently seek to tame the LME, verbally at least. Policy-makers expect that, as soon as the control crisis diminishes – or is dislocated by a different crisis scenario (as we will see in Germany) – a more open embrace of liberal recruitment might recur:

> It would be difficult to convince ... [the public] of the benefits until they felt that we had migration under control. Once that happens ... we can start espousing the virtues a little bit more, but it's tough at the moment. (UK Border Agency official, November 2010)

4.2. *'When we saw no recession ... we were able to open up rhetorically'[7]: expanding the CME as a cure for the German demographic 'crisis'*

Before the economic crisis in Germany, the vision of a self-sufficient EU labour market that would automatically limit non-EU migration demand for workers was wide-spread among policy-makers. [8] The need to create a 'true EU labour market', which included EU-wide recruitment and coordination mechanisms took priority over labour migration from outside the EU (Labour Ministry official, December 2009). The self-proclaimed need to think and regulate migration issues in accordance with EU labour supply was accompanied, of course, by a timid approach to enlargement toward the East.

Given the recent liberalisations, labour migration increasingly operates alongside, rather than complementing, intensified EU mobility and recruitment coordination. In policy-makers' justification of the liberalised policy arrangement, 'crisis' features as an explanatory factor in two interrelated ways:

- Most importantly, the now dominant *demographic crisis* frame has gained relevance as a catalyser for intensified EU mobility and liberalised LMP alike. It has muted welfare and distributional concerns.
- Secondly, the perceived *good weathering of the financial crisis* in Germany allows the country to 'sell' policy liberalisations, become more attractive as a destination country, cushion crisis effects in other EU countries, and increase VET-skilled and academic workforce supply as a response to the demographic crisis.

The notion of a fundamental *demographic crisis* which fuels systemic skills shortages has gradually established itself as a scenario which trumps shorter term economic and social concerns in German policy-making. In response to demographic change in Germany, the 2011 'Fachkräftekonzept' (concept for skilled workers) was created by the Federal Government and mainstreamed labour migration along one of five 'pathways' to secure skilled labour supply. Migrants' equal access to vocational training, lower earnings thresholds in high-skilled jobs, job search visas and several exceptions regarding the resident labour market test for more skilled professions became key tools to combat the demographic crisis. The same policy expert who stated a limited need to operate LMPs beyond strict demand satisfaction in late 2009 justifies the introduction of supply-driven instruments four years later:

> The demographic development issue is always operating in the background. This means that migration has to be considered as a means of solving the skills shortage issue. .. Germany wants to attract *perpetually more* labour migration in the future. … The role of migration in the demography strategy of the government clearly highlights that … we need *continuous migration from third countries* to cushion the demographic problem. … We ought to stop always leering at specific shortages … and need to arrive at a stronger mix of supply- and demand-driven migration. (Labour Ministry official, September 2013)

The sudden supremacy of the demographic rationale – and its increasing use as 'a mantra' in ministerial rhetoric (senior Labour Ministry official, October 2013) – cannot be underestimated as driver for recent German LMP change. Unlike Britain, Germany experiences a considerable shrinking of the overall population. Low fertility rates paired with ageing particularly reduce the relative share of the working age population. While population projections estimate a growth of more than three million in the UK between 2010 and 2050, the German population is expected to shrink by around eight million (almost 10%). Already in 2010, the German share of the population aged 65 and over has been much higher (20.4%) than in the UK (16.6%) (Eurostat 2008). Newspapers do not get tired reporting that Germany needs annual net inflows of 400,000 migrants to sustain its skills base (Die Zeit 2014). In this scenario, the successful labour market integration of foreign workers also becomes a stabiliser for the social insurance system (senior Labour Ministry official, December 2013). Policy experts therefore predict the policy liberalisations between 2009 and 2013 to be rather sustainable and robust: 'I believe that the demographic problem is independent from economic cycles. … I can hardly imagine rolling back liberalisations based on economic developments' (Labour Ministry official, September 2013).

If the internal demographic crisis serves as a key rationale for LMP liberalisations, the *German experience with the financial crisis* has provided a fertile ground for putting a more liberal mobility and migration policy into practice – all the while without considerable contestation from party competition or public opinion. [9] Arguably, CME skills formation processes have been actively expanded to new migrant groups and exported to crisis-struck parts of the common market. In the second round of interviews led in 2013, the financial crisis tellingly features as a crisis of other EU countries. Given the perceived stability of the German economy and the weakness of others, higher EU entries in Germany are described as 'a matter of European solidarity' (senior Labour Ministry official, December 2013). Mobility becomes part of the bundle of stability mechanisms for weaker common market economies.

This is not just altruism. Rather, German policy-makers see remedies to the demographic crisis in heightened and more coordinated EU mobility. Programmes such as MobiPro-EU, an EU funding programme that is meant to cushion crisis effects for young free movers seeking vocational training or employment in Germany, is described as a win-win (Labour Ministry official, September 2013).

> With high unemployment over there and demand of specialists here, it is normal that one helps each other. … The mutual benefits are accepted now, I think, even if Spain criticised us first, fearing that we wanted to 'steal' their young people. (Senior Labour Ministry official, October 2013)

Such programmes are welcomed precisely because they increase the quality-controlled skills supply for German businesses who would otherwise suffer from the demographic crisis:

> That would be a great deal, winning young people who do their vocational education in Germany, as they would gradually learn the culture and the language alongside the curricula. Meaning that our past courting of academic graduates to stay in Germany after their degrees could be expanded to the realm of vocational training. (Labour Ministry official, September 2013)

However, intensified EU mobility is no longer seen as the sole remedy for skilled labour needs. Exceptions from the EU labour market self-sufficiency claim were already in effect in bilateral recruitment agreements with non-EU countries, mostly for some lower-skilled jobs in high demand areas such as geriatric care. With the demographic crisis narrative on the horizon, policy-makers not only discuss the benefits of introducing supply-driven migration tools; they have increasingly focused their efforts on PR campaigns which can 'sell' the opening-up for migrant workers and raise Germany's attractiveness as a destination country for EU and non-EU workers alike.

In the initial months of the financial crisis, during the first interview phase in late 2009, policy-makers saw the need to sell liberalisations cautiously in order to avoid recoil in public opinion. The hope for a 'pragmatic policy' which would 'polish our reputation abroad as a very open migration country' (senior Labour Ministry official, December 2009) was already powerful then, but the time was not ripe for further liberalisations or PR campaigns:

> During the crisis 2008–2010 we have deliberately waited and have not 'sold' the new liberal tools yet, as we feared that a restrictive public opinion during the crisis could destroy the new approach. As soon as we saw that no recession was taking place [in Germany], we were able to open up rhetorically and start communicating the legal facilitations more offensively. (senior Labour Ministry official, October 2013)

In the spirit of this interpretation, both the Labour Ministry and the Ministry for the Economy and the Federal Office for Employment have jointly started a large-scale PR campaign online in 2013 (www.make-it-in-germany.com). The portal takes pains to sell the advantages of the country's labour market, vocational training and social security systems, rental market, and university landscape. It portrays the country as an attractive, tolerant and secure place to live and work. The government promotes the portal in selected sending countries – at the moment with India, Indonesia, and Vietnam – to ensure that it helps shaping Germany's reputation in the world as an open and agreeable labour-importing country (Labour Ministry official, September 2013).

The relatively optimistic economic atmosphere in Germany during the crisis – unlike in most of its EU neighbours – has arguably kept anti-immigrant voices at bay to some extent (cf. Kim 2010). As in Britain, the key to ensuring acceptance of a liberal migration approach, however, is seen in a 'manageable' number of newcomers. Low entry figures, especially when compared to Britain, seemingly allow for a process of gradual societal enculturation into a more liberal LMP philosophy:

> Well, the numbers [of annual newcomers] are still within manageable scope. The focus is more on 2060, I would say, recognising that a migration model has to be grasped in people's minds first, that structures have to develop – that all takes years, decades even … I don't think it depends so much on the economic situation. (Labour Ministry official, September 2013)

As soon as numbers are considered to be 'too high' from the viewpoint of local residents and public service providers (the current rocketing number of refugees from the war-struck middle East provide a litmus test), the acceptance of the economically liberal migration approach might suffer. As their British homologues in 2010, German policy-makers feeling unencumbered by their present demography-related economy-drive may come to find that 'economic arguments don't work' anymore if a control crisis frame were to gain discursive weight. The recently much heightened numbers of refugees – almost 450,000 new asylum applications were issued in 2015 – constitute the first litmus test for the country's liberal LMP approach then (Bundesamt für Migration und Flüchtlinge 2015).

5. Crisis and the negotiation of capitalism through labour migration policies

This paper problematised the assumption that LMPs neatly support dominant capitalist coordination models empirically. As an alternative explanatory venue for recent policy change, it examined the ways in which policy-makers' crisis frames challenge and reconstruct economic coordination models in LMP change. This concluding section discusses key findings.

Firstly, the analysis suggests that the close theoretical association of reactivated LMPs and VoC might have been premature and somewhat tautological in its argumentation. We rehearse Deborah Stone's remark that policies have the ability to 'view the world in a particular way when other visions are possible' (2012, 380). At the time of policy liberalisation in the late 1990s and early 2000s, decades after an official recruitment stop, economic efficiency arguments had seemingly muted competing migration policy goals. As Section 2 indicates, British and German policy-makers had clearly chosen to embrace the economic benefits of LMPs while ignoring other concerns. It is not really surprising then that policies, which were explicitly justified as boosters of economic growth and companies' competitiveness, followed national institutional patterns of capitalist coordination. This does not mean, however, that competing policy goals such as economic distribution, social and cultural cohesion, public order or national security disappeared. Rather, they were temporarily sidestepped by powerful economic rationales (see also Carmel 2011; Ruhs 2013).

Secondly, the paper highlights the value of a cultural political economy approach to explaining policy change. Crisis frames expose the shifting relevance of competing discourses and institutional arrangements within the twenty-first century LMPs; for instance between dominant economic utility rationales in a given capitalist variety and the social cohesion promises of electoral politics. This is most evident in the British case where the increasingly powerful notion of a migration control crisis has invalidated the previous policy choice of economic openness to EU free movers and migrant workers, thus leading to restrictive policy changes. In Germany, the rise of the demographic crisis frame to the realm of factual knowledge beyond political dispute ('a mantra') has favoured the increasing dominance of CME-driven economic utility rationales and disrupted previously severe social cohesion and unemployment concerns. These findings highlight the instability of policy arrangements as preliminary inevitable winner stories, which concern the best ordering of social and economic relations (cf. Paul 2015; Sum and Jessop 2013).

Just as suggested in the issue's editorial, the economic crisis plays only a marginal role for LMP changes. Both Britain's migration control crisis and Germany's demographic crisis operate independently from the financial turmoil of 2008/2009. If anything, the relatively better or worse weathering of the economic crisis is integrated into the respective dominant crisis frame as additional support. As Section 4 showed, the justification for partial closure in Britain's control crisis scenario ('economic arguments don't work at the moment') and additional liberalisations in Germany's demographic crisis situation ('when we saw no recession, we were able to open up rhetorically'), gained extra credit through references to the national economy's performance during the financial crisis. The German case especially seems to confirm a relative resilience and adaptability of liberal policy ideas, notwithstanding the financial crisis (Schmidt and Thatcher 2013).

Thirdly and directly linked to the previous two points, the recorded policy responses to national crisis frames showcase governments' attempts to negotiate the economic coordination models[10] which underpin firms' staffing and skilling strategies. British policy-makers treat the LME's openness to foreign workers of all skill levels as root cause for the deeply felt migration control crisis. Indeed, the initially and rather enthusiastic facilitation of labour recruitment of the late 1990s has come under sharp attack. The policy answer is to tame firms' typical flexible recruitment strategies with restrictive tools such as closely monitored sponsorship licences, more demanding skills profiles and earning conditions, quotas and more restrictive visas. German decision-makers have, cautiously but steadily, come to view the skills provision mechanisms of the CME as key cure to the perceived demographic crisis. They streamline more skilled and also lower skilled admission routes along the economic coordination model, try to export their vocational training approach to other EU countries, and even enable German firms to recruit non-EU school leavers as vocational trainees. This approach is also maintained during the current refugee 'crisis' which set off after research for this article was conducted: while seeking to limit entries of asylum seekers overall (pursuing a control impulse that seems not dissimilar from the British one described in this article) the German government also facilitates access to vocational training for young refugees and offers a residence perspective to those in training.

Overall, the paper's findings suggest that capitalist varieties should not be mistaken for neutral informants of LMPs. Statutory policies play a much more important role than that of facilitating a distinct capitalist model. Rather than being unidirectional shapers of policies, firms' profitability and competitiveness strategies are themselves under negotiation in LMPs. Depending on their specific crisis discourse, policy-makers marginalise firms' standard skills provision approaches for the sake of competing policy goals, where they can be facilitated, promoted and diffused to new realms. Capitalist varieties may be significantly structurally bound to LMPs, but LMPs entail both the aim and capacity to negotiate national capitalisms according to shifting notions of crisis.

Notes

1. The analysis is inductive and does not prescribe a definition of crisis. While all policy-makers were inquired about the role of the financial crisis in 2008/2009, their answers often entailed other notions of crisis: control crisis, demographic crisis, skills provision crisis, etc.
2. The anonymised list of interviewees can be requested from the author.
3. For example, jobs such as meat-cutter, chefs, and cooks or care assistants have been taken off the shortage list in 2011. Jobs such as purchasing officers, IT operations technicians, and paramedics fell victim in 2012.
4. Former UK Border Agency official, February 2014.
5. 182,000 in 2009 as compared to a negative net balance of 13,000 in Germany (Huddleston and Niessen 2011).
6. As New Labour never fundamentally disagreed with the new Government's stance, party-political cleavages cannot explain policy shift though.
7. Senior official in Federal Ministry of Labour, December 2013.
8. This was much in contrast to the migration debate for high-skilled and specialist labour markets, which were seen as part of a global competition logic and responded to with equally global recruitment strategies (Paul 2012).
9. 'It's become almost boring: everybody agrees', relates a Labour Ministry official in an interview in September 2013.
10. Beyond the focus of this paper lays the question whether these negotiations have the potential to actually change firms' recruitment preferences. British evidence suggests that more restrictive LMPs coexist with a 'wilful negligence' of informal migrant recruitment (Wilkinson and Craig 2011), or what Boswell and Geddes (2011) would call 'policy malintegration' of talk and action. Our point is that policies also have the power to shape firms' opportunities for formal recruitment options against their preferences.

Acknowledgements

Thanks are due to Steffen Mau for his support as a host. I am grateful for the valuable comments by anonymous reviewers, Christof Roos and Natascha Zaun, as well as for feedback by the participants of the final conference of the Collaborative Research Centre 597 'Transformations of the State' at the University of Bremen (4–5 April 2014). Thanks are further due to Jacob Reilley for thorough language editing.

Disclosure Statement

No potential conflict of interest was reported by the authors.

Funding

This research was funded with a post-doc reintegration stipend by the German Academic Exchange Service and conducted at the Bremen International Graduate School of Social Sciences.

References

Anderson, Bridget. 2013. *Us and Them. The Dangerous Politics of Immigration Control.* Oxford: Oxford University Press.

Anderson, Bridget, and Bernhard Ryan. 2011. "Playing the Numbers Game? Understanding the Coalition's Immigration Policy." Seminar organised by COMPAS and the Migration and Law Network, 5 September, London.

Boswell, Christina, and Andrew Geddes. 2011. *Migration and Mobility in the European Union.* Basingstoke: Palgrave Macmillan.

Bundesamt für Migration und Flüchtlinge. 2010. *Migrationsbericht 2009.* Nürnberg.

Bundesamt für Migration und Flüchtlinge. 2011. *Migrationsbericht 2010.* Nürnberg.

Bundesamt für Migration und Flüchtlinge. 2015. *Aktuelle Zahlen zu Asyl.* Nürnberg.

Bundesministerium für Arbeit und Soziales. 2008. *Beitrag der Arbeitsmigration zur Sicherung der Fachkräftebasis in Deutschland.* Berlin.

Bundesministerium für Wirtschaft und Arbeit. 2013. *Verordnung über die Zulassung von Neueinreisenden Ausländern zur Ausübung Einer Beschäftigung (Beschäftigungsverordnung, as Amended in June 2013).* Berlin.

Bundesrepublik Deutschland. 2004. *Gesetz zur Steuerung und Begrenzung der Zuwanderung und zur Regelung des Aufenthalts und der Integration von Unionsbürgern und Ausländern (Zuwanderungsgesetz).* Berlin.

Carmel, Emma. 2011. "European Union Migration Governance: Utility, Security and Integration." In *Migration and Welfare in the New Europe. Social Protection and the Challenges of Migration*, edited by Emma Carmel, Alfio Cerami, and Theo Papadopoulos, 49–66. Bristol: Policy Press.

Caviedes, Alexander. 2010. "The Sectoral Turn in Labour Migration Policy." In *Labour Migration in Europe*, edited by Georg Menz, and Alexander Caviedes, 54–75. Basingstoke: Palgrave Macmillan.

Devitt, Camilla. 2011. "Varieties of Capitalism, Variation in Labour Immigration." *Journal of Ethnic and Migration Studies* 37 (4): 579–96.

Die ZEIT. 2014. "Falscher Akzent". Newspaper article published on 4 December.

Durrant, Hannah. 2014. "Governing Good, Bad and Ugly Workplaces? Explaining the Paradox of State-Steered Voluntarism in New Labour's Skills Strategy for England." *Journal of Education and Work.* First online. doi:10.1080/13639080.2014.987736.

Dustmann, Christian, Tommaso Frattini, and Caroline Halls. 2010. "Assessing the Fiscal Costs and Benefits of A8 Migration to the UK." *Fiscal Studies* 31 (1): 1–41.

Düvell, Franck. 2007. "United Kingdom." In *European Immigration. A Sourcebook*, edited by Anna Triandafyllidou, and Ruby Gropas, 347–59. Aldershot: Ashgate.

Eurostat. 2008. *In the Spotlight. Demographic Change: Challenge or Opportunity?* Brussels: Eurostat.

Ford, Robert, Will Jennings, and Will Somerville. 2015. "Public Opinion, Responsiveness and Constraint: Britain's Three Immigration Policy Regimes." *Journal of Ethnic and Migration Studies* 41 (9): 1391–1411. doi:10.1080/1369183X.2015.1021585.

Green, Simon. 2004. *The Politics of Exclusion: Institutions and Immigration Policy in Contemporary Germany*. Manchester: Manchester University Press.
Green, Simon. 2007. "Zwischen Kontinuität und Wandel: Migrations- und Staatsangehörigkeitspolitik." In *Regieren in der Bundesrepublik Deutschland. Innen- Und Aussenpolitik Seit 1949*, edited by M.G. Schmidt, and R. Zohlnhöfer, 113–34. Wiesbaden: VS Verlag für Sozialwissenschaften.
Hall, Peter A., and David Soskice. 2001. "An Introduction to Varieties of Capitalism." In *Varieties of Capitalism: The Institutional Foundations of Comparative Advantage*, edited by Peter A. Hall, and David Soskice, 1–68. Oxford: Oxford University Press.
Héritier, Adrienne. 2008. "Causal Explanation." In *Approaches and Methodologies in the Social Sciences: A Pluralist Perspective*, edited by Donatella della Porta, and Michael Keating, 61–79. Cambridge: Cambridge University Press.
Home Office. 2005. *Controlling Our Borders: Making Migration Work for Britain. Five Year Strategy for Asylum and Immigration*. London.
Home Office. 2011. *Tier 1 and 2 Immigration Rules, Settlement and Asylum – Written Ministerial Statement*. London.
Home Office. 2014. *Tier 1 Applications*. London.
Huddleston, T. and J. Niessen. 2011. *Migrant Integration Policy Index III*. Brussels: MIPEX
Kim, A. 2010. "Foreign Labour Migration and the Economic Crisis in the EU: Ongoing and Remaining Issues of the Migrant Workforce in Germany." IZA Discussion Papers No. 5134, August.
Layton-Henry, Zig. 2004. "Britain: From Immigration Control to Migration Management." In *Controlling Immigration: A Global Perspective*, edited by Wayne A. Cornelius, Philip L. Martin, and James F. Hollifield, 297–333. Stanford: Stanford University Press.
Menz, Georg. 2009. *The Political Economy of Managed Migration: Nonstate Actors, Europeanization, and the Politics of Designing Migration Policies*. Oxford: Oxford University Press.
Menz, Georg. 2010. "Employers, Trade Unions, Varieties of Capitalism, and Labour Migration Policies." In *Labour Migration in Europe*, edited by Georg Menz, and Alexander Caviedes, 25–53. Basingstoke: Palgrave Macmillan.
Migration Advisory Committee. 2010. *Limits on Migration. Limits on Tier 1 and Tier 2 for 2011/12 and Supporting Policies*. London.
Migration Advisory Committee. 2013. *Immigration and the British Labour Market: The Role of the Migration Advisory Committee*. London.
OECD. 2012. *International Migration Outlook 2012*. Paris.
OECD. 2013. *International Migration Outlook 2013*. Paris.
Office for National Statistics. 2009. *Migration Statistics 2008, Annual Report*. London: ONS, Home Office and Department for Work and Pensions.
Parusel, Bernd, and Jan Schneider. 2010. *Deckung des Arbeitskräftebedarfs Durch Zuwanderung*. Nürnberg: Bundesamt für Migration und Flüchtlinge.
Paul, Regine. 2012. "Limits of the Competition State: The Cultural Political Economy of European Labour Migration Policies." *Critical Policy Studies* 6 (4): 379–401. doi:10.1080/19460171.2012.730764.
Paul, Regine. 2013. "Strategic Contextualisation: Free Movement, Labour Migration Policies and the Governance of Foreign Workers in Europe." *Policy Studies* 32 (2): 122–41. doi:10.1080/01442872.2013.767584.
Paul, Regine. 2015. *The Political Economy of Border-Drawing: Arranging Legality in European Labor Migration Policies*. New York, Oxford: Berghahn Books.
Ruhs, Martin. 2013. *The Price of Rights. Regulating International Labour Migration*. Princeton, NJ: Princeton University Press.
Ruhs, Martin, and Bridget Anderson. 2010. "Semi-Compliance and Illegality in Migrant Labour Markets: An Analysis of Migrants, Employers and the State in the UK." *Population, Space and Place* 16 (3): 195–211. doi:10.1002/psp.588.
Salt, John. 2009. *International Migration and the United Kingdom (Country Report to the OECD)*. Paris.

Salt, John. 2010. *International Migration and the United Kingdom (Country Report to the OECD).* Paris.
Schain, Martin. 2008. *The Politics of Immigration in France, Britain, and the United States: A Comparative Study.* Basingstoke: Palgrave Macmillan.
Schmidt, Vivien A., and Mark Thatcher, eds. 2013. *Resilient Liberalism in Europe's Political Economy.* Cambridge: Cambridge University Press.
Somerville, Will. 2007. *Immigration Under New Labour.* Bristol: Policy Press.
Stone, Deborah. 2012. *Policy Paradox: The Art of Political Decision Making.* New York: W.W. Norton.
Sum, Ngai-Ling, and Bob Jessop. 2013. *Towards a Cultural Political Economy. Putting Culture in Its Place in Political Economy.* Cheltenham: Edward Elgar Publishing.
Triadafilopoulos, Triadafilos, and Karen Schönwälder. 2006. "How the Federal Republic Became an Immigration Country. Norms, Politics and the Failure of West Germany's Guest Worker System." *German Politics and Society* 24 (3): 1–19.
UK Border Agency. 2010. *Limits on Non-EU Economic Migration. A Consultation.* London.
Wagenaar, H. 2011. *Meaning in Action: Interpretation and Dialogue in Policy Analysis.* Armonk, NY: M.E. Sharpe.
Wilkinson, Mick, and Gary Craig. 2011. "Wilful Negligence: Migration Policy, Migrants" Work and the Absence of Social Protection in the UK." In *Migration and Welfare in the 'New' Europe: Social Protection and the Challenges of Integration,* edited by Emma Carmel, Alfio Cerami, and Theo Papadopoulos, 177–90. Bristol: Policy Press.
Yanow, Dvora. 2000. *Conducting Interpretive Policy Analysis.* Thousand Oaks, CA: Sage.

Migration policy reforms in the context of economic and political crises: the case of Belgium

Sonia Gsir, Jean-Michel Lafleur and Mikolaj Stanek

ABSTRACT

A body of literature has examined the role of 'crises' on policy-making. Yet, we observe that endogenous or exogenous events called 'crisis-events' are often randomly chosen as sweeping explanations for reforms in migration and integration policy. Thus, we attempt to find answers for the question of how the latest financial and economic crisis affected policy-making in the area of migration and integration. We apply a combination of interest-based and ideas-based theories to the case of Belgium in order to question the role of crises in policy reforms in the field of migration and integration. Multiple political and economic crises have affected the country since 2007. Examining these crises and immigration politics we argue that electoral competition both between and within the Francophone and Flemish party systems continues to be the main driver of migration and integration policy reform. Yet, we also discover a cumulative effect of economic and political crises: while the intention of restricting immigration has remained largely unchanged over the years, the policy instruments employed to reach this objective have changed with the political and economic crises.

1. Introduction

Crises are generally considered as 'turning points' (Alink, Boin, and T'Hart 2001, 300) and the global financial crisis of 2008 was undoubtedly a crucial one in Europe. The crisis triggered many reforms in economic and financial policies all over Europe but its effect on migration policies is a research topic that has received surprisingly little attention. Part of the reason for this may be that, based on the observation of previous crises, the assumption is that economic crises are strictly considered as opportunities to implement restrictive immigration policies. For instance, the Great Depression of the 1920s and the Oil Crises of the 1970s were both occasions during which states implemented stronger barriers to immigration as a response to deteriorating labour market conditions. In the case of the current economic crisis, scholars have also noted that two kinds of impact have affected immigrants primarily (Papademetriou, Sumption, and Somerville 2009; Papademetriou and Terrazas 2009; Cerna 2010). Firstly, the economic crisis has tightened regulations on migration control as well as integration policies. Secondly, the crisis has greatly worsened labour market conditions which – together with rising xenophobia and protectionism in destination countries – has contributed to growing unemployment, a decrease in migration flow, as well as waves of return migration to certain countries of origin.

In this article, we intend to question the simplistic link between economic crises and the adoption of restrictive immigration policies. More precisely, we hypothesise that narratives built by policy-makers to justify reforms in the context of economic crisis may obscure broader social, economic or political variables that are equally or more relevant in understanding policy reform processes. Analysing the case of Belgium, this article explains in particular how political and economic crises conflate and create pressure for limited policy reforms while leaving policy objectives untouched.

Studying small open economies like Belgium is particularly relevant in understanding the effect of crises on policy reforms. According to the political economy literature, such economies are particularly vulnerable in the global economy since they are 'forced to expose themselves to the chill winds of world markets and global competition given the small size of their domestic markets' (Obinger et al. 2010, 6). The dependence of these economies on the world market thus makes them particularly exposed to global crises – like the 2008 financial and economic crisis – but also potentially more adaptable and reactive to changing socio-economic conditions. Belgium's federal structure and its ongoing ethno-linguistic conflict, however, significantly complicate the process of policy reform. Belgium has two party systems – Flemish and Francophone – and different parties compete within each political system exclusively for the votes of citizens belonging to their own ethno-linguistic community. [1] Over the years, these two party systems have revealed strong differences in the ideological preferences of Belgian citizens: Flemish voters prefer centre-right and nationalist parties, while centre-left parties dominate the Francophone party system. The devolution process in Belgium has granted Regions with important prerogatives in the field of integration (with the exception of nationality and voting rights) but most of the immigration policies are still designed at the national level.

Immigration and integration policies have undergone profound transformations since the beginning of the economic crisis in Belgium. Yet, we posit that policy objectives have remained largely untouched since the 1970s: that is, the goal is to restrict immigration. For this reason, we argue that the recession merely constituted an opportunity to adjust existing policy instruments and to adopt new ones to reach those same goals. Most importantly, we show below that the economic crisis in Belgium only partly explains the policy reforms that have been implemented. In 2007 and in 2010–2011, Belgium also went through two of the most severe political crises of its history, leaving the country without a government for several months. These political crises revealed major political divergences between the Flemish and Francophone parties, which eventually led to the formation of a government in 2011 that excluded the country's biggest political party (the National Flemish Alliance, hereafter the N-VA). This government, however, implemented the migration policy promoted by the oppositional N-VA in order to appeal to voters of the party.

In this article, our objective is twofold: first, to show how the context of double (economic and political) crises affects policy-making in the field of migration and integration and second, to examine a possible combined effects of the different crises. To achieve this goal, and in line with George and Bennett (2005), we use a 'process-tracing method' in order to identify the key mechanisms and interactions that reveal the causal process between the crises and the policy reforms. In the first section, we articulate interest-based and ideas-based approaches to policy-making and examine the broader literature on policy-making in times of crisis. As part of this analysis, we posit that while political competition remains the main driver of policy reforms, crises may alter the goals of those policies, alter the settings of policy instruments to reach those goals and even trigger the adoption of new policy instruments.

Second, we focus on the transformation of Belgium's immigration and integration policies in the context of the political and economic crises. We show that this led political parties to mobilise new frames in debates on migration and integration policies. More precisely, we show how three trends have clearly emerged from the diversity of reforms adopted in the last decade: (1) selectivity towards would-be migrants has increased, (2) policies are becoming more coercive as sanctions are made part of policies and (3) social policy has turned into a tool for migration control. Our analysis discusses numerous policy reforms in the 2007–2014 period, with a particular focus on three policies that affected most strongly immigrants themselves but that also generated the greatest number of political debates: (1) the 2011 law on family reunification, (2) the removal of residence permits from EU citizens using welfare and (3) the 2012 reform of nationality law. Using existing literature, parliamentary archives and sources from the press, we show how policy instruments rather than the overall objectives of migration and integration policies have been altered by the crises. Third, we conclude with a discussion on the contribution of the Belgian case study to the understanding of migration policy reforms in the context of crises. This article allows in particular to highlight the combined effects of multiple crises. In a context of the increased politicisation of migration and asylum issues in Europe since 2015, we argue that combining interest-based and ideas-based approaches to policy-making like we do could also be useful to analyse other European states facing economic, political and, humanitarian crises at the same time.

2. Theoretical insights on crises and migration policy reforms

At the outset of this article, we posited that in the aftermath of the global financial crisis, states have implemented protective measures and restrictive immigration policies. For authors such as Kuptsch (2012, 19), migration policy reforms in receiving countries during the global economic crisis consisted mostly of four types of measures: (1) making immigration more difficult, (2) protecting native workers, (3) employing more measures to increase return of immigrants and (4) clamping down on irregular migrants. Yet, while these changes are concomitant with the economic crisis, the question of causality remains. Has the economic crisis triggered the reforms or would they have happened anyway? In other words, how can we avoid endogenous or exogenous events being randomly chosen as sweeping explanations for migration and integration policy reforms?

Scholars have struggled for several decades both to define crises and to theorise their role in policy-making (Hall and Taylor 1996; Legro 2000). A point of departure is to determine whether our understanding of what constitutes a crisis has evolved due to the magnitude and length of the current economic and financial crisis. Nohrsted and Weible (2010, 3) have made a contribution to this debate, noting that crises are usually considered as 'periods of disorder in the seemingly normal development of a system and widespread questioning or discrediting of established policies, practices, and institutions'. The nature of a crisis may, however, differ according to certain variables. First, a crisis may be caused by either an internal or an external shock. While this basic 'external-internal' distinction may appear to be of limited use at first sight, it refers to the geographic scale at which stimuli for policy reforms occur, which, in turn, affects the ability and autonomy of policy-makers to react. This relates to the second axis of variation, which is the intensity of a crisis: not all crises – even when they are described as global (e.g. the 2008 financial and economic crisis) – are equally severe nor do they equally affect all states. However, there is still no agreement in the literature on possible correlations between the scale of a crisis and the importance of the reforms adopted in reaction to it. Third, crises also vary in the responses they provoke, according to the existing prerogatives of policy-makers and most importantly, according to their subjective interpretation of what constitutes an adequate response to the crisis. As observed with the reaction shown by several EU member states to the 2008 financial and economic crisis, the same external crisis with broadly similar effects on their socio-economic situations may lead two states to adopt different reforms in the same policy area or to even adopt reforms in different policy areas.

As mentioned previously, the specificity of the Belgian case study is that over the past decade, the country has gone through both internal and external crises: the financial and economic crisis represented a shock that was external to Belgian policy-makers, while the political crises were very much the result of internal strife between political parties defending the interests of different ethno-linguistic groups. For this reason, studying the Belgian case constitutes an ideal opportunity to identify both the differentiated effects of each type of crisis and the specific effects of their combination on policy-makers.

Because ethno-linguistic tensions between Francophone and Flemish political parties have been a defining feature of Belgian politics for several decades, we believe that an interest-based approach to migration policy reform has historically been the most appropriate choice to understand the evolution of Belgium's migration and integration policies. Following the pluralist model of migration policy-making, states act according to the interests defined by organised groups (e.g. trade unions, lobbies, political parties) guided by economic, political or humanitarian motives (Money 1999; Watts 2002). Following this approach, '[i]mmigration policy is the outcome of a political process through which competing interests interact within bureaucratic, legislative, judicial, and public arenas to construct and implement policies that encourage, discourage, or otherwise regulate the flows of immigrants' (Massey 1999, 307). Freeman's focus on the role of electoral competition in explaining policy reforms is of interest in our case. For Freeman, migration policies must be studied by observing voters, interest groups and their relations with the state: '[t]he optimal immigration policy […] is that preferred by the median voters where voters are utility-maximizers with complete information' (Freeman 1995, 883).

In spite of criticism of the neglect shown by this approach of the symbolic dimension of immigration (Boswell 2007), the role of institutions and ideologies (Hollifield 2000) and the role of judicial processes (Joppke 1998), Freeman's interest-based model seems particularly relevant to us because it is political competition that has framed Belgian migration and integration policies at two levels. First, within each political system, political parties have used migration and integration issues to differentiate themselves and to gain electoral support. Second, at the Federal level where migration policy and parts of the integration policy are designed, the Flemish and Francophone political systems compete with one another as parties are trying to impose their views on national policies. Because of the different ideological orientations between the Flemish and Francophone political systems and because these parties only respond to voters who belong to their own ethno-linguistic group, debates on migration and integration issues often become highly salient before coalition governments at the Federal level can reach a compromise (see, for instance, Jacobs 1999 on the debate on the enfranchisement of foreigners in local elections).

Even though an interest-based analysis aids our understanding of Belgian migration and integration policy in the context of devolution, it does not explain satisfactorily why policies have become increasingly selective and coercive in the context of the political and economic crises of the past decade. It is for this reason that we combine the interest-based perspective with ideas-based theories that stress the influence of ideas and perceptions on policy reforms. According to Muller and Surel (1998), public policies are not aimed at 'solving problems' but rather at constructing a new representation of the problem that puts in place the necessary socio-economic conditions for the problem to be resolved by public authorities. This entails a different vision of policy-making, which involves three central variables that are susceptible to being reformed in times of crisis: 'the overarching goals that guide policy in a particular field, the techniques or policy instruments used to attain those goals, and the precise settings of these instruments' (Hall 1993, 278).

As we will show in the next section, even though migration had been considered as a 'problem' by policy-makers previously, the recent economic crisis have allowed migration and integration reforms to be framed in a context of decreasing public finances and 'scarce resources'. Those frames have enabled policy-makers to adjust existing policy instruments and to adopt new ones, while leaving untouched the overall policy objective of further restricting immigration.

3. The evolution of Belgium's migration and integration policies in the context of double crisis

3.1. Pre-crisis immigration and integration policies in Belgium

Similarly to other European countries, Belgium started an active immigration policy after World War II by signing bilateral agreements with Southern European governments and later with non-European countries. Following the oil crisis and the subsequent economic recession of the 1970s, the Belgian government stopped actively recruiting low-skilled workers in 1974. Nevertheless, a limited work migration continued and, most importantly, family migration became the privileged avenue for foreigners wishing to move to Belgium. Parliament consequently adopted the law of 15 December 1980, regulating access to the territory as well as the sojourn, the settlement and the removal of foreigners (also known as the Aliens Law), with the aim of stopping new immigration and fostering the integration of those already present in the territory (Rea 2006, 193). In the mid-1980s, Belgium experienced renewed migration from Eastern Europe, Africa and Asia (see Bousetta, Gsir, and Jacobs 2007, 34; Martiniello et al. 2010) and in the 1990s, the number of applications for asylum increased rapidly, creating a growing undocumented population in the process. During the 2000s, with the same recurring objective of limiting new immigration, the Belgian government imposed transitional measures to limit access to its labour market for new EU citizens whose countries had joined the EU in 2004, 2007 or 2013 (with the exception of Maltese and Cypriot citizens). Nonetheless, Belgium still experienced a strong increase in inflows of EU migrants proceeding from Central and Eastern European member states (Table 1).

In the period between the Oil Crises of the 1970s and the 2008 economic crisis, immigration and integration policy reforms were continuously readjusting to changing socio-economic conditions and the changing institutional context, characterised internally by regional devolution and externally by the process of EU integration. However, Belgium never really questioned its 1970s' zero immigration doctrine. In line with interest-based approaches to migration and integration policy-making, scholars have noted that the presence of a strong extreme-right party – such as the Flemish Vlaams Blok (later called the Vlaams Belang) – explains the country's restrictive approaches to migration (Koopmans, Michalowski, and Waibel 2012). As a result of the electoral success of this party, migration and integration are becoming central topics that other parties also have to pick up on during electoral campaigns (Coffé 2005; Adam and Torrekens 2015). This explains the persisting restrictive approach in immigration policies adopted at the Federal level, where the pressure on the Flemish parties to appear strict on migration meets with the Francophone parties' traditionally less restrictive approaches on the issue. Most importantly, it explains the diverging paths of Flanders' and Wallonia's integration policies during this period.

Following the constitutional process of regional devolution, Belgium turned progressively into a federal state with prerogatives in the field of integration being transferred to subnational entities. Integration policies in the country's two biggest regions – Flanders and Wallonia – were originally based on two decrees, respectively the decree on the integration of foreigners or persons of foreign origin, signed in 1996 by the Walloon government, and the minorities decree, signed by the Flemish government in 1998. [2] The Flemish policy was initially based on the idea of the recognition of groups, even though particular ethnic groups were not formally recognised. In addition to this multicultural approach, a more assimilationist approach was initiated at the end of the 1990s and further developed

Table 1. Foreign regular residents in Belgium 1970–2013 (by nationality).

	1970	1981	1991	2000	2010	2013
Germany	22.956	27.619	27.924	34.328	39.421	39.745
France	86.658	103.512	93.363	107.240	140.227	153.413
The Netherlands	61.261	66.233	65.294	85.763	133.536	143.977
Italy	249.490	279.700	240.127	200.281	165.052	157.426
Spain	67.534	58.255	51.318	45.924	45.233	54.406
Portugal	15.340	23.080	23.129	25.563	33.084	38.812
Greece	22.354	21.230	20.461	18.389	14.798	15.513
Poland	18.370	7.642	4.871	7.760	43.085	61.524
Romania	n.d.a	n.d.a	n.d.a	2.424	23.383	50.906
Bulgaria	n.d.a	n.d.a	n.d.a	962	13.171	23.386
Turkey	20.312	63.587	85.303	72.064	39.551	37.989
Morocco	39.294	105.133	142.098	122.005	81.943	83.271
D. R. of Congo (Zaire)	5.244	8.575	11.828	14.307	18.056	20.066
Others	87.469	114.011	135.139	160.100	267.126	314.688
Total	696.282	878.577	900.855	897.110	1.057.666	1.195.122

Sources: Directorate General of Statistics and Economic Information, Poulain and Perrin (2002).

in the 2000s. In line with the decree on Flemish civic integration policy, [3] since 2004, the government has implemented compulsory civic integration programmes for all new immigrants settling in Flanders. In contrast to Flanders, Francophones have been reluctant to recognise ethnic minorities (Jacobs 2004, 282). In Wallonia, the party system is characterised by the absence of extreme-right and nationalist parties as well as by a stronger preference of voters for centre-left parties. In this region, integration policies were originally limited and characterised by a laissez-faire policy in which local integration centres were in charge of developing their own integration programmes adapted to their local realities (Adam 2013, 554). Immigrant integration was mostly perceived as an inherent part of broader social policies focusing on the disadvantaged strata of the population. Accordingly, priority was given to the fight against social exclusion by prioritising education and positive discrimination measures.

Overall, by the eve of the 2008 financial and economic crisis, Belgium had already undergone dramatic transformations of its migration and integration policies, as dictated by institutional transformations and, most importantly, by electoral competition within and between the two party systems. Yet, the overarching objective of limiting further immigration had not changed.

3.2. Political and economic crises in Belgium since 2007

Similarly to many other EU member states, Belgium was hit severely by the economic crisis. The peculiarity of Belgium, however, is that the economic crisis occurred during a period of acute political instability caused by a growing distrust between the Francophone and Flemish political parties.

A few months before the beginning of the economic crisis in Europe, Belgium experienced one of its longest political crises, as the country remained without a government for over 6 months following the 10 June 2007 federal elections. The main point of contention between the Flemish and Francophone political parties concerned the voting rights of Francophone minorities in Flemish municipalities around Brussels. As the parties eventually agreed to postpone debates on this issue until the next election, a new government was finally appointed in March 2008. The political crisis had, however, strongly affected the levels of trust between the parties and many observers predicted that its parliamentary majority would therefore be very fragile (Rihoux et al. 2011).

During the initial phase of the economic crisis in 2008, the recently appointed government was very rapidly put under significant pressure as three of Belgium's biggest banks (Fortis, Dexia and KBC) ran the risk of bankruptcy. In order to save these banks, the government invested about 20 billion euros in them (i.e. 5% of the country's GDP). Moreover, the decision to nationalise Fortis Bank overnight had considerable political implications, as it raised major opposition among shareholders and triggered an investigation that led to the eventual resignation of Prime Minister Leterme in December 2008 (Troupin, Stroobants and Steen 2013, 5).

The appointment of a new prime minister coincided with the further deterioration of economic indicators. By 2009, Belgian public finances registered a deficit of –5.6% of GDP and the public debt rose to 96.2% of GDP the same year. In addition, the economic crisis also affected seriously Belgium's labour market. Between 2008 and 2009, 20,000 jobs were destroyed (representing a net drop of 1.2%). In light of those different indicators, it is not surprising that Belgium was considered – along with Portugal, Spain, Ireland, Greece and Italy – as one of the countries most at risk of falling into a long-lasting and profound economic recession in the early days of the economic crisis.

As shown in Figure 1, the deterioration in economic conditions had a differential impact on several categories of workers. For instance, the immigrant population seemed to be especially affected (Høj 2013), even though their level of unemployment was already higher than that of native workers prior to the economic crisis. In addition, as shown in Table 2, the level of support for immigration by nationals significantly eroded between the early hours of the economic crisis in 2008 and its peak in 2010. [4] In other words, not only were immigrants in Belgium more affected by the crisis, nationals also increasingly questioned their social and economic 'added-value' as the effect of the recession became more visible.

The new government opted for several 'anti-crisis' policies, mainly consisting of measures facilitating access to temporary unemployment and specific reductions of the value-added-tax (VAT). After the dramatic setbacks of 2008 and 2009, Belgium began to gradually recover and by 2011, the labour market situation improved as unemployment reached its pre-crisis level.

The Federal legislative elections of 23 June 2010 initiated the second political crisis as electoral results confirmed the growing divide between Flemish and Francophone voters. In Flanders, the right-wing nationalist party (N-VA) became the largest party (29%), while in Wallonia, the incumbent Socialist Party (PS) maintained its leadership. As these two parties had vowed not to govern together because of their irreconcilable positions on the future of Belgium as a unitary state and on decisions regarding the socio-economic reforms that ought to be implemented, a long period of political instability opened up. After 17 months (the longest period of government negotiation in history), the

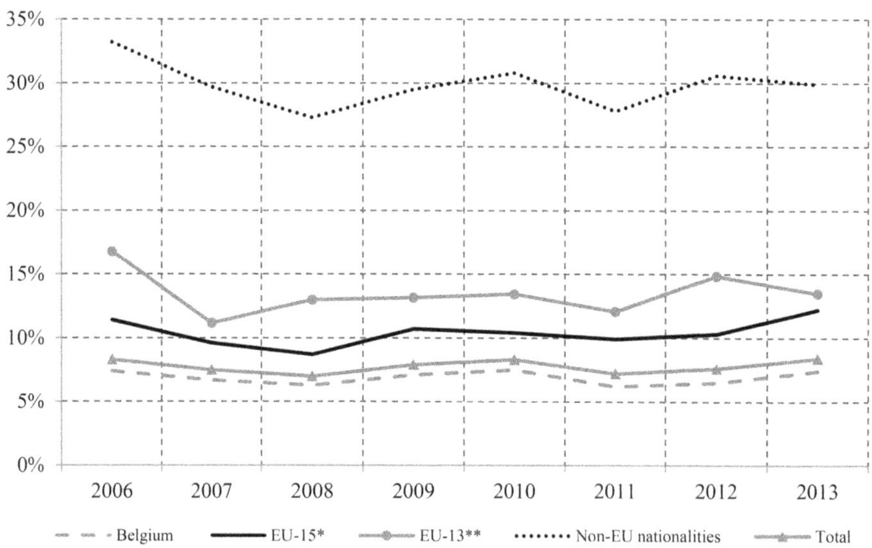

Figure 1. Evolution of unemployment rates in the EU by nationality 2006–2013. *EU member states prior to 2004 enlargement. **2004, 2007 and 2013 accession member states. Source: EU Labour Force Survey 2005–2013.

Table 2. Belgian nationals' attitudes towards immigrants 2006–2014.[a]

	2006	2008	2010	2012	2014
Immigration bad or good for country's economy	4.56	4.68	4.37	4.48	4.4
Immigrants make country worse or better place to live	4.58	4.8	4.55	4.66	4.69

[a]Average scores on a scale from 0 (highly negative view on immigration) to 10 (highly positive view on immigration)
Sources: European Social Survey—Waves 3, 4, 5, 6, 7.

French-speaking socialists managed to convince the Flemish parties to form a coalition government without the N-VA.

3.3. Migration and integration policy reforms in times of crisis

Starting in 2011, the combination of the long-lasting effect of the economic crisis and the perceived political instability of the country shared by most policy-makers has provided for an interesting context for the study of migration and integration policy reforms. On the one hand, an interest-based analysis of the reforms adopted in this period confirms the role of electoral competition in migration and integration policy-making: the political crisis strongly affected voters' confidence in the political parties and significantly increased political competition both within and between the two party systems. Indeed, the decision to govern without the country's largest party (N-VA) pushed other Flemish parties to support increasingly restrictive reforms at the Federal level in order to regain this share of the electorate. This position was in direct contradiction to the approach of another large member of the governing coalition – the Francophone PS – which had historically defended a more favourable stance on immigration.

On the other hand, an ideas-based approach to these reforms invites us to consider them as only a partial continuation of the past. Even though the objectives of national and regional immigration and integration policies are still very much in line with the restrictive approach that has prevailed since the 1970s (especially at the national and Flemish level), the context of economic crisis has led policy-makers to adjust existing policy instruments as well as to create new policy instruments in order to reach those same goals. In other words, the political crisis did not alter the goals of migration and integration policies but rather the means to achieve them.

3.3.1. Policy objectives: continuing to keep undesirable migrants out

In the last decade, Belgian migration law has been modified repeatedly at the initiative of the governing coalitions or in order to comply with EU directives. These reforms were passed with specific goals, such as combating the fraudulent misuse of the right to family reunion, combating forced marriage, and accelerating the asylum procedure and promoting the voluntary return of migrants (European Migration Network 2014). Important reforms implemented in this period, however, all share the overarching goal of making it harder for foreigners to come to Belgium when they are perceived to be 'non-economically productive' or 'undesirable'. By contrast, access for those that are highly skilled has been facilitated in Belgium and even encouraged. Indeed, the Belgian scheme for highly skilled migrants offers more favourable provisions than the so-called Blue Card Directive, [5] that was transposed into Belgian law in 2012[6] (Cerna 2013, 192).

In the field of family migration, the law on family reunification of 8 July 2011 introduced minimum income requirements for sponsors seeking family reunification in

Belgium with family members residing abroad. The required level of income now has to be at least equivalent to 120% of the social integration income but this cannot come from social assistance (European Migration Network 2013). Even though it offered one of the few remaining options for migrating to Belgium, this reform was designed explicitly to make family reunification harder. In the words of MP Theo Francken (N-VA), it was meant to put an end to years of misuse of the 1980 Foreigners Law, epitomised by a 'laissez-faire and open-door approach' (La Chambre, Compte-rendu integral, 26 May 2011). On the Francophone side, MP Ducarme (Francophone Liberal Party, hereafter MR) confirmed that the governing coalition saw this reform as crucial to restore voters' confidence after the political crisis: 'the Belgian people needs to know that its Parliament is working even in the current context of crisis, in spite of which we have managed to pass this important reform' (La Chambre, Compte-rendu integral, 26 May 2011).

Reforms of family reunification procedures measures were accompanied by reforms on marriages and legal cohabitations of convenience in 2013 (European Migration Network 2014).[7] In addition, information campaigns against forced marriage were conducted, targeting explicitly the Moroccan, Turkish, Algerian and Tunisian communities in Belgium.

With regards to labour migration, measures have also been taken to protect native workers in reaction to a fear of a large influx of EU workers following the enlargements to Central and Eastern Europe: Belgium extended transitional measures to restrict workers' access to the labour market until 31 December 2013 and later the Royal Decree of 24 June 2013 installed a transitory period regarding the free movement of Croatian workers until 30 June 2015 (European Migration Network 2013). In practice, this meant that workers arriving from those new EU countries had to apply for work permits in order to be able to work in Belgium.

Lastly, as mentioned above, Belgium transposed the EU return directive[8] into Belgian law[9] and modified its law on expulsion and detention (e.g. extending the deadline for leaving the territory from 5 to 30 days and encouraging the voluntary return of refused asylum seekers).

As demonstrated in this brief overview, the Belgian migration policy reforms of the past decade have exhibited a consistent trend of keeping undesirable migrants out of the country. However, this trend, in spite of the rhetorical arguments used during the debate, does not constitute a new focus in the objectives followed by migration policies since the 1970s. It is rather a deepening of existing restrictive policies already in place. This trend is consistent with the competition between and within the political systems in Belgium, characterised in the last decade by the growing influence of Flemish right-wing nationalists (the N-VA). Similar to the Vlaams Blok before, the consequence of the N-VA's electoral success was that migration and integration issues have remained publicly highly salient, forcing other Flemish parties to adopt a similar line to the N-VA on those issues.

3.3.2. Adjusting existing policy instruments: towards a coercive approach to integration

While the objectives of policy-makers seem to have remained unchanged with the economic and political crises of the past decades, policy instruments designed to reach these goals have been modified. This is most clearly visible with the reforms of integration policies at the Federal and Regional levels. These reforms support the objective of restricting further migration of non-economically active foreigners, but the instruments to achieve this (i.e. nationality law and integration courses) have taken a more coercive turn. Indeed, migrants who do not comply with integration goals that are set for them increasingly risk sanctions under the new legal provisions. In the implementation of these reforms, the desire to protect the Belgian welfare state from potential abusers makes a recurrent appearance. The crisis therefore offers policy-makers a unique opportunity to stress the idea that when public finances are under pressure, receiving country authorities can no longer justify access to welfare for all migrants, even when this population has been the most affected by the economic crisis.

The law of 4 December 2012, modifying the Belgian nationality code, represents the largest modification of citizenship rules in Belgium since the 1980s. It provided stricter conditions for accessing nationality and extended the minimum period of residence before applying for citizenship from 3 to 5 years. This represents a major shift compared to the last modification in 2000, which was designed to facilitate access to nationality as a means to encourage integration. Contrarily to the previous legislation, the 2012 law contained a series of criteria designed to assess whether migrants are 'integrated enough' to be granted Belgian citizenship. Foreigners who have resided in Belgium for 5 years can apply for citizenship but must prove their knowledge of one of the three national languages. They must also demonstrate their social integration (e.g. with a school diploma, certificate of attendance of integration courses, etc.) and their economic integration (i.e. with evidence that they have worked for at least 468 days in the past 5 years). Similarly to the above-mentioned reforms, the tightening of conditions of access to Belgian citizenship has been justified by the fear of abuse and the necessity to protect the welfare state. These concerns were made particularly clear by the two largest Flemish parties of the governing coalition (Christen-Democratisch en Vlaams known as CD&V and Open Vlaamse Liberalen en Democraten known as VLD) during parliamentary debates. Both parties insisted that abusers – defined as anyone who does not respect the economic criteria – be barred from accessing Belgian citizenship (La Chambre, Compte-rendu intégral 26 May 2011).

Reforms of the regional integration policies in Wallonia and Flanders also epitomise the increasing use of conditionality and sanctions to force immigrants to adopt certain practices. In Flanders, where conditionality and sanctions had already been in place since the *Inburgering* reform of 2004 with the implementation of a compulsory civic integration programme for newcomers, the decree on the reform of the Flemish 'civic integration policy' of 21 December 2012, only confirmed this trend.

In Wallonia, by contrast, a major step was taken with the adoption of the 27 February 2014 decree on the Immigrant Integration Pathway which, for the first time, provides for some obligatory steps to be taken by newcomers arriving in Wallonia (i.e. meeting with a social worker and following a course on the rights and obligations of citizens in Belgium). The decree also provides for fines against immigrants refusing to participate in the initial steps of the Integration Pathway. The outcome of parliamentary debates on the Immigrant Integration Pathway was strongly determined by competition within Wallonia's party system. On the one hand, the PS was concerned to limit the obligatory and coercive nature of the scheme in order to protect its popularity among Belgian voters of foreign origin. To this end, it mostly used rhetorical arguments on Wallonia's 'tradition of welcoming foreigners' to justify the reform (Parlement wallon, Compte-rendu integral, 26

March 2014). On the other hand, many within the Francophone Social-Democratic party called Centre Démocrate Humaniste (CDH) – the coalition partner of the PS in the Walloon Region – were convinced that voters were expecting a tightening of integration policies in line with the reforms adopted at the Federal level. They were thus concerned that the Liberal Party (MR) would benefit electorally from legislation appearing too lax in the eyes of voters. Overall, the context of economic and political crisis appears therefore far less relevant than electoral competition in understanding Wallonia's mild shift to a more coercive approach to immigrant integration.

3.3.3. New policy instruments: social policy as migration and integration policy

Alongside the adjustments made to existing instruments, new policy instruments also arose with the policy reforms adopted in the context of economic and political crises. The main instrument has been social policy – and welfare in particular – which increasingly became a yardstick for determining whether individual migrants are economically valuable or not to the country. The first step in instrumentalising social policy to regulate migration has been the creation of the position of the State Secretary for Asylum, Migration and Social Integration, grouping those portfolios under the leadership of one single minister. Working with the new State Secretary Maggie De Block, the government has been able to develop a more comprehensive – but equally restrictive – approach towards the different legal and illegal avenues for migrating to Belgium. Most importantly, however, the inclusion of the social integration policy in her portfolio enabled the new State Secretary to use social policies as a means to regulate immigration.

The use of social policy for migration control arose in the context of budget cuts imposed during the economic crisis in order to meet budget deficit reduction plans. Public spending to support employment policies has been compensated for by cuts in other areas such as health care, education and pension schemes along with an imposed rise in taxation (Castanheira, Rihoux, and Bandelow 2014). In addition, more stringent controls and the supervision of welfare recipients have been introduced with the stated objective of reducing 'misuse and fraudulent access to benefits' (Nelson 2011).

Several restrictions and control measures have targeted the immigrant population and particularly EU citizens. Since 2012, newly arrived EU citizens have not been entitled to social benefits during the first 3 months of stay in Belgium. Also, EU citizens who are seeking work are not entitled to social benefits as long as they retain the status of job seeker (Mussche, Corluy, and Marx 2013). The most controversial measure was, however, implemented in 2011 and consisted of the large-scale withdrawal of residence permits from non-economically active EU citizens, who were claiming non-contributory social benefits in Belgium. This policy did not result from a new legal provision adopted in Parliament but rather from the restrictive interpretation made by the State Secretary for Asylum, Migration and Social Integration of the EU Directive 2004/38/EC on the right of citizens of the Union and their family members to move and reside freely within the territory of the member states. According to the directive, member states are allowed to withdraw the residence permit of EU citizens legally residing in the territory if they represent an 'unreasonable burden' on the public finances of the host state. In other words, this provision allows member states to expell undesirable EU migrants.

Citizens targeted by this measure are not the workers and self-employed but rather inactive EU citizens. These EU citizens, who had been granted residence permits in

Belgium after they demonstrated that they had health coverage and sufficient resources to live autonomously, were expelled because – at some point after becoming official residents in Belgium – they received some form of welfare assistance. It is striking to note that the number of EU citizens expelled on this basis has exploded since 2011. That year, the Minister for Social Integration instigated the automatic exchange of information between the Social Security Administration and the Belgian Immigration Office. The consequence of this flow of information is visible in the sudden increase in the number of residence permits that were removed (Table 3).

As documented in the press, EU citizens who applied for a living allowance or asked for social assistance to deal with a specific difficulty (e.g. unexpected hospital or utility bills) were recurrently among those considered as a 'burden' and were accordingly targeted by this policy. Yet, the definition used by the administration to define an 'abusive use' of social assistance is extremely lax. For instance, EU citizens hired under specific activation schemes financed by the Social Security Administration to work in schools or hospitals were initially also expelled under this policy. The rationale was that publicly-financed jobs were not real jobs but rather a hidden form of social assistance. The legality of such an interpretation was nevertheless challenged (Mormont and Neven 2014). Most importantly, however, the European Commission itself expressed concerns over the sudden and dramatic increase in the removal of residence permits. It also reminded Belgium that it needed to pay more attention to the specific circumstances of each case, since expulsions should never be the automatic consequence of claiming benefits (European Commission 2014).

Targeting directly EU citizens is a major policy turn in Belgian politics. Indeed, such a stance against the freedom of circulation of EU citizens damages the country's image as an advocate of a deeper EU integration process. Heightened political competition following the political crisis, however, explains why political parties are willing to take such a risk. Similarly to other reforms, competition within the Flemish party system pushed the two Flemish coalition partners at the Federal level (VLD and CD&V) to appear tough on the issue of migration in order to appeal to N-VA voters.

The economic crisis provided those parties with a unique opportunity to frame those reforms as indispensable in the context of decreasing resources for social programmes. For the State Secretary, 'undeserving EU migrants' represent a threat to Belgium's welfare system and her policies were designed 'to avoid immigrants being here only to take advantage of the social system' (RTL info 2013). She received significant support in implementing this policy, including from the Flemish coalition partner of the Christian Democrats (CD&V), who considered that Belgium should not become 'Europe's welfare

Table 3. Number of residence permits removed by nationality on the basis of directive 2004/38/EC.

	Spain	Italy	The Netherlands	France	Romania	Slovakia	Poland	Bulgaria	Other	Total	Change in %
2008	n/a	n/a	n/a	n/a	n/a	n/a	n/a	n/a	n/a	8	–
2009	n/a	n/a	n/a	n/a	n/a	n/a	n/a	n/a	n/a	61	+662.5
2010	75	5	60	21	43	91	11	31	6	343	+462.3
2011	98	28	102	32	96	108	n/a	261	817	1542	+349.6
2012	207	75	161	109	402	73	70	236	585	1918	+24.4
2013	323	265	305	176	816	60	66	393	308	2712	+41.4

Source: Office des Etrangers (2008, 2009, 2010, 2011, 2012, 2013).

agency' (Het Nieuwsblad, 5 June 2013). But support also came from the Flemish nationalist opposition party N-VA, who denounced the cost of welfare for EU citizens as 'unbearable in times of economic crisis' (La Chambre, Compte-rendu integral, 23 October 2012).

Overall, while the policy of expelling non-economically active EU citizens constitutes a new instrument within Belgium's migration policy, its objective is fully consistent with the long-term goal of keeping undesirable migrants out.

4. Migration policy reforms in times of crisis: conclusive lessons from Belgium

At the outset of this article we argued that – while crises are often described as stimuli for migration policy reforms – little is still known about the extent to which they affect migration and integration policies, about the mechanisms that lead to specific policy reactions or about the interaction with other variables that may equally affect policy-making during crises. Drawing on the case of Belgium, which experienced two crises in combination over the same period of time, we therefore wish to conclude this article by stressing the importance of combining interest-based and ideas-based approaches to migration and integration policy-making.

Because of its focus on electoral competition, the interest-based approach has been useful in our analysis in determining whether crises are serious enough to change a party's perception of the salience of migration issues for voters. In the case of Belgium, we have shown that crises only served to reinforce that perception. Moreover, this approach did not allow us to determine the exact impact of crises on policies. However, the ideas-based approach we presented did offer an interesting complement in this regard. It prompted us to disaggregate policy-making in times of crisis as processes that can lead to three types of change: changes in policy goals, adjustments within existing policy instruments to reach these goals, and the adoption of new instruments. With the Belgian case study, we showed that electoral competition remained a central variable in migration and integration policy-making processes but that crises triggered adjustments to policy instruments and the adoption of new policy instruments.

4.1. Crises and policy objectives

As disruptive and challenging as they were, the political and economic crises that affected Belgium did not dramatically change the goals of the country's migration and integration policies. Since the 1970s, Belgium has developed policies whose objectives were to keep economically inactive migrants out, and those objectives have been maintained and reaffirmed throughout the crises.

The absence of alterations to policy objectives has been justified by the fact that the crises did not profoundly alter the state of electoral competition in Belgium. The presence of a strong xenophobic party in Flanders in the 1990s (Vlaams Belang) and the emergence of a strong right-wing nationalist party in the 2000s (N-VA) have maintained the high saliency of migration issues in the public throughout the crises. Electoral competition within Flanders therefore dictated that Region's stricter stance on integration. Yet, it also explained the importance for Flemish parties of imposing their views on migration and integration policies at the national level where, historically, they have had to find a compromise with the Francophone parties (which traditionally lean towards the centre left).

This is not to say, however, that crises have no effect on policy objectives in the field of migration and integration. Political crises, in particular, create a sense of political emergency that increases electoral competition. It also forces parties to act in policy areas where they believe they can gain credit among voters. Within the context of a political crisis, policy-makers therefore perceive that the electoral cost of inaction or failure is substantially higher than in a non-crisis environment. The specificity of large-scale political crises such as Belgium's – in which the political class has become entirely discredited – is that policy-makers are unable to blame external factors. The choice of policy areas in which reforms are likely to be received positively by the majority of voters therefore becomes of critical importance in restoring confidence. Migration and integration are very appropriate policy areas to focus on for two reasons. First, they affect primarily foreigners who usually have no or limited voting rights. Second, reforms in this area touch upon fundamental prerogatives of the state: for example, Who is a citizen? Who has access to the territory? Who is entitled to receive welfare? It is therefore a privileged policy area for policy-makers, where appearing firm and in control is likely to reaffirm the authority of the state in the eyes of citizens; especially when support for immigration had declined with the economic crisis. In the case of Belgium, this has meant explicitly maintaining and even reinforcing the objective that has been in place for over 30 years – that of keeping undesirable migrants out.

4.2. Crises and policy instruments

While the political crisis explained the urge to act in the area of migration and integration and the importance for political parties to appear to be adopting strict policies, it did not offer a satisfactory explanation for the choice of policy instruments to be adopted or reformed in order to reach this objective. Examining those precise changes, however, allowed us to distinguish the effects of the political crisis from those of the economic crisis.

The case of Belgium shows that numerous existing policy instruments have been reformed and that a selected number of new policies have been adopted in the dual context of economic and political crises. Existing policies, particularly in the field of integration, have been modified to include or strengthen coercive measures and sanctions (e.g. the nationality law and regional integration policies). New policy instruments, on the other hand, are characterised by the instrumentalisation of social policy, and welfare in particular, to serve the objectives of migration and integration policies.

The economic crisis and associated budget cuts to welfare programmes adopted in Belgium (and throughout Europe) have allowed political parties to develop a discourse about the 'threatened European welfare state'. Rhetorical arguments about the survival of the welfare state have served to reform social policies but also migration and integration policies. In both cases, reforms have been generally characterised by a decrease in accessibility and an increase in sanctions faced by individuals deemed undeserving of social assistance. Most importantly, however, such a discourse has legitimised the use of welfare policies as instruments for migration control, and more precisely, to keep undesirable migrants out. While this process had been observed in other national contexts before, the case of Belgium has, however, demonstrated that the economic crisis provided political parties with a powerful narrative to implement restrictions on immigrants' access to welfare under the guise of protecting the welfare state. This, in turn, strongly differentiated the effects of the economic crisis from those of the political crisis in the case of Belgium.

Overall, this article has stressed the peculiar situation of Belgium as a federal state under economic and political tension. Further comparative work with other federal states and more centralised states, as well as the study of Southern European states more deeply affected by contexts of multiple crises, would undoubtedly deepen our understanding of migration policy reforms in times of crisis. Indeed, states like Greece or Spain have been confronted to various crises (economic, political, humanitarian) which develop at different levels of governance. More recently, several other EU Member States have also had to deal with combined political and humanitarian crises following the increase in flows of asylum seekers in 2015. Nevertheless, our study of the continuities and transformations of recent migration and integration policies offers three key lessons. First, combining interest-based and ideas-based approaches to migration and integration policy-making helps disentangle the effects of crisis from those of broader and longer-term variables such as electoral competition. Second, it is crucial to look both at the objectives and policy instruments in the migration and integration policy-making process in order to be able to determine what type of change or continuities are triggered by crises. Third, economic and political crises have differentiated effects, and their interaction, as shown in Belgium, creates stronger pressure for the reform of migration and integration policy instruments. In other words, the effects of the economic and political crises are not only differentiated, they are also cumulative.

Notes

1. In Brussels, competition between the Flemish and Francophone parties is partly possible but because of the demographic structure of the region, the Francophone parties continue to win an overwhelming majority of the votes.
2. Décret relatif à l'intégration des personnes étrangères ou d'origine étrangère adopted by the Walloon Government on 4 July 1996. Decreet Etnisch-culturele minderheden adopted by the Flemish Government on 28 April 1998.
3. Decreet van 28 februari 2003 betreffende het Vlaams inburgeringsbeleid.
4. Decrease in support for immigration was equally observed in Flanders, Wallonia and Brussels between 2008 and 2010.
5. Council Directive 2009/50/EC of 25 May 2009 on the conditions of entry and residence of third-country nationals for the purposes of highly qualified employment.
6. Law of 15 May 2012 and Royal Decrees of 15 August 2012, 17 July 2012 and 3 August 2012.
7. The law of 2 June 2013 provided a legal definition of legal cohabitation of convenience and in November 2013, another measure making information regarding marriages and legal cohabitations of convenience accessible via the National Register was approved (European Migration Network 2014).
8. Directive 2008/115/EC of the European Parliament and of the Council of 16 December 2008 on common standards and procedures for returning illegally staying third-country nationals.
9. Law of 19 January 2012 amending the Aliens Law (Belgian Official Journal of 17 February 2012). This law came into force on 27 February 2012.

Disclosure statement

No potential conflict of interest was reported by the authors.

References

Adam, I. 2013. "Immigrant Integration Policies of the Belgian Regions: Sub-state Nationalism and Policy Divergence after Devolution." *Regional & Federal Studies* 23 (5): 547–569. doi:10.1080/13597566.2013.789024.

Adam, I., and C. Torrekens. 2015. "Different Regional Approaches to Immigration Related Cultural Diversity. Interpreting the Belgian Cultural Diversity Policy Paradox." *Régionalimse et Fédéralisme* (online only). http://popups.ulg.ac.be/1374-3864/index.php?id=1526.

Alink, F., A. Boin, and P. T'Hart. 2001. "Institutional Crises and Reforms in Policy Sectors: The Case of Asylum Policy in Europe." *Journal of European Public Policy* 8 (2): 286–306. doi:10.1080/13501760151146487.

Boswell, C. 2007. "Theorizing Migration Policy: Is There a Third Way?" *International Migration Review* 41 (1): 75–100. doi:10.1111/j.1747-7379.2007.00057.x.

Bousetta, H., S. Gsir, and D. Jacobs. 2007. "Belgium." In *European Immigration: A Sourcebook*, edited by A. Triandafyllidou and R. Gropas, 33–44. Aldershot: Ashgate.

Castanheira, M., B. Rihoux, and N. C. Bandelow. 2014. *Belgium Report*. Sustainable Governance Indicators 2014 Project. Gütersloh: Bertelsmann Stiftung. http://www.sgi-network.org/docs/2014/country/SGI2014_Belgium.pdf.

Cerna, L. 2010. *Policies and Practices of Highly Skilled Migration in Times of the Economic Crisis*. International Migration Papers 99. Geneva: International Labor Organization. http://www.ilo.org/wcmsp5/groups/public/—ed_protect/—protrav/—migrant/documents/publication/wcms_179666.pdf.

Cerna, L. 2013. "Understanding the Diversity of EU Migration Policy in Practice: The Implementation of the Blue Card Initiative." *Policy Studies* 34 (2): 180–200. doi:10.1080/01442872.2013.767587.

Coffé, H. 2005. "Do Individual Factors Explain the Different Success of the Two Belgian Extreme Right Parties." *Acta Politica* 40 (1): 74–93. doi:10.1057/palgrave.ap.5500078.

European Commission. 2014. *Libre circulation: la Commission demande à la Belgique de respecter les règles de l'UE*. Brussels: European Commission.

European Migration Network. 2013. *Annual Report on Asylum and Migration Policy in Belgium 2012*. Brussels: EMN-Belgian Contact Point. http://ec.europa.eu/dgs/home-affairs/what-we-do/networks/european_migration_network/reports/docs/annual-policy/2012/be_emn_policy_report_2012_-_final_en.pdf.

European Migration Network. 2014. *Annual Report on Asylum and Migration Policy in Belgium 2013*. Brussels: EMN-Belgian Contact Point. http://www.emnbelgium.be/sites/default/files/publications/be_policy_report_2013_on_migration_and_asylum_emn_0.pdf

Freeman, G. 1995. "Modes of Immigration Politics in Liberal Democratic States." *International Migration Review* 29 (4): 881–902. doi:10.2307/2547729.

George, A., and A. Bennett. 2005. *Case Studies and Theory Development in the Social Sciences*. Cambridge: MIT Press.

Hall, P. A. 1993. "Policy Paradigms, Social Learning, and the State: The Case of Economic Policymaking in Britain." *Comparative Politics* 25 (3): 275–296. doi:10.2307/422246.

Hall, P. A., and R. Taylor. 1996. "Political Science and the Three New Institutionalisms." *Political Studies* 44: 936–957. doi:10.1111/j.1467-9248.1996.tb00343.

Høj, J. 2013. *Enhancing the Inclusiveness of the Labour Market in Belgium*. OECD Economic Department Working Paper (2013)1. Paris: OECD. http://www.oecd.org/eco/labour/2013-1.pdf.

Hollifield, J. 2000. "The Politics of International Migration. How can we 'Bring the State back in'?" In *Migration Theory: Talking Across Disciplines*, edited by C. Brettel and J. Hollifield, 137–185. London: Routledge.

Jacobs, D. 1999. "The Debate Over Enfranchisement of Foreign Residents in Belgium." *Journal of Ethnic & Migration Studies* 25 (4): 649–663. doi:10.1080/1369183X.1999.9976708.

Jacobs, D. 2004. "Alive and Kicking? Multiculturalism in Flanders." *International Journal on Multicultural Societies* 6 (2): 280–299.

Joppke, C. 1998. "Why Liberal States Accept Unwanted Migration." *World Politics* 50 (2): 266–293. doi:10.1017/S004388710000811X.

Koopmans, R., I. Michalowski, and S. Waibel. 2012. "Citizenship Rights for Immigrants: National Political Processes and Cross-National Convergence in Western Europe, 1980–2008." *American Journal of Sociology* 117 (4): 1202–1245. doi:10.1086/662707.

Kuptsch, Ch. 2012. "The Economic Crisis and Labour Migration Policy in European Countries." *Comparative Population Studies* 37 (1–2): 15–32. doi:10.4232/10.CPoS-2011-17en.

Legro, J. 2000. "The Transformation of Policy Ideas." *American Journal of Political Science* 44 (3): 419–432. doi:10.2307/2669256.

Martiniello, M., A. Rea, C. Timmerman, and J. Wets, eds. 2010. *Nouvelles migrations et nouveaux migrants en Belgique*. Gent: Academia Press and Politique Scientifique Fédérale.

Massey, D. 1999. "International Migration at the Dawn of the Twenty-First Century: The Role of the State." *Political and Development Review* 25 (2): 303–322. doi:10.1111/j.1728-4457.1999.00303.x.

Money, J. 1999. *Fences and Neighbors: The Political Geography of Immigration Control in Advanced Market Economy Countries*. Ithaca, NY: Cornell University Press.

Mormont, H., and J.-F. Neven. 2014. "Le droit à l'aide sociale et le droit à l'intégration sociale en faveur des étrangers: questions d'actualité." In *Questions spéciales de droit social Hommage à Michel Dumont*, edited by J. Clesse and J. Hubin, 13–172. Bruxelles: Larcier.

Muller, P., and Y. Surel. 1998. *L'analyse des politiques publiques*. Paris: Montchrestien.

Mussche, N., V. Corluy, and I. Marx. 2013. "Migrant Access to Social Security – Policy and Practice in Belgium." Study for the Belgian National Contact Point of the European Migration Network. Brussels: European Commission. http://www.emnbelgium.be/publication/migrant-access-social-security-policy-and-practice-belgium-and-eu-emn.

Nelson, K. 2011. *Improving the Efficiency of Social Protection*. Brussels: European Commission. http://ec.europa.eu/social/images/icons/pdf.gif

Nohrsted, D., and Ch. M. Weible. 2010. "The Logic of Policy Change after Crisis: Proximity and Subsystem Interaction." *Risk, Hazards, & Crisis in Public Policy* 1 (2): 1–32. doi:10.2202/1944-4079.1035.

Obinger, H., P. Starke, J. Moser, C. Bogedan, E. Gindulis, and S. Leibfried. 2010. *Transformations of the Welfare State: Small States, Big Lessons*. Oxford: Oxford University Press.

Office des Etrangers. 2008. *Rapports d'activités 2008*. Bruxelles: SPF Intérieur.

Office des Etrangers. 2009. *Rapports d'activités 2009*. Bruxelles: SPF Intérieur.

Office des Etrangers. 2010. *Rapports d'activités 2010*. Bruxelles: SPF Intérieur.

Office des Etrangers. 2011. *Rapports d'activités 2011*. Bruxelles: SPF Intérieur.

Office des Etrangers. 2012. *Rapports d'activités 2012*. Bruxelles: SPF Intérieur.

Office des Etrangers. 2013. *Rapports d'activités 2013*. Bruxelles: SPF Intérieur.

Papademetriou, D., M. Sumption, and W. Somerville. 2009. *Migration and the Economic Downturn: What to Expect in the European Union*. Migration Policy Institute Working Paper. Washington, DC: Migration Policy Institute. http://www.migrationpolicy.org/research/migration-and-economic-downturn-what-expect-european-union.

Papademetriou, D., and A. Terrazas. 2009. *Immigrants and the Current Economic Crisis: Research Evidence, Policy Challenges, and Implications*. Migration Policy Institute Working Paper. Washington, DC: Migration Policy Institute. http://www.migrationpolicy.org/pubs/lmi_recessionJan09.pdf.

Poulain, M., and N. Perrin. 2002. "The Demographic Characteristics of Immigrant Populations in Belgium." In *The Demographic Characteristics of Immigrant Populations*, edited by W. Haug, P. Compton, and Y. Courbage, 57–130. Strasbourg: Council of Europe Publishing.

Rea, A. 2006. "Les politiques d'immigration: des migrations ordonnées aux migrations débridées." In *Penser l'Immigration autrement. Une initiative belge inter-universitaire*, edited by B. Khader, M. Martiniello, A. Rea, and C. Timmerman, 177–207. Bruxelles: Bruylant.

Rihoux, B., P. Dumont, L. De Winter, S. Deruette, and D. Bol. 2011. "Belgium." *European Journal of Political Research* 50 (7–8): 913–921. doi:10.1111/j.1475-6765.2011.02013.x.

RTL Info. 2013. *Maggie De Block: 'Il faut éviter que des gens profitent de notre système social'*. Brussels: RLT. http://www.rtl.be/info/belgique/politique/maggie-de-block-il-faut-eviter-que-des-gens-profitent-de-notre-systeme-social-video–396658.aspx

Troupin, S., J. Stroobants, and S. Trui. 2013. "The Impact of the Fiscal Crisis on Belgian Federal Government: Changes in the Budget Decision Making Process and Intra-governmental Relations." Paper presented at the Conference on the Impact of the financial crisis on public administration, Tallinn, May 3–4.

Watts, J. 2002. *Immigration Policy and the Challenge of Globalization. Unions and Employers in Unlikely Alliance*. Ithaca, NY: ILR Press, an imprint of Cornell University Press.

Citizenship in the shadow of the Euro crisis: explaining changing patterns in naturalisation among intra-EU migrants

John Graeber

ABSTRACT

The Euro crisis has transformed the European political and economic landscape. Amidst lingering political uncertainties, austerity, high unemployment, and diminished levels of trust in the European project, how has the Euro crisis affected the institution of citizenship within the European Union? While the development of EU citizenship and the number of rights and freedoms attached to it since the 1990s has progressively reduced the incentive of intra-EU migrants to acquire citizenship in other member states, I argue that the Euro crisis and its political and economic consequences have reinvigorated the perceived value of national citizenship. In its wake, many intra-EU migrants, and especially those from the most crisis-stricken countries, may have a renewed incentive naturalise in other member states. Using data collected for 14 Western European countries from 2000 to 2013, I demonstrate how a growing lack of trust in political institutions and economic hardship since the Euro crisis has inspired surprising new naturalisation trends across Europe. Rather than perpetuate a further decline of national citizenship in Europe, the Euro crisis appears to have rendered national citizenship once again politically consequential.

The Euro crisis has profoundly altered the European political and economic landscape. Austerity, slow growth, and persistently high unemployment plague countries such as Spain, Greece, and Italy and have upended governments in many of them. Many Eurozone countries still cannot escape the Brussels-inspired spending cuts that continue to weight heavily on their economies. Fears of Grexits, a greater Eurozone demise, and even exaggerated predictions of the collapse of the European Union (EU) continue to bring political and economic uncertainty to citizens and governments across the continent. Trust in national governments and EU institutions has bottomed out in many EU countries, especially in those hardest hit by the recession.

In this context, the effects of the Euro crisis on the intra-EU mobility of Europeans have generally conformed to theoretical expectations. Since the formal advent of European Union citizenship in the 1992 Maastricht Treaty and broadening of the Schengen zone, most nationals of the EU-28 and of a few non-EU Schengen states today fully enjoy rights of free movement, settlement, and employment across Europe. Recent Eurobarometer surveys have revealed that moving and living freely within the EU is the right most frequently associated with EU citizenship.[1] Indeed, while EU enlargement to the 12 accession countries of Eastern Europe (henceforth A-12) rapidly increased intra-EU mobility and had positive effects on gross domestic product (GDP) and labour markets,[2] the Euro crisis and subsequent recession have greatly reduced the inflows of A-12 nationals into a number of Western European states, and redirected many intra-EU migrants from Europe's southern periphery to the countries of the northern core whose economies have suffered less economically (Orrenius and Zavodny 2009, 1–2; Papademetriou et al. 2010; Bräuninger 2014; Eurostat 2015d, own calculations).

But despite the increased mobility, whether the crisis affects intra-EU citizenship acquisition is much less straightforward. As a result of a series of European Court of Justice decisions expanding the economic and social rights of EU citizens living in other member states (Kostakopoulou 2012), the value of one's status as an EU citizen has only increased in recent years. Because of EU citizenship, nationals of EU member states enjoy a panoply of rights in other EU member states by virtue of their status. In what Joppke (2010) calls the 'inevitable lightening' of national citizenship through this court-driven empowerment of EU citizenship, the content of national citizenship has been progressively hollowed out a consequence. In this setting, European nationals have every incentive to move to and settle in another member state today without ever considering the acquisition of citizenship there. Yet on the other hand, because of lingering uncertainties, economic difficulties, and diminished trust in political institutions in recent years, Europe's citizens may have good reason to question the legal and political value of EU citizenship today compared to its national equivalent. In the shadow of the Euro crisis, has the value of national citizenship continued to decline among intra-EU migrants, or has the crisis reinvigorated it?

As I demonstrate by examining naturalisations across Western Europe, the Euro crisis has apparently weakened the pre-crisis disincentive to acquire national citizenship that the rise of EU citizenship previously engendered. Rather than undermining the motivation for intra-EU migrants to naturalise in other member states, the Euro crisis is actually provoking new interest in citizenship acquisition among them, particularly those from the most crisis-stricken countries. The Euro crisis, in other words, has reaffirmed the value of national citizenship, suggesting that, at least in difficult times, its content is not as empty as previously assumed.

The article proceeds as follows. First, I situate my theory and explanation of the Euro crisis's effects on intra-EU citizenship acquisition within extant theories of naturalisation, especially as applied to the EU. In the context of political and economic crisis in many migrants' countries of origin, I contend that national citizenship acquisition may confer certain political and economic advantages to migrants that exist beyond what EU citizenship provides. Generally, I theorise that immigrant demand for citizenship should increase with the severity of the crisis in migrants' countries of origin. Specifically, aggregate acquisitions should be positively related with both rising levels of political distrust in the EU and with a worsening economic situation in the country of origin. To test my theoretical framework, I then present an empirical analysis of citizenship acquisition across 14 Western European countries in the years before and after the Euro crisis began in 2009. The analysis reveals that the Euro crisis and its economic and political consequences seem to be re-incentivizing intra-EU migrants to acquire citizenship in other member states, despite the rights and benefits derived from EU citizenship. The final section summarises the results of the analysis and concludes with a discussion of future implications for citizenship in Europe and possible extensions for future research.

Explaining citizenship naturalisation in Europe

Explanations of immigrant citizenship acquisition have drawn from a diverse literature but generally focus on either individual or aggregate-level institutional or structural factors. Individual-level factors have received arguably the most attention. At the individual level, as Yang (1994) notes, the 'costs, benefits and meaning of naturalization are the most immediate considerations in immigrants' decisions to naturalize' (451). There are a number of political, civic, economic, and social rights and privileges that accrue to citizens that are often denied permanent residents, as well as commensurate costs of acquiring citizenship. As successful economic, social, and cultural adaptation to the receiving country deepens and those same ties to the country of origin diminish, the benefits of acquiring political membership in the receiving country increasingly outweigh the costs of severing former country ties. By this logic, individuals with higher income, occupational status, education level, language proficiency, and length of time in residence have been shown to increase the likelihood of naturalisation (Portes and Curtis 1987; Yang 1994; Jones-Correa 2001; Dronkers and Vink 2012; Vink, Prokic-Breuer, and Dronkers 2013).

More contextual determinants of citizenship acquisition have received relatively less attention. Of these, many have considered factors such as level of political and economic development in immigrants' country of origin (Jasso and Rosenzweig 1986; Bueker 2005; Chiswick and Miller 2009; Vink 2013). Others have examined socioeconomic context in the settlement country as a factor in citizenship acquisition, often in conjunction with the country of origin, but have found mixed empirical support. Dronkers and Vink (2012), for example, test GDP per capita in the receiving country as a 'pull factor' affecting naturalisation but find it has no significant effect on citizenship acquisition, while Vink, Prokic-Breuer, and Dronkers (2013) conversely find that employment status matters for naturalisation, but only for immigrants from less developed countries. The legal-institutional diversity of citizenship policies that structure access to citizenship across settlement countries has arguably received the least attention, although Janoski (2010) and Dronkers and Vink (2012) find evidence that accessible citizenship policies are associated with higher naturalisation rates.

The introduction of formal European Union citizenship in 1992 and the incorporation of the Schengen *acquis* into the Treaty of Amsterdam in 1997 is one unique institutional context that has challenged the traditional understanding of citizenship in Europe and altered the context for the acquisition of citizenship among intra-EU migrants (Hansen and Weil 2001). EU citizenship has always been conceived as a means to foster popular support and allegiance to the EU as well as a sense of European identity beyond the nation-state. The Commission on Citizenship of the Union (2001) described it as

> both a source of legitimation of the process of European integration, by reinforcing the participation of citizens, and a fundamental factor in the creation among citizens of a sense of belonging to the European Union and of having a genuine European identity.[3]

In its report on the Year of the Citizen in 2013, the Commission proclaimed that its citizens 'are and must be at the heart of European integration' still proceeding rapidly beyond a reformed Economic and Monetary Union toward eventual political union.[4]

Many scholars and policy-makers initially greeted, and continue to treat, European citizenship with a degree of scepticism, considering it as purely symbolic and more representative of the EU's market-oriented character than a viable alternative to national citizenship (Everson 1995; Downes 2001). Others have viewed it as an ideological and political effort to address the democratic deficit or simply inspire stronger identification with Europe (Jessurun d'Oliveira 1995; O'Leary 1996, 1999; Vink 2005). Weiler (1996, 11) boldly dismissed it as 'a cynical exercise in public relations' in that it conferred no new rights to intra-EU migrants. Hansen (2009) has likewise maintained that as 'a derivative status that creates no new rights, EU citizenship in no way challenges national citizenship' and is rather devoid of 'empirical content and theoretical importance' (6). Yet other scholars have countered that EU citizenship has matured over the years both in terms of legal status (Kostakopoulou 2001, 2008, 2012; Joppke 2010) and as embodiment of post-national citizenship (Soysal 1994; Jacobson and Kilic 2003; Bosniak 2006). The European Court of Justice (ECJ) has been instrumental to this evolution. Through a series of court decisions, the ECJ has endowed European nationals with an ever-widening scope of economic and social rights that may be exercised beyond national borders within the wider EU polity. The 2004 Citizenship Directive (2004/58/EC), the entry into force of the Charter of Fundamental Rights in 2006, and the establishment of a EU Fundamental Rights Agency to monitor those rights have all formalised this development. These accessory rights have furthermore developed alongside and beyond its secondary status to national citizenship, being transformed from a derivative status into a source of rights in itself. As Joppke (2010) argues, EU citizenship is 'reinforcing the lightening of citizenship that is happening independently at member state level ... the future of citizenship is bound to be light, and lighter still with the help of "Europe"' (22).

If, as Yang (1994) maintains, demand for citizenship is premised on the tangible benefits it confers to those acquiring it, then many of the conventional benefits of naturalisation have disappeared for intra-EU migrants. Alongside the freedom of movement and facilitated right to permanent residence, EU citizens are entitled to a number of other benefits in other EU states, from non-discrimination protections to varied forms of social assistance to voting for and standing in local municipal elections. By this reasoning, European nationals today can move to and settle in another member state and enjoy a range of benefits in that member state by virtue of their EU citizenship. Even though a growing number of member states offer relaxed, or facilitated, naturalisation requirements for other EU nationals, acquiring citizenship would be a relatively costly behaviour with relatively inconsequential benefits for most intra-EU migrants. This logic seems to hold empirically as well. For example, Dronkers and Vink (2012, 395) hypothesise that acquiring citizenship in another EU member state 'would provide relatively little in terms of substantive benefits of citizenship' (395) and they indeed find that European citizens 'are clearly less motivated to acquire another European citizenship' in their country of residence (409). Naturalisation rates also tend to decrease among intra-EU migrants whose countries join the EU (Eurostat 2015a, own calculations).

How has the Euro crisis affected these citizenship acquisition dynamics in Europe? Does national citizenship continue to lose its relative value among intra-EU migrants, or has the crisis reaffirmed it? I contend that the Euro crisis has in fact altered this incentive structure among European citizens and has reaffirmed the importance of national citizenship and inspired a renewed interest in acquiring the citizenship of another member state. There are several theoretical reasons for this expectation that in part build on previous research focused on the context of origin and settlement countries. First, in the aftermath of the crisis, Europeans are ever more uncertain and distrustful of national-level and EU-level political elites and institutions. As Figure 1 shows, distrust in EU institutions across all populations began reaching historic highs in 2010, immediately corresponding with the eruption of the Greek debt crisis. On a nearly daily basis, Europeans have heard countless reports about the precarious future of the Eurozone, speculations about a possible 'Grexit' or other club departures, and even exaggerated fears 'that the euro crisis may end up destroying the European Union'.[5] Anti-immigrant policies and xenophobic public sentiment, much of it directed toward intra-EU migrants, is also on the rise in a number of European countries. In the context of mounting political uncertainty and distrust of institutions back home, which countries may or may not belong in the future, and the status and acceptance of EU migrants living abroad, holding EU citizenship may provide little comfort. If the EU benefits deriving from their own national passport may soon be curtailed or dissipate entirely, intra-EU migrants have every incentive to acquire the citizenship of their country of residence.

As we see in Figure 2, furthermore, these changing political sentiments vary in magnitude between pre-crisis and post-crisis years among different European subpopulations. Whereas average pre-crisis distrust differs only moderately among all EU nationals from post-crisis distrust, it more than doubled among populations in Europe's periphery – Greece, Italy, Ireland, Portugal, and Spain (henceforth the GIIPS) – and nearly so in the A-12 countries. In fact, before the crisis, only two countries – Sweden and the UK – had average distrust levels that exceeded 50%, whereas 13 countries, including all the GIIPS countries, have exceeded this level in the post-crisis years. This variation clearly suggests that increasing distrust is a political sentiment strongly associated with the temporal onset and geographic severity of the crisis in the EU.[6] By this logic, sharply rising uncertainty and distrust in those countries of origin hit hardest by the crisis may most strongly incentivize naturalisation abroad. For example, it may be that a Greek citizen would acquire

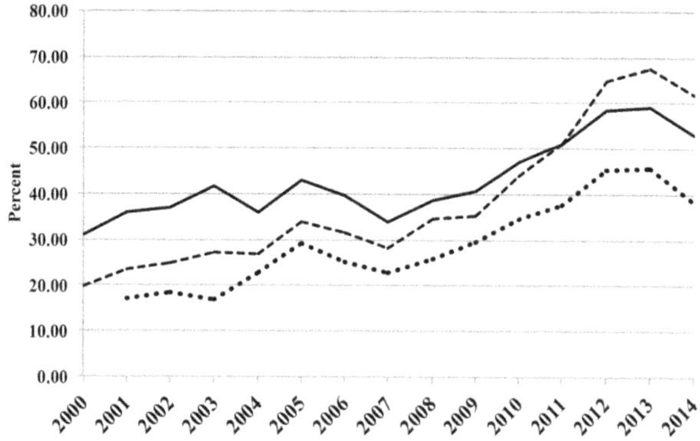

Figure 1. Distrust of EU, by select region.
Source: European Commission (1995–2014). *Standard Eurobarometer*, Nos. 54–57, 59–82. Brussels; European Commission (2001–2004). *Candidate countries Eurobarometer (CCEB)*, ||Nos. 2001, 2002, 2003.2, 2003.3, 2004.1. Brussels.

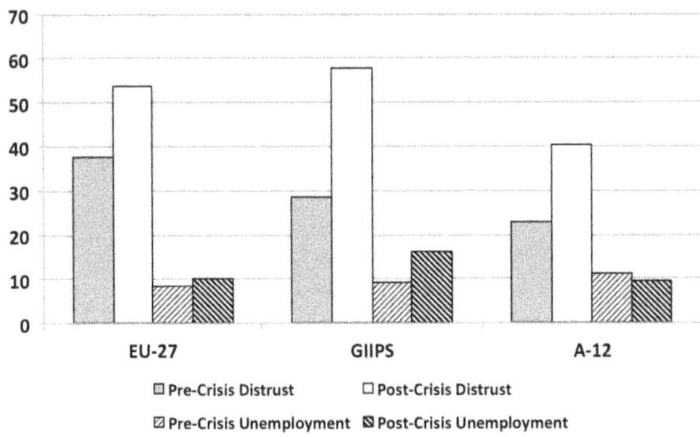

Figure 2. Average pre- and post-crisis distrust and unemployment rates, by region. Sources: Distrust levels from Standard Eurobarometer and Candidate Countries Eurobarometer, European Commission (1995–2014) and European Commission (2001–2004); Unemployment rates from Eurostat (2015f). Pre-crisis averages reflect years 2000–2009, post-crisis years reflect years 2010–2014.

citizenship abroad to safeguard against the potential loss of the rights and privileges of EU citizenship among persistent fears of a Grexit from the Euro zone, or to escape the political and economic uncertainty rampant in Greece in recent years. Naturalisation may also then be a form of political and economic insurance should the hitherto advantages of EU citizenship diminish or disappear. In this context, holding a new national passport may be more valuable for some intra-EU migrants than relying on the rights and privileges of EU citizenship derived from one's old passport.

Second, the acute effects of the Euro crisis may have increased the economic benefits of naturalisation for many immigrants within the EU. Although migration flows are also often closely tied to the business cycle and migrants are among the most vulnerable during recessions like the Euro crisis (Orrenius and Zavodny 2009, 1–2), many intra-EU migrants may be less inclined to return home. Because many European countries continue to suffer under the yoke of austerity, anaemic growth, and high unemployment, the return migration that often occurs during times of recession may be an undesirable option, as the economies of many countries of origin may be even worse off than those in the country of residence (Papademetriou et al. 2009). Indeed, as Figures 2 and 3 reveals, the unemployment rate in many EU migrants' region of origin makes the prospect of returning home relatively unappealing in the post-crisis years. Furthermore, in terms of access to welfare assistance, EU migrants may also qualify for more social benefits by naturalising in their country of residence than remaining bound to precarious welfare systems back home. Rather than return to dismal economic prospects at home, many EU migrants with established lives in another member state may rationally opt for new citizenship, perceiving little value in the rights afforded them by their national passport or EU citizenship abroad.

Third and relatedly, drawing on a growing literature on the economics of citizenship, there may be more informal but very tangible benefits that derive from citizenship acquisition. Many immigrants may perceive that naturalisation confers a 'citizenship premium' in a host country that non-citizens do not receive. If citizens are perceived to earn more, achieve higher status, or are more upwardly mobile in a competitive labour market than non-citizens, the economically motivated migrant may opt for naturalisation to earn this

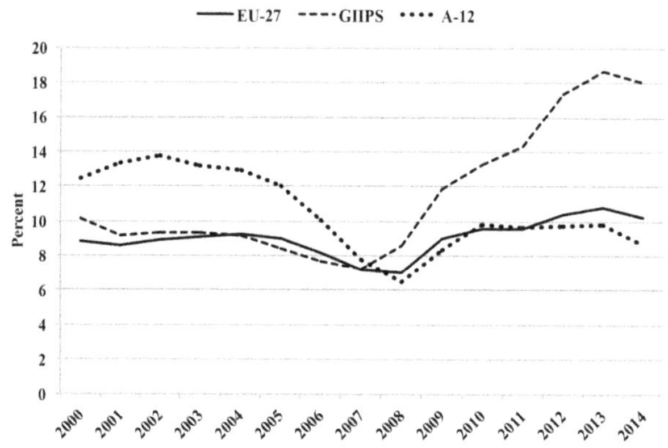

Figure 3. Unemployment rate, by select region. Source: Eurostat (2015f). 'Unemployment rate by sex and age groups, annual average, % [une_rt_a].' Accessed on 1 June 2015.

potential premium (DeVoretz 2008; OECD 2011, 17–18).[7] The rights and privileges of EU national abroad may not be enough during a time when post-crisis competition for stable and upwardly mobile employment is fierce. Holding a country's citizenship also signals one's commitment to the labour market and to the country in a way that a foreign passport does not. If signalling one's commitment to a strong economy is a better prospect than returning home to a faltering one, then EU migrants may find the acquisition of citizenship alluring.

Because it punctuated recent European history so dramatically and had such continental economic and political effects, the Euro crisis serves as a unique critical juncture within which to evaluate the relative importance of citizenship acquisition for intra-EU migrants today. If national citizenship and the attendant rights and privileges of EU citizenship continue to trump the relative value once attached to naturalisation abroad, we should observe that the Euro crisis has done little to alter declining citizenship acquisition trends among intra-EU migrants. If however these are insufficient, and holding the appropriate nationality retains its practical importance in spite of the rights and privileges of European citizenship, then we should observe that the crisis and its consequences have had discernible and significant effects on citizenship acquisition trends.

With this theory and context in mind, I offer the following hypotheses. First, the crisis has unleashed unprecedented levels of political uncertainty and distrust across much of the EU.[8] As uncertainty and distrust of political institutions in one's country of origin increases, especially in response to the Euro crisis, migrants should be less inclined to remain politically attached to these institutions. I thus expect increased aggregate demand for citizenship among EU migrants in their respective countries of residence. However, distrust in the country of residence should be associated with fewer acquisitions, since this may indicate depressed confidence in the political stability or status of that country and its passport within the EU. Thus the two should have opposite effects. If political distrust of the EU is positively associated with demand for citizenship abroad where distrust of national-level institutions is not, this would suggest that the perceived value of EU citizenship itself has declined and not simply one's national citizenship. Confirmation of this hypotheses would offer some support to the idea that the crisis has renewed interest in national citizenship and increased its relative value.

Second, the crisis has yielded economic recession and distressingly high levels of unemployment in migrants' countries of origin compared to the years before it, which should likewise incentivize citizenship acquisition among intra-EU migrants. Specifically, the economic context in the country of origin should be inversely related to citizenship acquisition. Economically stronger countries of origin should be associated with fewer naturalisations, not only because in these contexts there is less economic and political incentive to be gained from naturalisation, but also because the prospects of returning home to such an economy are not as discouraging. As the economy of origin becomes worse, however, migrants should have greater incentive to naturalise because the perceived gains from naturalising abroad increase over the benefits of remaining a national tied first and foremost to their economy of origin. Reversing the logic, as the economy of one's country of residence worsens, return migration may be a more viable strategy for intra-EU migrants than putting down roots in an economically unstable country. Confirmation of these hypotheses would also lend credence to the broader theory that the economic benefits of acquiring another national citizenship trump the current value of EU citizenship.

Finally, I hypothesise that the effects of the crisis should be highly contingent on the countries of origin and destination during the crisis. This means first and foremost that the effects of the crisis should vary across different groups of intra-EU migrants, with the strongest effects associated with migrants from the most crisis-stricken parts of Europe, and no effect for those from less affected regions. In destination countries, I expect that aggregate acquisitions among intra-EU migrants should increase in the years following the crisis in countries that have weathered the crisis most successfully. However, in the GIIPS countries – those most severely affected countries of the European periphery – we should observe overall relatively fewer acquisitions during the crisis years. This is because the crisis has left a level of economic and political uncertainty in its wake that largely negates any economic or political advantage of acquiring new national citizenship. Other strategies like return migration or migration to more stable countries should be most beneficial than citizenship acquisition in an economically and politically precarious country context.

Assessing the effects of the Euro crisis on naturalisation

To compare how naturalisation trends have changed as a consequence of the Euro crisis, I collected data on migration flows, stocks of foreign population, and citizenship acquisitions in fourteen Western European countries between 2000 and 2013 ($n = 196$).[9] Most of this demographic data comes from a combination of national statistical offices, Eurostat (2015a, 2015d, 2015e), and the OECD's (2014) *International Migration Database.* While some sources were more or less incomplete for certain selected countries, for the most part the significant comparability among them corroborated the reliability of the data gathered. Unfortunately, for a few country-years in the sample, notably France and the UK, there were higher levels of missing data in the population statistics whose omission might bias the estimates in the following analysis. Rather than omit these two important European countries and lose observations in an already small sample, I used the Amelia II programme by Honaker, King, and Blackwell (2009, also Honaker and King 2010) appropriate for time series cross-sectional analyses to multiply impute the missing values ($m = 15$). With the completed datasets, I conducted a series of pooled OLS and fixed effects regressions in these countries over the period in question. To deal with potential heteroskedasticity across country-years, I employ robust standard errors.[10] Below I describe how I operationalise the variables in my analysis.

I gathered data for three groups of immigrants: all EU migrants, GIIPS nationals, and A-12 nationals. Assessing citizenship acquisition among these subgroups of intra-EU migrants enables an important test of the potentially disparate effects of the Euro crisis on different migrants. If the benefits of EU citizenship have largely eliminated the incentive to acquire the citizenship of another EU state, we should observe few significant effects among the explanatory variables in all-EU migrant models. Because post-crisis political and economic trajectories of the GIIPS and A-12 countries have differed before and after the crisis, and have been observably worse among the former, we might reasonably expect that the theorised dynamics of the Euro crisis to be more observable among the former and less so among the latter.

For methodological reasons, I use the number of citizenship acquisitions in a given country-year rather than the naturalisation rate as my dependent variable, with size of the respective immigration population included as a control variable.[11] My primary independent variables represent measures of specific economic and political correlates of the crisis that best approximate its nature. Variables for distrust of the EU, distrust of national parliaments, national unemployment rates, foreign unemployment rates, and change in GDP per capita in each country-year for the country of settlement seem to be reasonable indicators of the Euro crisis generally. The distrust variables are drawn from annual Eurobarometer surveys and are percentages of the national population expressing distrust of the EU in a given year.[12] Economic variables were drawn from Eurostat (2015b, 2015c, 2015f). From these I calculate a series of weighted distrust, unemployment, and GDP change measures for the EU, GIIPS, and A-12 regions that adjust these figures according to the size and composition of the immigrant population in that country-year.[13] Aggregate levels of distrust and unemployment in the region of origin (country of residence) should be positively (negatively) associated with acquisitions abroad, while annual GDP change in the region of origin should be inversely related. In one model I include a Crisis categorical variable with three levels: 0 for all country-years from 2000 to 2008, 1 for non-GIIPS country-years from 2009 to 2013, and 2 for GIIPS country-years from 2009 to 2013. If the theory is correct, we should observe a positive effect in non-GIIPS post-crisis country-years as migrant demand for citizenship increases, and a negative effect for GIIPS post-crisis country-years where migrant demand falls, compared to the baseline country-years before the crisis. To capture any independent effects of the GIIPS countries on citizenship acquisition, I include a GIIPS dummy variable for the Spain, Italy, and Portugal observations in several models.

To control for institutional context, I include values from the Integration Cost of Citizenship Index (Graeber 2016), a quantification of citizenship policies according to eight different acquisition requirements, such as dual citizenship and duration of residence, and reflects the institutional costliness of citizenship acquisition in a given country-year.[14] Acquisitions should decrease with higher values of the index. I control for the size of the corresponding immigrant population, given very disparate population sizes across countries, as well as the migrant inflow in each country-year where appropriate.[15] I include logged GDP per capita for the country of residence as an economic control as well. For the all-EU and A-12 models, a final dummy variable represents the two recent rounds of Enlargement during which demand for citizenship may have changed more idiosyncratically, coded for the years 2004/2005 and 2007/2008 respectively.

Analysis and results

The models for all immigrants, GIIPS nationals, and A-12 nationals are summarised in Tables 1 and 2. Model 0 in Table 1 represents the baseline model for each group without any of the main explanatory variables included, while subsequent models add the explanatory variables of interest to test the various hypotheses generated by the theory.

In the first table, Model 1 for each group captures broadly the average aggregate differences in acquisitions across various country-years after the Euro crisis compared to the pre-crisis country-years. For the most part these differences are significant across the different EU national populations. Acquisitions in non-GIIPS countries during crisis years are significantly higher for all EU migrants and GIIPS nationals compared to pre-crisis years, while among all intra-EU, GIIPS, and A-12 nationals in Spain, Portugal, and Italy, there are significantly fewer acquisitions compared to pre-crisis years. The years after the Euro crisis are thus associated with more acquisitions on average in the northern European countries, and fewer in the more troubled periphery. These two findings together suggest that the intervention of the Euro crisis has affected the incentive to acquire another nationality among intra-EU migrants, despite their status as EU citizens. While the difference in A-12 acquisitions in GIIPS post-crisis country-years is on average lower than before the Euro crisis, it is neither positive nor significant. Instead, the crisis years seem to shift the number of acquisitions downward, regardless of destination. This result is unsurprising, given that many A-12 migrants were recent post-enlargement arrivals and thus not yet eligible for citizenship. Also, since the crisis has not been as devastating for many A-12 countries as it has for the GIIPS countries, many A-12 nationals simply considered return migration a better option, regardless of country of residence.

The remaining models in Table 1 report various estimated effects of distrust on citizenship acquisition during the period. The distrust hypotheses find strong confirmation in the results. For both all-EU migrants and GIIPS migrants, increasing levels of distrust in the EU reported in other EU countries and in the GIIPS region are associated with statistically significant increases in citizenship acquisitions, while the opposite association results from increasing levels of distrust in the EU reported in the country of residence (Model 2). It is especially striking that this phenomenon is statistically significant among all EU migrants, which supports the more general hypothesis that acquiring national citizenship still matters in spite of the legal and political evolution of EU citizenship in recent years. Furthermore, the seemingly small coefficients are not inconsequential. For example, for every additional percentage point increase in weighted aggregate distrust in the GIIPS countries, we should expect 31 more acquisitions among GIIPS nationals abroad in an average country-year, holding all other variables constant. Given that distrust of the EU in the GIIPS countries increased by roughly 33 percentage points from 2008 to 2013, as seen in Figure 1, this is in fact a quite sizable number of acquisitions.[16] The estimate for origin region distrust among intra-EU migrants is also significant in the fixed effects model which controls for individual countries (Model 5). However, distrust also seems to have had little effect on acquisitions among A-12 nationals. This result could likewise

Table 1. Estimated effects of region and distrust on intra-EU migrant citizenship acquisitions.

DV: Citizenship acquisitions among:	All EU migrants							GIIPS migrants					A12 migrants				
	(0)	(1)	(2)	(3)	(4)	(5, FE)	(6, FE)	(0)	(1)	(2)	(3)	(4)	(0)	(1)	(2)	(3)	(4)
Migrant Population	0.0046***	0.0047***	0.0048***	0.0049***	0.0042***	0.0033***	0.0030***	0.0055***	0.0067***	0.0052***	0.0055***	0.0052***	0.0051***	0.0029**	0.0065***	0.0061***	0.0062***
	(0.00058)	(0.00050)	(0.00054)	(0.00058)	(0.00068)	(0.00095)	(0.00095)	(0.00063)	(0.0012)	(0.00061)	(0.00061)	(0.00070)	(0.00086)	(0.0011)	(0.00077)	(0.00080)	(0.00086)
Citizenship Policy	−299.3***	−339.1***	−354.9***	−336.3***	−426.4***	−31.3	−217.5	−194.4***	−169.3***	−218.6***	−217.9***	−212.1***	37.6	−72.8**	−10.3	0.63	−9.20
	(65.2)	(60.2)	(53.8)	(56.9)	(76.3)	(141.1)	(159.9)	(39.7)	(37.9)	(36.8)	(36.7)	(38.4)	(51.1)	(32.9)	(39.5)	(39.2)	(47.1)
Country GDPpc (Log)	1567.6***	181.6	−1460.7**	−1115.2	−2293.9***			387.8***	−24.2	−856.2***	−817.5***	−720.8**	−109.7	97.4	−2432.2***	−2287.3***	−2549.9***
	(405.3)	(415.5)	(660.6)	(695.5)	(808.4)			(146.3)	(161.0)	(242.4)	(264.5)	(314.5)	(269.6)	(248.4)	(404.9)	(401.5)	(503.4)
Enlargement	241.8		564.4	300.6	411.8	557.9*	155.4						75.6	−582.1*	134.2	193.5	171.0
	(512.2)		(483.9)	(518.7)	(478.5)	(304.2)	(306.8)						(339.6)	(296.2)	(283.7)	(288.5)	(319.3)
GIIPS			−4446.9***	−4072.4***	−4808.0***					−1831.5***	−1621.0***	−1168.1***			−3895.8***	−3645.6***	−3779.3***
			(1094.1)	(1036.5)	(1060.3)					(288.7)	(301.3)	(305.2)			(604.2)	(562.4)	(541.9)
Crisis (Non-GIIPS)		1528.0***							542.4*					−363.7			
		(456.0)							(276.6)					(260.7)			
Crisis (GIIPS)		−3532.0***							−559.3***					−1867.2**			
		(1344.9)							(184.8)					(844.6)			
Distrust of EU, Country of Residence			−48.6			−15.3				−42.5***					−8.92		
			(30.7)			(30.2)				(10.7)					(18.5)		
Weighted Distrust of EU, Region of Origin			91.6**			77.0*				31.4***					−7.31		
			(40.0)			(45.2)				(7.62)					(17.3)		
Trust in EU, Country of Residence				44.4*							53.7***					−14.4	
				(25.2)							(9.54)					(13.4)	
Weighted Trust in EU, Region of Origin				−38.9							−30.4***					26.3	
				(43.3)							(8.64)					(20.2)	
Distrust of Parliament, Country of Residence					−29.0†		−70.5**					−8.09					−0.37
					(41.1)		(29.4)					(14.2)					(16.9)
Weighted Distrust of Parliament, Origin					105.7***		106.1***					15.5					4.07
					(40.3)		(29.0)					(9.91)					(14.6)
Inflows									−0.034					0.019***			
									(0.024)					(0.0034)			
Constant	−13216.9***	1284.1	17699.3**	15331.5**	24361.4***	−2338.2	−870.4	−2516.0*	1578.6	11696.1***	9552.2***	8881.8**	1758.3	387.6	27249.7***	24215.7***	27637.9***
	(4173.2)	(4360.3)	(7149.1)	(7132.4)	(8478.7)	(1756.2)	(1913.1)	(1489.7)	(1638.0)	(2786.7)	(2811.7)	(3548.9)	(2683.3)	(2547.8)	(4239.6)	(4391.6)	(5165.4)
Observations (*n*)	196	196	196	196	196	196	196	196	196	196	196	196	196	196	196	196	196

Number of Imputations (*m*)	15	15	15	15	15	15	15	15	15	15	15	15	15	15	15	15	15
Average R-squared	0.51	0.57	0.59	0.58	0.60	0.82	0.83	0.56	0.62	0.60	0.62	0.58	0.41	0.65	0.58	0.58	0.57
Adjusted Average R-squared	0.50	0.56	0.57	0.57	0.58	0.80	0.81	0.56	0.61	0.59	0.61	0.57	0.39	0.64	0.56	0.56	0.56
F	29.79 (4, 187.3)	37.15 (5, 187.1)	27.95 (7, 184.5)	26.61 (7, 184.8)	29.41 (7, 184.9)	57.55 (17, 172.1)	63.96 (17, 171.9)	31.20 (3, 186.8)	12.58 (6, 140.4)	26.67 (6, 180.9)	22.52 (6, 183.2)	22.04 (6, 179.5)	9.23 (4, 189)	33.43 (7, 185.7)	18.53 (7, 186.0)	20.62 (7, 185.9)	18.44 (7, 186.0)

Note: Standard errors in parentheses.
*$p < .10$.
**$p < .05$.
***$p < .01$.
†Estimated coefficients achieve significance at the $p < .05$ level in the equivalent non-imputed model.

Table 2. Estimated effects of economic factors on intra-EU migrant citizenship acquisitions.

DV: Citizenship acquisitions among:	All EU migrants						GIIPS migrants				A12 migrants			
	(1)	(2)	(3)	(4)	(5, FE)	(6, FE)	(1)	(2)	(3)	(4)	(1)	(2)	(3)	(4)
Migrant Population	0.0048***	0.0046***	0.0045***	0.0045***	0.0041***	0.0031***	0.0051***	0.0050***	0.0051***	0.0050***	0.0072***	0.0067***	0.0064***	0.0063***
	(0.00046)	(0.00049)	(0.00052)	(0.00051)	(0.0011)	(0.00080)	(0.00061)	(0.00059)	(0.00059)	(0.00059)	(0.00065)	(0.00064)	(0.00072)	(0.00072)
Citizenship Policy	−429.8***	−327.2***	−315.8***	−314.8***	88.1	18.3	−205.4***	−181.3***	−199.7***	−206.3***	−60.6	−53.7	−0.49	−7.44
	(62.8)	(59.3)	(61.3)	(60.2)	(130.3)	(138.1)	(39.4)	(37.7)	(38.3)	(38.4)	(41.8)	(39.5)	(39.8)	(39.3)
Country GDPpc (Log)	−2164.7***	−1256.9	−1082.1	−1205.8*			−611.5**	−247.0	−473.6*	−699.7**	−2844.8***	−3134.6***	−2511.1***	−2454.6***
	(634.8)	(820.9)	(681.3)	(679.9)			(259.3)	(274.3)	(269.7)	(273.5)	(407.5)	(431.2)	(375.6)	(370.7)
Enlargement	576.2	259.8	312.0	476.4	118.0	453.4					178.8	112.2	100.3	22.3
	(467.5)	(467.0)	(480.9)	(485.8)	(314.7)	(284.5)					(328.4)	(297.5)	(299.6)	(302.6)
GIIPS	−2648.4***	−3761.6***	−3751.8***	−3788.1***			−1234.3***	−1149.9***	−1192.4***	−1313.5***	−3196.5***	−4023.0***	−3707.7***	−3749.9***
	(949.2)	(993.6)	(987.3)	(997.4)			(279.5)	(291.5)	(272.8)	(280.2)	(490.6)	(524.8)	(515.2)	(516.3)
Unemployment, Country of Residence	−334.5***				−201.2*		−13.6				−207.9***			
	(106.2)				(114.2)		(24.8)				(69.0)			
Weighted Unempl. Region of Origin	732.9***					324.3**	46.6**				65.0			
	(160.6)					(139.9)	(22.0)				(50.7)			
Foreign Unemployment, Country of Residence		−32.1						40.2**				−94.8***		
		(59.7)						(18.1)				(32.6)		
Country GDP Change			−18.6						−28.7				90.7*	
			(78.8)						(39.4)				(49.7)	
Origin Weighted GDP Change				−122.7						−90.9**				61.2
				(98.4)						(45.3)				(43.7)
Constant	23004.8***	17486.4*	15232.1**	16682.1**	−445.4	−3156.8*	7867.4***	3805.5	6840.1**	9313.2***	31760.4***	35477.9***	27282.2***	26688.6***
	(6700.1)	(9142.0)	(7162.3)	(7170.2)	(1569.1)	(1728.7)	(2869.4)	(3013.5)	(2926.0)	(2987.2)	(4573.1)	(4650.0)	(3795.7)	(3759.7)
Observations (n)	196	196	196	196	196	196	196	196	196	196	196	196	196	196
Number of Imputations (m)	15	15	15	15	15	15	15	15	15	15	15	15	15	15
Average R-squared	0.64	0.58	0.58	0.58	0.82	0.81	0.58	0.59	0.58	0.59	0.62	0.61	0.58	0.58
Adjusted Average R-squared	0.63	0.56	0.56	0.57	0.80	0.80	0.57	0.58	0.57	0.58	0.60	0.59	0.57	0.57
F	33.44	29.76	29.99	30.18	73.82	78.81	18.44	19.51	17.59	20.95	26.60	29.67	21.64	21.49
	(7, 183.6)	(6, 184.9)	(6, 185.7)	(6, 185.5)	(16, 174.0)	(16, 174.1)	(6, 178.7)	(5, 181.8)	(5, 177.5)	(5, 178.9)	(7, 186.0)	(6, 187.0)	(6, 187.0)	(6, 187.0)

Note: Standard errors in parentheses.
*$p < .10$.
**$p < .05$.
***$p < .01$.

be due to the fact that levels of reported distrust remain much lower in the A-12 countries than in the EU or GIIPS countries, as Figure 1 demonstrates, or they may constitute large populations in countries like Italy and Spain where distrust of the EU is an even stronger deterrent to naturalisation than origin country distrust is an incentive.

How do we know that the culprit is a lack of confidence in the EU as an institution rather than a general lack of confidence in the country of origin? In other words, it may be that these estimated effects on changes in the number of citizenship acquisitions actually result from growing uncertainty about political institutions back home, such as parliaments, rather than specific misgivings about the EU. Unfortunately, these two sentiments are highly correlated, and therefore comparing their relative effects in the same model is not possible. Nonetheless, to provide an indirect comparison, I rerun the same models with similar weighted distrust measures of the national parliaments in the regions of origin, and if this alternative hypothesis were true, we would expect the results to at least approximate the previous results. The results are reported in Models 4 and 6 for all EU migrants and Model 4 for the GIIPS and A-12 nationals.[17] Beginning with all EU migrants, let us first compare Models 2 with 4. The estimated effects of the two pairs of variables are indeed very similar. Holding all else constant, for a one percentage point increase in aggregate weighted distrust of national parliaments we can expect a significant increase of approximately 106 additional acquisitions by intra-EU nationals, which is slightly larger in magnitude than the predicted acquisitions associated with a similar increase in distrust of the EU. Comparing fixed effects Models 5 and 6 reveal similar correlations, although distrust of the parliament in the country of residence is also significant in Model 6. From this we might tentatively conclude that general distrust and uncertainty about the political situation at home – regardless of institution – is a plausible alternative explanation for the corresponding changes in broad acquisition trends among EU migrants as a consequence of the crisis.

However, comparing Models 2 and 4 for both the GIIPS and A-12 nationals casts some doubt on this alternative hypothesis. Changing levels of distrust of the national parliament in neither the region of origin nor country of residence are associated with a change in citizenship acquisitions among these populations. While this non-finding is expected in the respective A-12 model, it is quite surprising in the model for GIIPS nationals: after all, this is precisely the region of the EU where we would most expect distrust and uncertainty of all forms to be most salient and observable. Rather, it appears that distrust of only the EU has a statistically significant correlation with citizenship acquisitions by GIIPS nationals. We can therefore interpret this as evidence, albeit tentative, that among those hardest hit by the Euro crisis, it is not simply general distrust and uncertainty wrought by the crisis, but specific distrust and uncertainty directed *toward the EU in particular*, that is associated with changes in their citizenship acquisitions.

Turning to Table 2, which reports the estimated effects of economic factors on citizenship acquisitions, the economic hypotheses seems to find confirmation as well. From Model 1, we see that the weighted EU and GIIPS unemployment rates are associated with a large and significant increase in citizenship acquisitions among EU nationals. While the weighted unemployment rate in the A-12 region is also signed as expected, the association does not achieve significance. In the country of residence, conversely, there is a significant negative correlation between the unemployment rate and acquisitions for all EU migrants and A-12 nationals, yet not for GIIPS nationals. This further strengthens the notion that high unemployment in the country of residence inspires return migration rather than naturalisation, with immigrants exiting difficult economic times rather than weathering them as new citizens. This may especially explain the significant finding for A-12 nationals, the population whose migratory patterns in Western Europe have been so highly responsive to enlargement and the subsequent Euro crisis. However, it may also reflect the fact that many European countries include financial conditions, such as employment, income, and welfare use, in their requirements for citizenship acquisition, and thus many immigrants may be indirectly disqualified by these policies as a side effect of the Euro crisis. Foreign unemployment rates in the country of residence seem to offer a more mixed picture. For A-12 nationals, a higher foreign unemployment rate is still associated with a lower number of naturalisations, suggesting unemployment disincentivizes citizenship acquisition. Yet among all EU nationals, the estimated effect is not significant, and for GIIPS nationals, the foreign unemployment rate is even positive and significant, which runs counter to the theorised direction.

Finally, only annual GDP change in the GIIPS region has a significant effect on acquisition. In this case, for a one percent increase in annual GDP growth in the GIIPS region, there are approximately 90 fewer naturalisations among GIIPS nationals in a country-year, if all other variables are fixed. Conversely, as GDP growth falls – due to the Euro crisis or otherwise – we can expect a corresponding increase in naturalisations among these migrants. Given the sharp negative growth rates in this region after 2008, this result is most expected and offers some confirmation of the hypothesis, even if the effect is not significant among the other two populations. In terms of changes in resident country GDP growth, this factor only achieves significance among A-12 nationals, suggesting stronger economic growth might incentivize citizenship acquisitions. However, this variable's lack of significance among the other populations suggests it is not an important predictor of citizenship acquisition among most Europeans generally.

Discussion and conclusion

This paper has examined the relationship between the Euro crisis and citizenship acquisition trends across the EU and performed one of the first analyses of citizenship acquisition explicitly among intra-EU migrants. The prevailing assumption in the literature has been that Europeans prior to the Euro crisis were much more disinclined to acquire the citizenship of another EU country, whether due to the freedom of mobility made possible by Schengen or the slow but steady accumulation of rights that derive from EU citizenship. Regardless of the theoretical reason, this disincentivising effect of EU citizenship on naturalisation among intra-EU migrants has not been surprising. However, the statistical analysis in this article reveals that the Euro crisis and its political and economic consequences seem to have *re-incentivised* citizenship acquisition among EU nationals living in other European countries. Many of the consequences of the crisis – rising levels of political distrust, economic uncertainties about the future of the Eurozone or a country's future in it, continued economic malaise and austerity – have apparently reaffirmed the value of national citizenship acquisition among all intra-EU migrants. However, it seems the effects vary by the population. On the one hand, distrust of the EU in both the region of origin and country of residence has observable and significant effects on most populations under study. On the other hand, poor economic indicators in the regions of origin seem to incentivize citizenship acquisition among most intra-EU migrants, while the same indicators in the country of residence have more ambiguous effects. Compared to the other populations, A-12 nationals appear either less sensitive to potential economic incentives of citizenship acquisition, or simply more prone to return to their country of origin.

In the absence of individual-level data, systematic qualitative evidence from these different migrant populations would be necessary to identify the precise causal mechanisms at work and further substantiate the conclusions drawn here. Given the reliance on aggregate-level data, then, how can we be certain that individual-level demographic profiles of the intra-EU migrants in question are not driving these trends? This was partly accounted for in the use of three different migrant populations, since migrants from each region of analysis share very similar demographics. However, in the wake of the Euro crisis, might simply young, highly educated migrants be moving to these more stable countries of the European core and naturalising in higher numbers, thus accounting for the trends observed here? This is plausible, but there are two reasons to doubt this is driving the findings in the analysis. First, by my calculation using existing citizenship laws, the average length of residence required to acquire citizenship in the 14 countries under analysis is between 5 and 6 years. Hence, even if a wave of young, educated GIIPS nationals began migrating into these countries in 2009, the earliest they would be eligible for naturalisation would be 2014 (notwithstanding some exceptions for familial relations). The same reasoning generally holds for A-12 nationals who first began migrating in large numbers throughout the EU in 2006–2007: this wave would first achieve eligibility for citizenship in 2011 or 2012 at the earliest. These dates are generally too late to have any observable effect on acquisitions in the period under analysis. Instead, by this logic, it is ostensibly permanently settled long-term migrants driving these citizenship acquisition patterns rather than highly mobile, short-term migrants.

Second, even if this new post-crisis wave of young, educated economic migrants were driving some component of the findings here, most were inspired to migrate by the crisis itself and its political and economic effects, not by the allure of acquiring new nationality abroad. Thus even if they were eligible for citizenship after the crisis began, the more relevant variables accounting for their acquiring of citizenship derive from conditions in their country of origin and country of destination rather than their demographic profile per se. Without the political and economic incentives fostered by the crisis, neither their migration nor naturalisation would arguably have occurred. It thus seems unlikely that demographic variables correlated with the crisis itself and omitted in the aggregate-level analysis account for the findings here.

One could also question whether it is the changing value of the citizenship rights of intra-EU migrants in the country of settlement, or the growing insecurity of these citizenship rights, that is driving the results. In other words, recent legal limitations on social and economic rights enjoyed by intra-EU migrants in a growing number of EU countries, rather than the renewed value of such rights associated with national citizenship, may be the cause of the naturalisation trends observed here. Indeed, a number of countries, such as the UK and Belgium, have attempted in recent years to prevent the full exercise of rights by intra-EU migrants. The European Commission (2013a) has also recognised the need for 'robust safeguards' that ensure intra-EU migrants do not abuse the rights afforded to them and that protect the member states from 'unreasonable financial burdens' from claims of intra-EU migrants (5), leading some member states to consider restrictions on such benefits. To my knowledge, however, only in late 2013 did the UK government begin to plan and formulate limitations on EU migrant benefits, coinciding with similar policy discussions in other countries around the same time. The UK's bans on in-work benefits for intra-EU migrants would also only apply to arrivals after the law would come into effect. Furthermore, the Court of Justice of the European Union (2014) in *Florin Dano v Jobcenter Leipzig* on Germany's right to refuse welfare benefits to economically inactive EU migrants was issued only in November 2014. However, the period of analysis of this paper temporally precedes these national-level discussions and court proceedings on citizenship rights restrictions, as well as any legal implementation that would be applicable for the naturalisation trends I assess. Thus such concerns about the limited implementation of EU citizenship rights and growing restrictions on those rights may be a reasonable explanation as part of this naturalisation story as the EU moves forward, but this does not seem to undermine the mechanism stressed here about the shifting value of perceived rights intensified by the crisis.

Finally, the qualitative research I have conducted across several northern European countries supports the general theoretical mechanism advanced here: acquiring the citizenship of the country of settlement may be a strategic form of political and economic insurance as well as a source of socioeconomic advantage in a difficult post-crisis labour market. According to one naturalisation official in Berlin,

> long-time residents from the EU's crisis countries have often explained that they don't want to be viewed as those immigrants now coming from those countries ... they want to set themselves apart from those now arriving for work. This has meant more applications filed by long-term residents from Greece and Spain, for example.[18]

Other interviews conducted among naturalisation officials from different cities in the Netherlands, Germany, and Austria confirmed this discernible uptick in naturalisation inquiries and applications from individuals from Greece, Italy, and Spain despite often diminishing numbers of applications overall. Several Greek- and Italian-born naturalising residents of Germany, for example, also affirmed to me that their primary motivation for naturalisation was the discouraging prospect of returning to either country of origin in the wake of the Euro crisis.[19] Similar trends, for ostensibly similar strategic reasons, seem to be occurring in the wake of a potential Brexit, as British migrants throughout Europe begin applying for additional passports while intra-EU migrants in Britain have done similarly.

What does this analysis reveal about the importance of citizenship in the shadow of the Euro crisis? Does national citizenship continue to lose its relative value for intra-EU migrants, or has the crisis reaffirmed it? The analysis performed in this article suggests that the crisis has at least moderated the aversion of intra-EU migrants toward acquiring citizenship in another European country. The findings are certainly in line with previous literature, whereby acquisition patterns reflect economic and political dynamics in one's country of origin and settlement. By this logic, the economic and political factors captured in the models represent many EU migrants' uncertainty and loss of confidence in their own country, or confidence in their country of settlement. Hence a new citizenship abroad apparently offers more net value than one's previous citizenship status, for an intra-EU migrant would only bear the additional hassle of acquiring another EU member state's citizenship if that new status offered a benefit not already guaranteed by the previous nationality and EU citizenship.[20]

Although the findings here prevent us from broader conclusions about the relative value of EU citizenship today, we can safely deduce that the attendant rights and privileges of EU citizenship abroad are an insufficient replacement for national citizenship acquisition among intra-EU migrants, at least in difficult times such as these. In addition, the results indicate that growing distrust towards political institutions back home and towards the EU in particular may both be plausible determinants of intra-EU migrants' acquisition abroad, at least for those most affected by the crisis. It thus seems likely that the value of acquiring citizenship among intra-EU migrants today derives from the political and economic prospects in the country of residence, the lack of them back home, and a growing lack of confidence in the EU or in one's EU citizenship rights to have an impact on either. At a minimum, then, acquiring another state's citizenship has assumed renewed consequence over and above one's status simply as an intra-EU migrant from elsewhere. EU citizenship may still have much to offer, but the crisis reveals that it is not yet a sufficient replacement of its national equivalent.

This analysis also speaks to a number of broader debates about the meaning of citizenship today and the determinants of citizenship acquisition among immigrants. The empirical evidence strongly supports an instrumentalist and highly strategic view citizenship acquisition, at least among intra-EU migrants, rather than one based on cultural or identity-related motivations. Relatedly, the findings here also offer clear evidence of certain economic and political determinants of citizenship acquisition that have either been overlooked or found to be relatively insignificant in previous analyses. Nonetheless, additional research will be required to disentangle the theorised causal mechanisms outlined in this article, whether they interact or operate in isolation, and which among them account for the observed dynamics. Furthermore, future analyses might extend the theoretical framework to non-EU immigrants, both within and beyond the context of the Euro crisis.

That more intra-EU migrants are naturalising in other EU states does also challenge the continued 'lightening' of national citizenship in a post-national Europe that some scholars have predicted in recent years (Joppke 2010). Whether this reincentivizing of citizenship is a short or long-term effect of the Euro crisis remains to be seen, and likely depends on how quickly a permanent resolution to the ongoing debt crisis in Greece can be reached. But in any case, this is a rather troubling development for the broader European project. If proponents of an 'ever closer union' among the peoples of Europe increasingly imagine a truly European citizenry rather than a European collection of disparate nationalities, then the crisis has seemingly undermined the complex and ever evolving relationship between everyday Europeans, the nation-state, and greater Europe. Instead, it seems again that the nation-state maintains its traditional importance in the eyes of its citizens when political and economic obstacles emerge on the road to an integrated Europe, as is often the case. In the shadow of the Euro crisis, national citizenship in Europe is once again politically consequential, even among EU nationals, and potentially to the detriment of its EU counterpart.

Notes

1. Special Eurobarometer 75.1 – The European Ombudsman and Citizens' Rights – July 2011.
2. See for example European Commission (2011) *Employment and social developments in Europe 2011*, "Chapter 6: Intra-EU labour mobility and the impact of enlargement", 256.

3. *Third Report from the Commission on Citizenship of the Union*, COM (2001) 506 final (9 July 2001).
4. *EU Citizenship Report 2013 from the Commission*, COM(2013b) 269 final (8 May 2013).
5. George Soros, "How to Save the EU from the Euro Crisis," *The Guardian*, April 9, 2013. Examples of less exaggerated speculations include *The Economist*, "Is Grexit good for the euro?" June 16, 2012, and Ralph Atkins, "Trichet warns on dangers of Greek eurozone exit," *Financial Times*, February 24, 2015.
6. This is not to claim that manifest distrust of the EU as a phenomenon is only associated with the Euro crisis in any one country. Indeed, persistent and deep-seated Euroskepticism has long existed to varying degrees across many countries, and uncertainty and distrust may certainly be caused by longer term factors that may precede or extend beyond the crisis. While existing data do not permit one to fully disentangle these deeper forms of distrust from crisis-induced distrust, distrust of the EU nonetheless seems to be a proximate and short-term phenomenon and one direct and observable consequence of the Euro crisis. Thus its use as a proxy variable for the crisis and its effects on naturalization seem conceptually appropriate.
7. Although few political scientists have examined the economics of naturalization, a number of economists have explored this citizenship premium in both the North American and European context. However, the evidence is so far mixed. Bratsberg, Ragan, and Nasir (2002) find that the wage premium associated with naturalization is greater for immigrants from poorer countries, while DeVoretz and Pivnenko (2004) find in the Canadian case that acquiring citizenship increased the naturalized immigrant's earnings. Fougère and Safi (2009) analyze longitudinal data and uncover a large citizenship premium earned with naturalization in France, particularly for economically disadvantaged immigrants. In another study of immigrants in the Netherlands, Bevelander and Veenman (2008) conclude that naturalized immigrants earn more generally than non-naturalized immigrants in the Netherlands, but other demographic and labor market variables tend to wash out its statistical effect.
8. Of course, the crisis has unleashed and exacerbated many political sentiments in addition to uncertainty and political distrust, and uncertainty and distrust may also be caused by factors other than the crisis. However, from the evidence presented above, measuring political distrust as one sentiment to capture the political consequences of the Euro crisis in home and destination member states seems conceptually justifiable and highly relevant to the years under analysis.
9. The countries are Austria, Belgium, Denmark, Finland, France, Germany, Italy, Luxembourg, the Netherlands, Norway, Portugal Spain, Sweden, and the UK. While Norway is admittedly not a member of the European Union, it is a member of the Schengen area and EU and Norwegian nationals may travel passport-free across their shared border. For this reason its inclusion in this analysis is not theoretically problematic.
10. In addition to using robust standard errors, I re-run the same analyses on the smaller, non-imputed dataset using panel-corrected standard errors (PCSE) advocated by Beck and Katz (1995). Although not shown, the conclusions from this alternative specification are broadly similar to the findings using the presented models unless otherwise noted.
11. The choice to rely on the number of acquisitions per country-year rather than naturalization rates per country-year (total number of citizenship acquisition/intra-EU migrant population) may seem questionable, in that it could bias the analysis due to differences in relative sizes of intra-EU migrant populations. However, there two methodological reasons that using naturalization rates as a dependent variable here is less suitable than the method employed here. First, many of the variables used to predict naturalization – unemployment, trust, political conditions, policy, annual inflows, migration rates, and so forth – affect not only the numerator of the dependent variable (number of naturalizations in a given country-year), but also the denominator (size of the respective population in that year) as well. This means that both the numerator and denominator are correlated to differing degrees with different predictors, rendering the statistical relationship unpredictable and difficult to estimate. Second, with OLS regression, the model would predict values that are beyond the acceptable range of

values, that is, below 0 or above 1. As a consequence of these truncations, the predicted relationship also becomes non-linear. Both problems would require less straightforward model specification than OLS, such as a tobit regression, with little gain methodologically. Rather than including population size as a control in the denominator of the dependent variable, I therefore include it as an independent control variable, which should address concerns about bias.

12. The survey question reads, 'I would like to ask you a question about how much trust you have in certain institutions. For each of the following institutions, please tell me if you tend to trust it or tend not to trust it: The European Union?' Because Eurobarometer did not conduct its surveys in Norway, the distrust scores were included as either imputed values or as averages of the other Scandinavian countries in the sample. Neither specification changed the results. A-12 trust levels were drawn from the separate Candidate Countries Eurobarometer surveys from 2001 to 2003 and from Standard Eurobarometer surveys for the remaining years.
13. For example, the weighted GIIPS distrust value for Germany in a given year is the average of the distrust levels in Greece, Italy, Ireland, Portugal, and Spain weighted by the relative size of each population of nationals living in Germany in that year. In this way, we capture a respective distrust level perceived by that population of GIIPS nationals in their region of origin. This makes no assumption that naturalizing GIIPS migrants share this same degree of distrust as co-nationals at home, but rather that the reported levels of distrust at home are at least perceptible to these migrant abroad and sufficient enough to inspire some of them to acquire citizenship acquisition abroad. For country-years for which data was unavailable, the relative weights were interpolated based on relative population figures and projections in available adjacent years. Although interpolation results in more imprecise country-year weights, there is no reason to expect that the loss of precision in a given country-year introduces bias into the relative weighting of the variables.
14. While a number of citizenship policy indices currently exist in the literature, none to my knowledge are coded on an annual basis for the period of investigation, which limits the ability to control for variation over the period of analysis. For details about the index and coding rules, see the author's website.
15. Immigrant inflows are highly correlated with and are often predicted by other explanatory variables in the models, especially immigrant population size, which introduces multicollinearity into the many of the models. This variable is therefore omitted in models where this is the case.
16. As a robustness check, I ran the same models (Model 3) with aggregate weighted trust variables instead of distrust and the results are very similar. In addition, to address concerns that measuring distrust in the EU may be a conceptually problematic indicator of the crisis and to disentangle it from preexisting distrust sentiments, I ran these models with a variable measuring the difference between the annual distrust level and the baseline level in 2000. This also had little significant effect on the conclusions drawn from these results.
17. This variable was drawn from the same Eurobarometer surveys and coded equivalently. The survey question reads, 'I would like to ask you a question about how much trust you have in certain institutions. For each of the following institutions, please tell me if you tend to trust it or tend not to trust it? The [Nationality] Parliament?'
18. Personal recorded interview #1001 with anonymous naturalization officer, Staatsangehörigkeitsbehörde Friedrichshain-Kreuzberg (Berlin, July 5, 2014).
19. Anonymous semi-structured interviews with naturalizing immigrants were conducted in the summer of 2013 and 2014.
20. As one reviewer very helpfully noted, the mechanism underlying intra-EU naturalization patterns might actually be one based on intra-EU migrants seeking not to gain particular rights but to avoid particular obligations. Specifically, intra-EU migrants may be responding to increased tax obligations in their countries of origin, and naturalization in other EU countries provides a means to avoid such financial obligations. In Greece, for example, governments of various political orientations beginning in 2010 have passed tax increases in attempts to boost government revenues and to qualify for additional bailout funds from EU and International

Monetary Fund lenders. Although my empirical analysis is agnostic on the question of rights versus obligations and does not test for this possibility directly, these increases in tax rates themselves can be explained by the economic crisis in countries of origin, and hence my theoretical explanation about the crisis' impact on naturalization only becomes stronger.

Disclosure statement

No potential conflict of interest was reported by the author.

References

Beck, Nathaniel, and Jonathan N. Katz. 1995. "What to do (and not to do) with Time-Series Cross-Section Data." *The American Political Science Review* 89 (3): 634–647.

Bevelander, Pieter, and Justin Veenman. 2008. "Naturalisation and Socioeconomic Integration: The Case of the Netherlands." In *The Economics of Citizenship*, edited by Pieter Bevelander and D. J. DeVoretz, 65–88. Malmö: Malmö University.

Bosniak, Linda. 2006. *The Citizens and the Alien: Dilemmas of Contemporary Membership*. Princeton: Princeton University Press.

Bratsberg, B., J. F. Ragan, and Z. M. Nasir. 2002. "The Effect of Naturalization on Wage Growth: A Panel Study of Young Male Immigrants." *Journal of Labor Economics* 20 (3): 568–97.

Bräuninger, Dieter. 2014. *EU Monitor: The Dynamics of Migration in the Euro Area*. Frankfurt am Main: Deutsche Bank Research.

Bueker, Catherine Simpson. 2005. ""Political Incorporation Among Immigrants from Ten Areas of Origin: The Persistence of Source Country Effects." *International Migration Review* 39 (1) (Spring): 103–140.

Chiswick, Barry R., and Paul W. Miller. 2009. "Citizenship in the United States: The Roles of Immigrant Characteristics and Country of Origin." *Research in Labor Economics (Ethnicity and Labor Market Outcomes* 29: 91–130.

Court of Justice of the European Union (ECJ). 2014. "Economically Inactive EU Citizens Who go to Another Member State Solely in Order to Obtain Social Assistance may be Excluded from Certain Social Benefits." Press Release No 146/14. Luxembourg, November 11, 2014.

DeVoretz, Don J. 2008. "The Economics of Citizenship: A Common Intellectual Ground for Social Scientists?" *Journal of Ethnic and Migration Studies* 34 (4): 679–693.

DeVoretz, Don J., and Pivnenko, Sergiy. 2004. *Economics of Canadian Citizenship*. Willi Brandt Working Paper 3/04. Malmö: University of Malmö.

Downes, Tony. 2001. "Market Citizenship: Functionalism and Fig-leaves." In *Citizenship and Governance in the European Union*, edited by R. Bellamy, & A. Warleigh, 93–106. New York: Continuum.

Dronkers, Jaap, and Maarten Peter Vink. 2012. "Explaining Access to Citizenship in Europe: How Citizenship Policies Affect Naturalization Rates." *European Union Politics* 13: 390–412.

European Commission. 1995–2014. *Standard Eurobarometer*, Nos. 54–57, 59–82. Brussels.

European Commission. 2001. *Third Report from the Commission on Citizenship of the Union*. COM (2001) 506 final (July 9, 2001).

European Commission. 2001–2004. *Candidate Countries Eurobarometer (CCEB)*, Nos. 2001, 2002, 2003.2, 2003.3, 2004.1. Brussels.

European Commission. 2011. *Report from the European Commission: Employment and Social Developments in Europe 2011*. Brussels.

European Commission. 2013a. Communication from the Commission to the European Parliament, The Council, the European Economic and Social Committee and the Committee of the Regions: Free movement of EU citizens and their families: Five actions to make a difference. COM (2013) 837 final (25 November 2013).

European Commission. 2013b. *EU Citizenship Report 2013 from the Commission*. COM (2013) 269 final (May 8, 2013).

Eurostat. 2015a. "Acquisition of Citizenship by Sex, Age Group and Former Citizenship [migr_acq]." Accessed April 20, 2015.

Eurostat. 2015b. "GDP and Main Components - Current prices [nama_gdp_c]." Accessed May 15, 2015.

Eurostat. 2015c. "GDP and Main Components - Volumes [nama_gdp_k]." Accessed May 15, 2015.

Eurostat. 2015d. "International Migration Flows [migr_imm1ctz]." Accessed April 20, 2015.

Eurostat. 2015e. "Population on 1 January by Five Year Age Group, Sex Group and Citizenship [migr_pop1ctz]." Accessed April 20, 2015.

Eurostat. 2015f. "Unemployment Rate by Sex and Age Groups, Annual Average, % [une_rt_a]." Accessed June 1, 2015.

Everson, Michelle. 1995. "The Legacy of the Market Citizen." In *New Legal Dynamics of European Union*, edited by J. Shaw, & G. More, 73–90. Oxford: Oxford University Press.

Fougère, Denis, and Mima Safi. 2009. "The Effects of Naturalisation on Immigrants' Employment Probability, France, 1968–1999." *International Journal of Manpower* 30 (1–2): 83–96.

Graeber, John. 2016. "The Causes and Consequences of Citizenship Policy in Europe." Unpublished PhD thesis, University of Texas at Austin, Austin, Texas.

Hansen, Randall. 2009. "The Poverty of Postnationalism: Citizenship, Immigration, and the New Europe." *Theoretical Sociology* 38: 1–24.

Hansen, Randall, and Patrick Weil. 2001. *Towards a European Nationality: Citizenship, Immigration and Nationality Law in the EU*. Houndmills: Palgrave.

Honaker, James, and Gary King. 2010. "What to do About Missing Values in Time Series Cross-Section Data." *American Journal of Political Science* 54 (2): 561–581.

Honaker, James, Gary King, and Matthew Blackwell. 2009. "Amelia II: A Program for Missing Data". Copy at http://j.mp/1F3g330.

Jacobson, D., and Z. Kilic. 2003. "European Citizenship and the Republican Tradition." *The Good Society* 12 (1): 31–34.

Janoski, Thomas. 2010. *The Ironies of Citizenship: Naturalization and Integration in Industrialized Countries*. Cambridge: Cambridge University Press.

Jasso, Guillermina, and Mark R. Rosenzweig. 1986. "Family Reunification and the Immigration Multiplier: U.S. Immigration Law, Origin-country Conditions, and the Reproduction of Immigrants." *Demography* 23 (3): 291–311.

Jessurun d'Oliveira, Hans Ulrich. 1995. "Union Citizenship: Pie in the Sky?" In *A Citizens' Europe: In Search of a New Order*, edited by Rosas and Antola, 58–84. New York: Sage.

Jones-Correa, Michael. 2001. "Under Two Flags: Dual Nationality in Latin America and its Consequences for Naturalization in the United States." *International Migration Review* 35 (4): 997–1029.

Joppke, Christian. 2010. "The Inevitable Lightening of Citizenship." *European Journal of Sociology* 51 (1): 9–32.

Kostakopoulou, Dora. 2001. *Citizenship, Identity and Immigration in the European Union*. Manchester: Manchester University Press.

Kostakopoulou, Dora. 2008. "SYMPOSIUM: The Evolution of European Union Citizenship." *European Political Science* 7: 285–295.

Kostakopoulou, Dora. 2012. "The European Court of Justice, Member State Autonomy, and European Union Citizenship: Conjunctions and Disjunctions." In *The European Court of Justice and the Autonomy of the Member States*, edited by B. de Witte and Hans-W. Micklitz, 175–203. Leiden: Intersentia.

OECD. 2011. *Naturalisation: A Passport for the Better Integration of Immigrants?* Paris: OECD.

OECD. 2014. International Migration Database. Accessed February 1, 2015. http://stats.oecd.org/Index.aspx?DataSetCode=MIG.

O'Leary, Siofra. 1996. *European Union Citizenship: The Options for Reform*. London: Institute for Public Policy Research.

O'Leary, Siofra. 1999. "Putting Flesh on the Bones of European Union citizenship." *European Law Review* 24: 68–79.

Orrenius, Pia M., and Madeline Zavodny. 2009. *Tied to the Business Cycle: How Immigrants Fare in Good and Bad Economic Times*. Washington, DC: Migration Policy Institute.

Papademetriou, Demetrios G., Madeleine Sumption, and Aaron Terrazas with Carola Burkert, Steven Loyal, and Ruth Ferrero-Turrión. 2010. *Migration and Immigrants Two Years after the Financial Collapse: Where Do We Stand?* Washington, DC: Migration Policy Institute.

Papademetriou, Demetrios G., and Aaron Terrazas. 2009. *Immigrants and the Current Economic Crisis: Research Evidence, Policy Challenges, and Implications*. Washington, DC: Migration Policy Institute. http://www.migrationpolicy.org/pubs/lmi_recessionJan09.pdf.

Portes, A., and J. W. Curtis. 1987. "Changing Flags: Naturalization and Its Determinants among Mexican Immigrants." *International Migration Review* 21 (2): 352–371.

Soysal, Yasmin. 1994. *The Limits of Citizenship*. Chicago: University of Chicago Press.

Vink, Maarten Peter. 2005. *The Limits of European Citizenship: European Integration and Domestic Immigration Policies*. Basingstoke: Palgrave Macmillan.

Vink, Maarten Peter. 2013. *Immigrant Integration and Access to Citizenship in the European Union: The Role of Origin Countries. INTERACT RR 2013/05*. San Domenico di Fiesole: European University Institute, 2013.

Vink, Maarten Peter, Tijana Prokic-Breuer, and Jaap Dronkers. 2013. "Immigrant Naturalization in the Context of Institutional Diversity: Policy Matters, but to Whom?" *International Migration* 51 (5): 1–20.

Weiler, Joseph H. H. 1996. *The Selling of Europe: The Discourse of European Citizenship in the IGC 1996*. Harvard Law School. Jean Monnet Working Paper Series, 3.

Yang, P. Q. 1994. "Explaining Immigrant Naturalization." *International Migration Review* 28 (3): 449–477.

Mobilities in the crisis and post-crisis times: migration strategies of Poles on the EU labour market

Anna Janicka and Paweł Kaczmarczyk

ABSTRACT

In the post-enlargement period, hundreds of thousands of 'new Europeans' from the New Member States embarked on their migration journeys in search of better jobs and living conditions. With over two million citizens staying temporarily abroad, Poland became one of the most important migrant sending countries in Europe. A few years after the 2004 enlargement round, most of the EU-15 labour markets and immigrants themselves were confronted with the most severe economic crisis since the 1930s. Such circumstances are presented as a test of how migration flows respond to changes in economic conditions and to what extent they may increase the adjustment capabilities of labour markets. Against this background, this article takes the migration of Poles as a case study in exploring the ways in which migrants respond to crisis-driven changes in the socio-economic environment. Based on two complementary data sets, we analyse the structural features of Polish migration and the strategies of mobile Poles on the EU labour market. The results indicate that links between the crisis and migration are more nuanced than suggested by economic theory. Furthermore, we show that labour market impulses can be effectively realigned by other factors of both economic and social nature such as access to welfare benefits or family-related strategies.

1. Introduction

The role migration flows play in the economies of sending and receiving countries has gained considerable attention in the literature. The conclusions are seldom unequivocal and usually depend on specific characteristics of both the incoming migrants (such as their skill level), and the receiving countries' labour markets (such as their level of segmentation, social security systems). Hence, any change of setting, such as the outburst of a crisis, brings the need to reassess the existing state of knowledge.

In the post-enlargement period, hundreds of thousands of 'new Europeans' from the New Member States (NMS) embarked on their migration journeys in search of better jobs and living conditions. With over two million citizens staying temporarily abroad after 2004, Poland became one of the most important migrant sending countries in Europe (Holland et al. 2011).

In 2008, the economic setting changed abruptly. The ensuing crisis is sometimes portrayed as symmetrical (Kahanec and Zimmermann 2009) due to the fact that it is global in nature and affected countries at different stages of development. Nonetheless, most authors describe the shocks as asymmetric (see e.g. Beine, Bourgeon, and Bricongne 2013; Jauer et al. 2014), since they resulted in significant differences in the output of particular economies. The years 2008–2009 saw a radical drop in GDP growth rates for most EU economies and the EU-27 as a whole. On the contrary, during the first phase of the crisis (2008–2010), Poland did exceptionally well and was the only economy which did not experience even a single quarter of negative growth. Signs of an economic decline in Poland only became visible in 2012/2013 (the 'second wave of the crisis'), but even then the downturn was much less severe than in many other EU Member States.

Determining crisis-induced changes in the mobility of Poles presents an important step towards assessing the overall impact of mobility flows on the crisis-struck economies of the EU, and answering the question whether these flows had a buffering effect. This is due both to the scale of contemporary migration from Poland and the recent changes in the economic setting in favour of Poland. We argue that since existing research results regarding the role of mobility are highly context-specific, it is also the context, that is, particular features of migration and underlying factors, which are key to understanding the outcomes of the post-accession migration of Poles. Among such crucial features of mobility, we especially recognise migration strategies understood as statistically traceable patterns of behaviour with respect to orientation towards return or settlement, labour market integration, etc. In our analysis, we will track the crisis and post-crisis changes in the strategies of Polish migrants in order to provide insight on the role of mobility from Poland in alleviating the effects of the crisis, that is, acting as a buffer on the labour markets.

We hypothesise that the reaction of migration from Poland to the crisis was far more limited than suggested by classic economic theory, and thus its role as an adjustment mechanism is low or moderate. This is due to: (1) a strong structural demand for foreign labour at main destination countries, and (2) the fact that the factors shaping the migration strategies of Poles are complex, involving family considerations and welfare benefits, causing migrants to sometimes act contrary to purely economically driven expectations. Moreover, as the share of settlers among all migrants increases, the role of non-economic strategies will grow in importance, and thus the mobility of Poles is expected to become less buffering in nature.

Based on quantitative Labour Force Survey data for the most important destination countries, we show that indeed, the actual flows between Poland and major destinations are not necessarily consistent with migration theories nor do they reflect changes in the economic setting. As we demonstrate further, this is mostly attributable to the fact that the strategies of Polish migrants altered significantly during the crisis. Thus, our findings question the adjustment capacity and the role mobility may play during the crisis.

This article is structured as follows: in the next section, we will outline the theoretical considerations on the effects of crises on mobility flows and provide an overview of existing research regarding migration strategies of Poles. In Section 2, we will briefly review related empirical literature on the recent developments in the EU, concentrating on the economic conditions and corresponding trends in the mobility of Poles during the crisis (2008–2009) and post-crisis (2010 onwards) periods. Section 3 is devoted to a statistical analysis of recent changes in the migration strategies of Poles. The last section concludes.

2. Crisis, mobility and migration strategies: theoretical predictions and empirical results

In a free mobility regime, unconstrained labour force flows are, just like capital flows, expected to respond to changing economic conditions in the sending and receiving countries. Workers are expected to relocate from areas with excess labour supply to locations providing more job opportunities (Holland and Paluchowski 2013; Kahanec, Pytlikova, and Zimmermann 2014). This mechanism should work both in times of stability and crises. Especially in times of a crisis and increasing disparities, migration flows are expected to be reactive and to play the role of an adjustment mechanism. In this section, we will briefly outline the theoretical considerations describing the adjustment mechanism, focusing on the importance of migration strategies in this context.

2.1. Theoretical predictions

Theoretical predictions related to the adjustment capacity of migration flows are derived primarily from basic neoclassical macroeconomic theories, pointing to the importance of the absolute wage differential (Hatton and Williamson 2002; Massey et al. 1993). From the perspective of a sending country, such as Poland, these predictions are straightforward. In response to unfavourable economic conditions, citizens who have the possibility of employment abroad should consider the option of leaving their home country to benefit from better opportunities (if institutional barriers do not exist). On the receiving end, the stock of migrants residing in a host country may change both due to diminishing inflows and to return migration. One commonly expects that in times of crisis, new immigrants are not welcome. Recruitment ceases and migrants currently residing in a country advise potential newcomers from their social networks not to migrate, which affects the inflows (Martin 2009; Papademetriou, Sumption, and Somerville 2009). Additionally, in case of lay-offs, it is migrants who are going to lose their jobs first, being often unskilled workers, employed in the secondary sector or sectors which are the first to be affected by an economic downturn (Beets and Willekens 2009; Martin 2009). Since immigrants are often neither eligible for the standard welfare benefits nor have strong ties with the host country, they may be more inclined to leave when losing their job (Papademetriou, Sumption, and Somerville 2009).

This picture changes, however, if we consider other, particularly microeconomic approaches. In this setting, a lay-off due to a crisis is not necessarily equivalent to the migrant returning to the home country. First, the possibility of finding new employment, conditional on skill level, age, and other factors, and/or having incurred large migration costs, may lead to an inclination to wait out the unemployment period in the host country – migrants may apply a 'wait-and-see' strategy and delay movement (further or return migration) (Burda 1995). Second, return migration may not be the best option if relative, rather than absolute, wage differentials and uncertainty are also considered (Duvell 2009; Stark and Bloom 1985). As the New Economics of Labor Migration (NELM) argues, migration should be understood not only as profit (wage) maximisation behaviour, but also as a risk-diversification strategy (Stark and Bloom 1985). This diversification may very well include also access to social benefits at destination. If migrants have incurred social rights, such as unemployment benefits, similar to the host society, they may not have incentives to return to the home country too quickly, especially if the level of benefits surpasses expected wages in the country of origin[1] (Benton and Petrovic 2013; Bratsberg, Raaum, and Roed 2014).

Third, contrary to the basic human capital approach (Sjaastad 1962), the NELM and sociologically founded theories argue that it is families, rather than individuals, who are the main decision-making units. A large number of theoretical and empirical studies point to the marital status and the family situation as the key determinants of migration strategies/trajectories (Castles and Miller 1993; Fawcett 1987; Massey et al. 1993). This is particularly valid if mobility becomes part of a broader contractual intra-family arrangement, which may imply allocation of labour and regular transfers of remittances. Last but not least, the traditional approaches to migration assume that the migrant settles in the host country or returns to the place of origin (Lee 1966; Massey et al. 1993). In reality, however, there is a plethora of temporary or circular movements, which may result from risk-diversification strategies, can be a function of differences in purchasing power, consumption preferences, legal issues, and family-related considerations (Dustmann and Görlach 2015; Stark and Bloom 1985). Additionally, such short-term or circular migration can easily create complex relations between mobile and immobile persons commonly described in terms of transnational families, transnational communities, or transnational social spaces comprising sets of economic, social, and symbolic ties (Faist 2015; Faist and Ozveren 2004; Glick Schiller, Basch, and Szanton Blanc 1992; Pries 2001). The existence of transnational social spaces is particularly important at the time of a crisis as transnational ties can be used as risk management measures.

All in all, we argue that the traditional economic migration theories, commonly used as a basis for analysing links between migration and crisis, overemphasise the role of economic factors and greatly underestimate and overlook the importance of migration strategies. Even if some additional aspects (such as access to welfare benefits or the obligation to remit) are taken into consideration when making predictions, this is still not enough. Migration strategies as such, we argue, are crucial in understanding migrants' responses to crisis.

2.2. Migration strategies of Poles

Polish migration in the aftermath of the crisis seems to follow patterns prevailing since 2004. The UK remains the most important receiving country followed by Germany, which is traditionally an important target for Polish migrants due to its proximity and well-established networks, and which maintained good economic performance in the crisis period. Even though the majority of Polish migrants nowadays target Anglophone countries, they are present in most of the EU Member States (Fihel et al. 2015). Similarly to previous migration waves, recent migration from Poland has been driven by differences in economic conditions and employment opportunities, networks, and social ties, as well as institutional changes (e.g. the introduction or relaxation of transitional arrangements). Nonetheless, it differs from pre-2004 migration in structural terms: migrants are more often young and relatively well educated (Grabowska and Okólski 2009; Kaczmarczyk

2013; Kaczmarczyk and Okólski 2008). Studies completed in the destination countries show a positive selection of post-accession migrants with respect to skill level and, at the same time, significant over-qualification (Clark and Drinkwater 2008; Drinkwater, Eade, and Garapich 2009).

The most recent studies point to a gradual diversion of the behaviour of Poles staying abroad. Based on the Norwegian case, Friberg (2012) suggests the migration project of Polish migrants comprises three stages: from an initial stage of temporary work abroad, through transnational commuting, to (permanent) settlement. This framework seems adequate for a large number of migration processes, even those that have been initiated as short-term or seasonal schemes, often fuelled by active recruitment as in the case of Norway or the Netherlands (Engbersen et al. 2013; Trevena, McGhee, and Heath 2013). Nonetheless, the line between those stages is fragile and the underlying factors may be very diverse. This is why researchers who attempted to identify the strategies of Polish migrants in the post-accession period often failed to present them in an unequivocal way. Eade, Drinkwater, and Garapich (2007) were the first who introduced the term 'intentional unpredictability' to describe the behaviour of Polish migrants in the UK which often did not fit the common understanding of the term 'strategy'. Such behaviour, highly dependent on volatile external conditions and characterised by keeping all possible options open, has been further described in other national contexts as 'liquid migration' (Engbersen et al. 2013) or 'deliberate indeterminacy' (Moriarty et al., 2010).

This 'indeterminacy' is to a large extent attributable to the fact that purely economic factors shaping the behaviour of Polish migrants (level of earnings, quality of job, and access to social benefits) intermix with socio-cultural elements (friends, family, etc.). In fact, a number of studies document that apart from 'traditional' labour migrants, Poles staying abroad could also be classified as mobile persons for whom the decision to migrate was related to lifestyle choices and long-term professional career (self-development) (Drinkwater and Garapich 2015; Krings et al. 2013; Parutis 2014). Isański, Mleczko, and Seredyńska-Abou Eid (2014) describe these migration strategies as 'Project: ME', where mobility is treated as part of a broader strategy of self-development and a means towards social and economic upward mobility, and the migration experience is used to enrich the migrant's own identity. Even if the majority of Polish migrants were clearly motivated by traditional economic factors, these relatively new migration strategies may be of importance during the economic recession as the impact of economic conditions is cushioned by other considerations. Ryan et al. (2009) question the 'individualistic' approach and claim that focus on individual migrants underestimates the complex roles of families and households in migration decision-making. Along the same line, White (2011) notes that 'families do not return'.

Available studies show that in the case of intra-EU mobility, the distinction between mobility, commuting, and settlement has become very subtle. New travel opportunities, communication technologies, and the free movement regime allow home communities to remain an important point of reference even for permanent migrants (Favell 2008). Importantly, recent studies document a growing tension between individualistic attitudes described in terms of 'intentional unpredictability' and family-oriented long-term and settlement strategies. This aspect becomes especially important when analysing the response of mobility to the crisis. If migrants do not centre on purely economic considerations, their proceedings and responses to the crisis will not be described well by economic theory. In such cases, predictions or expectations based predominantly on economic assumptions will not come true.

3. Mobility of Poles in the crisis and post-crisis periods

In this section, we test whether the actual migration flows in the EU reflect changes in the economic setting. We distinguish the crisis and post-crisis phases and focus on the mobility from Poland.

3.1. Trends in the EU since 2007

A crisis need not necessarily inflate or change the directions of migratory flows. The change in the flow volumes depends, *inter alia*, on the relative situation of the sending and receiving countries. It is possible that the situation at a crisis-struck destination is still better than the situation at the country of origin. This in turn signifies that a simple empirical analysis of the magnitude of migratory flows will not convey the full picture of the migratory response to the crisis.

The reservation regarding the usability of overall flow data notwithstanding, the available figures suggest that both permanent and temporary migration flows to the EU have, in aggregate, fallen significantly since 2007, and have only rebound just recently (2013) although without reaching levels observed in the pre-crisis period (Dhéret et al. 2013; European Commission 2014; OECD 2014).[2] The post-2008 migration flows can be divided into two phases with distinct mobility patterns. The first phase, from the outburst of the crisis until 2010 (the crisis phase), is characterised by a decline of migration flows, connected with the deterioration of pull factors, notably income differentials, and a rise in the significance of unemployment as a push factor. The second phase, since 2010 (the post-crisis phase), is characterised by increasing mobility, which Dhéret et al. (2013) link to the simultaneous process of the emergence of push factors in Southern Europe (mainly unemployment) and the economic recovery in other countries such as Germany. Zaiceva and Zimmerman (2012) and Barrett et al. (2014) suggest a positive buffering effect of the migration of NMS' citizens after the introduction of the free mobility regime. The commonly observed types of mobility among this group, namely repeat and circular migration, are expected to alleviate the potential negative impacts of the crisis particularly well, due to flexibility and the brain circulation aspects.

Many authors point to the dependence of emigration on local unemployment levels as a distinguishing feature of post-crisis mobility (see, among others, Bertoli, Brücker, and Fernández-Huertas Moraga 2013). Fihel et al. (2015) stress, however, that although migration does seem to react to push factors in the host country, such that when the conditions are unfavourable, individuals (both citizens and foreigners) leave the country, these migratory flows are not necessarily directed to the countries with the most favourable conditions, especially in terms of unemployment. Other authors also suggest that in case of the mobility of NMS citizens the business cycle of the destination country matters more than the economic situation in the country of origin (Kahanec, Pytlikova, and Zimmermann 2014).

When analysing recent flows from Poland to the EU, the data indicate worsening of the labour market situation in the most important destination countries, including the UK and Ireland (and in the EU-27 in general). In the case of the UK, the unemployment rate increased from around 5% in the pre-crisis period to around 8% in 2009/2010. In the case of Ireland, the situation was far worse: in 2010 the unemployment rate amounted to almost 14% (as compared to 4.5% in 2005–2007). Importantly, during the same period the rate of youth unemployment in Ireland rose from less than 10% to 30%. Even though the labour market performance was more favourable in the UK, youth unemployment also increased significantly, from 14% in 2006–2007 to around 20% in the post-crisis period.

Meanwhile, the situation on the Polish labour market has improved significantly after the EU enlargement: in 2002, that is, two years before accession, the unemployment rate in Poland was as high as 20%, and declined to around 7% over the next six years. Despite the crisis, the labour market situation in Poland in the late 2000s was still much better than in the first half of the decade. The same remains true in case of other indicators commonly presented as important pro-migratory factors in the post-accession period: the unemployment rates of young and well-educated persons (Grabowska and Okolski 2009; Kaczmarczyk and Okólski 2008). Both of these indicators declined significantly for Poland in the post-accession period, including the years 2008–2009, to increase slightly only after 2010. Based on these factors, we can say that the situation on the Polish labour market after the crisis was more favourable than in many EU-15 countries and other NMS.

One should not claim that economic reasons to migrate from Poland have disappeared, however. Even if accounting for the differences in costs of living, the wage gap between Poland and the West European countries remains high. In the case of Poland, the mean monthly earnings (in PPP EUR) in 2010 amounted to €1363 as compared to €2758 in Germany and €2899 in the UK, which means that a strong pull factor still existed. Additionally, in case of most EU economies, there is a stable demand for foreign workers that traditionally was and still is partly fulfilled by the Polish workforce (Clark, Drinkwater, and Robinson 2014; Kaczmarczyk 2013).

3.2. Crisis and post-crisis migration flows from Poland to the EU

The analysis of the macro-level migration trends in this section is based on the EU-wide Labour Force Survey (EU LFS) data. Due to methodological issues the presented outcomes are to be interpreted with caution,[3] but the EU LFS data presents a unique source of information on intra-EU mobility.

EU LFS data show that despite the economic downturn in most of the important EU destinations, there was no drop in the number of Polish migrants residing abroad (Figure 1). On the contrary, there is a slow, but steady, increase noted both during the crisis (2008–2009) as well as in the post-crisis period (2010 onwards).[4] Therefore, at the EU level, the stock of Polish migrants does not respond to changes in Poland's relative economic position as predicted by economic theory. The increasing scale of emigration coincides with gradual improvement of Polish GDP per capita and the conditions on the Polish labour market. The situation is more nuanced in case of particular destinations (Figure 2). The total stock of migrants seems to react to changes in labour market conditions, that is, relative unemployment rates. This is well visible in the case of two most important destinations, the UK and Germany, where the gradual improvement in conditions on domestic labour markets (relative to Poland) seems to fuel the stock of Polish migrants. The Netherlands also present an interesting case as a significant increase in the number of residing Polish migrants is correlated with the deterioration of relative

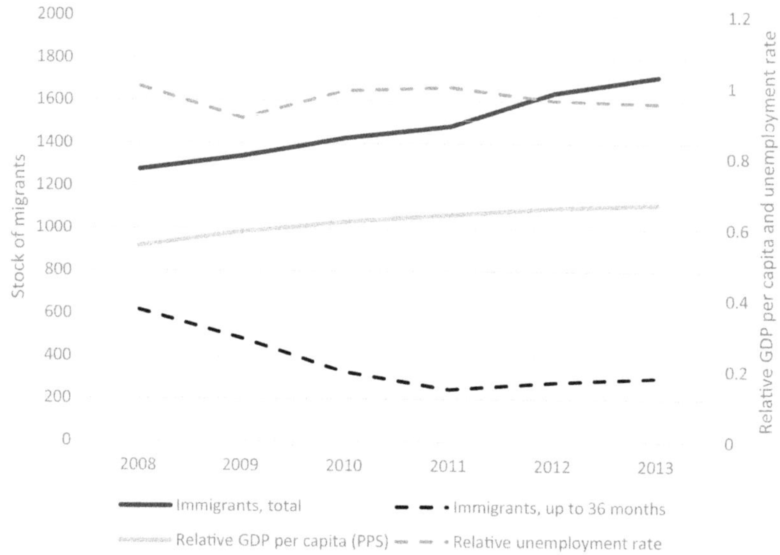

Figure 1. Stock of Polish migrants in the EU-27 and Polish GDP per capita and unemployment rate relative to the EU-27 average, 2008–2013.
Source: Own elaboration based on EU LFS data.

unemployment rates. This effect can be attributed to the opening of the Dutch labour market (in 2007) and gradual transformation of temporary migration into settlement (Engbersen et al. 2013).

Similarly to the Dutch case, in Germany the relatively high dynamics of changes in the migrant stock are attributable mainly to the fact that in 2011 Germany lifted restrictions resulting from the imposition of transitional arrangements concerning free access to the German labour market of Polish workers.

The EU LFS data show that, on the aggregate level, the economic downturn translated into changes in migrant stock only to a limited extent. The most significant changes have been noted in countries most severely hit by the crisis: Ireland and Southern European countries. In the case of Ireland, a 2% decrease in the stock of Polish migrants between 2008 and 2013 has been noted; in the case of Greece, which had hosted a much smaller population of Polish immigrants, this change was as high as 20%.

Unfortunately, it is not possible to use EU LFS data to trace migrant flows directly. To assess the short-term changes in mobility, we looked at those migrants who resided abroad for less than 36 months (see Figure 2). The behaviour of persons with the shortest 'migration tenure' is consistent with theoretical predictions. The economic downturn in the most important destinations and a relatively favourable economic situation in Poland are strongly correlated with a significant drop in the number of short-term stayers from Poland. An increase in the numbers of Polish migrants residing abroad up to 36 months is noted already in 2011 and 2012, suggesting a response to gradual recovery of the receiving economies (Kahanec 2013; Krause, Rinne, and Zimmermann 2014).

The tendency described above is visible particularly well in the case of Ireland where a dramatic drop in the number of short-term migrants has been noted. This change can be

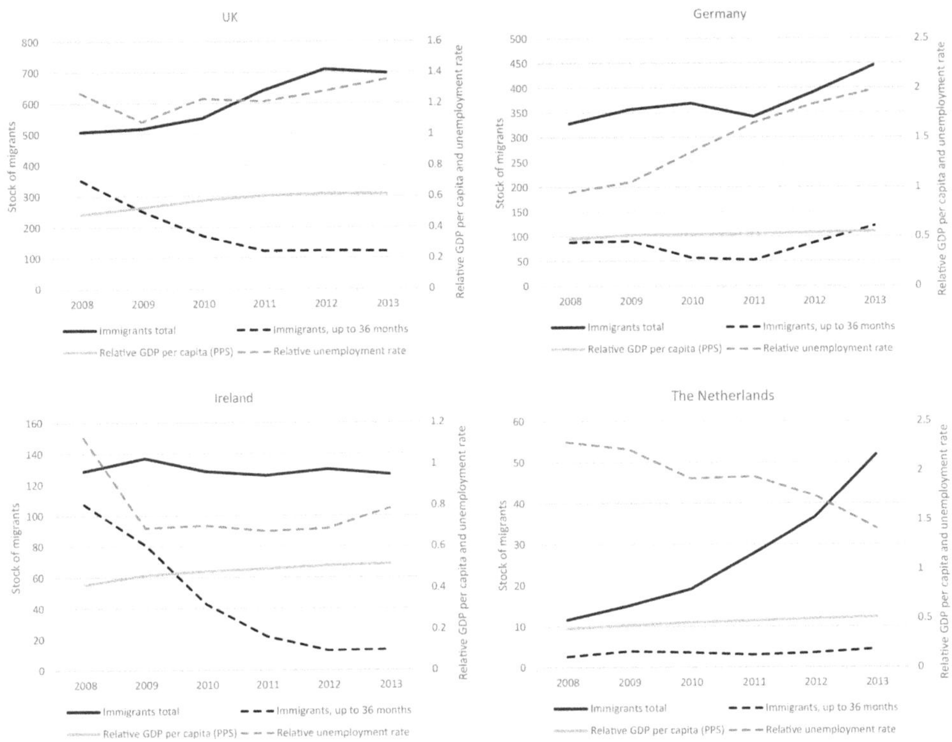

Figure 2. Stock of Polish migrants in the most important EU destinations and economic conditions in Poland (GDP per capita and unemployment rate relative to the level in a given destination country), 2008–2013.
Source: Own elaboration based on EU LFS data.

assigned to the deterioration of the labour market conditions in Ireland (as described above) both in absolute and relative terms. Between 2008 and 2009, that is, during the critical phase of the economic crisis, the unemployment rate among NMS migrants increased from 6.4% to 17.7% (among Irish nationals from 4.6% to 9.4%). These developments are largely attributable to the over-representation of NMS migrants in the construction sectors, which were severely hit by the crisis. Interestingly enough, there was only limited evidence suggesting that NMS migrants were to leave Ireland because of the crisis and thus the total stock of (long-term) Polish migrants remained almost unchanged. This resulted from: (1) continuous employment opportunities despite relatively high unemployment, (2) access to social benefits, and (3) the growing role of non-economic factors, including migrant networks acting as an insurance mechanism (Krings et al. 2013).

It is important to note, however, that relative unemployment rates as presented above are not necessarily a good proxy for factors influencing the situation (and decisions) of immigrants. Economic theory suggests that at the time of a crisis, immigrants are among those who lose their jobs first and face the biggest difficulties in finding new employment (see Section 1.1). Data on Polish migrants show that this is strongly conditional on the depth of the crisis and modes of labour market incorporation (the role of structural demand factors). A significant increase in the unemployment rate has

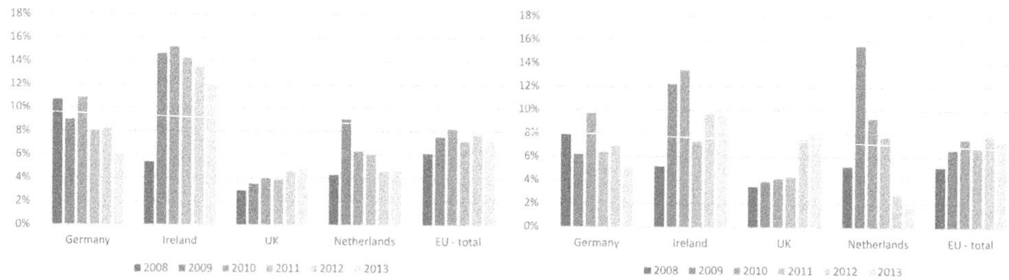

Figure 3. Unemployment rate of Polish migrants in the EU and selected destinations, total (left panel) and migrants residing abroad up to 36 months (right panel), 2008–2013, in %.
Source: Own elaboration based on EU LFS data.

been noted only in the case of Ireland, but even there (1) the rate of unemployment of Polish immigrants was comparable to the rate of the natives and (2) it started to decline as early as in 2011 (Figure 3).

In the case of other destination countries, the unemployment rates remained at relatively low levels (or even declined as it was in the case of Germany). Interestingly, there is no adverse effect visible in case of new arrivals. Unemployment rates of migrants residing abroad up to 36 months are comparable to the general unemployment rates (with the exception of the recent situation in the UK). This may suggest that in the case of Polish migrants, the labour market acts as an efficient filter: those having a job tend to stay or settle, those without employment tend to leave.

Moreover, the EU LFS data do not support the hypothesis that the crisis has led to sectoral re-allocation of immigrant workers from Poland.[5] In case of most sectors, the shares of employed Polish migrants remain almost constant over time (Figure 4). Slight decreases have been noted in the case of manufacturing (1.1 pp.) and construction (2.5 pp.), yet despite the crisis, in 2014 both sectors employed as many as 30% of the total number

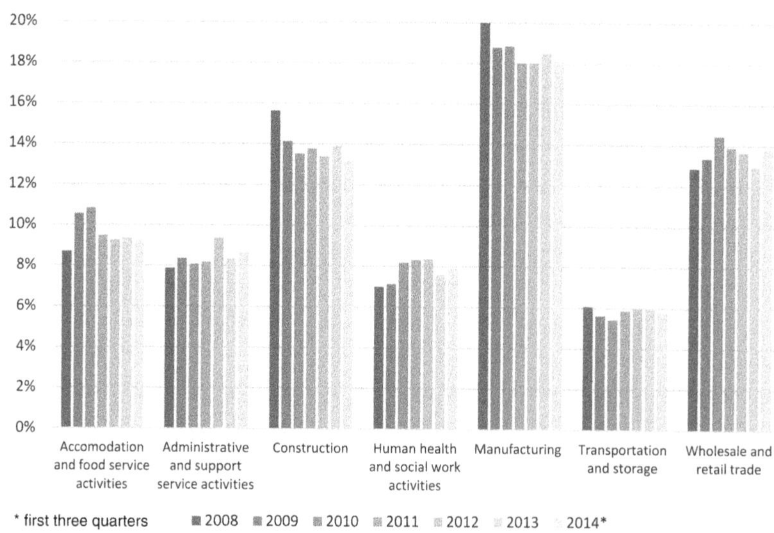

Figure 4. Polish migrants in the EU by economic activity, main categories (NACE1D), as % of the total.
Source: Own elaboration based on EU LFS data.

of Polish migrants working abroad, which presented a small decline as compared to 2008. Thus, data on Polish migrants are hardly consistent with the European Commission's report pointing to significant changes in the sectoral allocation of intra-EU movers in favour of high-skilled occupations and at the cost of employment in construction and manufacturing (European Commission 2014).

Similarly, the EU LFS data show that the occupational position of Polish migrants is also surprisingly stable in the crisis and post-crisis periods. Moderate changes have been noted only in the case of basic occupations such as plant and machine operators and assemblers, with a visible decline and well-skilled ones such as professionals and technicians, with an increase. These observations are in line with recent studies pointing to a slow but gradual process of occupational advancement of Polish and NMS migrants (see, among others, Parutis 2014).

The analyses presented above show that the recent crisis impacted the stock of Polish migrants in the EU to a limited extent only. This observation is in line with those theoretical predictions which emphasise that during a crisis immigrants may tend to postpone their return decisions because of prevailing possibilities of finding new employment, growing uncertainty and paid economic and social costs of integration. This feature is clearly identifiable even in the case of Ireland which was hit by the crisis most severely.

Many authors argue that the ability of NMS migrants to alleviate the negative impacts of the crisis are conditional on their flexibility, particularly on large shares of circular and temporary movements (see Barrett et al. 2014; Zaiceva and Zimmerman 2012). From the presented data, it follows that this feature of Polish migrants could have no longer been in place recently. In most countries under analysis, there were significant drops noted in the number of short-term migrants from Poland. Therefore, in view of research indicating a gradual diversion and individualisation of Poles' migration strategies (see Section 1.2), there is a need to deepen the macroeconomic analysis presented above by considering migration strategies.

4. Crisis-driven strategies?

As we have signalled, the situation of Polish migrants during the crisis phase seems far more complex than considered by existing theories. First, Poland was one of the few EU member states not having suffered from a severe economic downturn. Second, despite the relatively favourable economic situation in terms of GDP growth and labour market performance, there is still an income gap between Poland and major destination countries. Third, Polish migrants are indeed over-represented in typical immigrant sectors with construction and agriculture as the most prominent examples. At the same time, Poles are significantly overqualified. This last characteristic, theoretically, should increase their chances on the receiving labour market during an economic downturn. Fourth, in general, as EU citizens Poles do not face serious barriers to accessing social benefits in destination countries. Against this background, this section describes the crisis and post-crisis strategies of Polish migrants and provides insight into these migrants' role as an economic buffer on the labour market.

Findings from the EU LFS are complemented by data from cyclical quantitative surveys with Polish migrants conducted since 2009 in four main destination countries (the Netherlands, Ireland, Germany, and UK) by the National Bank of Poland (NBP).[6] Due to the fact that the survey results are not fully comparable year to year, we will illustrate the post-crisis trends with a comparison of results for 2009 and 2012 (Table 1). Contrary to data from the LFS, the NBP data do not provide information on the size of the migrant population, but allow analysing migrant characteristics and their changes.[7]

The basic findings are in line with EU LFS data. Between 2009 and 2012, the average time spent abroad by a migrant has increased significantly in all studied countries. The increase was the highest among migrants in Ireland, and relatively low in the Netherlands. The very high increase in case of Ireland indicates that new inflows were relatively low during the crisis period and that if migrants left, it was rather short-term and not long-term migrants who did so.

These observations are further confirmed by an analysis of the shares of migrants staying less than 12 and less than 36 months. In 2012, the shares of recent migrants were the highest in the Netherlands; but even there, they did not exceed 10% of the total stock, while in 2009, they ranged from 20% to 30%, depending on the destination. The fact that the shares of recent immigrants become somewhat lower is statistically natural even if no changes in migration patterns are observed as long as the stock of migrants in general increases proportionately, but this was not the case.

The findings from the NBP survey suggest that in view of the crisis in the destination countries, Poles have become less mobile. Those who were abroad and fairly settled stayed. Those who were less settled left. New arrivals became less frequent. The NBP data also show that during the studied period, the share of migrants for whom the surveyed migration episode was the only one *increased* significantly in all considered countries. This means that it was the most mobile ('fluid') individuals who have left the studied destination countries during the crisis. In view of the NBP data, these mobile individuals seldom relocated to one of the four countries under study. Although the shares of

Table 1. Selected characteristics of Polish migrants in the Netherlands, Ireland, Germany, and the UK, 2009 and 2012.

	The Netherlands		Ireland		Germany		The UK	
Category	2009	2012	2009	2012	2009	2012	2009	2012
Average length of stay abroad (months)	34.05	51.61	35.94	68.47	65.19	95.40	41.82	60.85
Share of migrants staying less than 36 months (%)	69.6	45.0	68.6	9.5	54.0	30.9	52.0	24.0
Share of migrants staying less than 12 months (%)	28.4	6.8	24.0	1.1	25.0	5.1	21.0	2.5
Share of migrants with one migration episode (%)	36.7	60.1	46.4	79	30.7	67.3	31.6	76.1
Share of migrants arriving from Poland (%)	97.3	93.7	94.3	94.6	93.3	95.6	95.6	94.7
Share of migrants planning permanent stay (%)	10.8	37.0	7.9	34.1	17.3	42.1	18.2	45.2
Share of migrants declaring no wage at origin would cause return (%)	6.5	16.1	4.9	13.6	6.7	25.2	8.0	15.7
Share of migrants without family members at destination (%)	51.0	44.4	47.1	24.5	57.6	42.8	45.6	31.1
Share of migrants owing real estate at destination (%)	6.2	8.4	2.9	5.0	10.0	11.6	8.2	9.5
Share of migrants with bank account at destination (%)	72.5	76.3	81.1	92.1	72.6	74.8	80.4	95.6
Share of migrants receiving welfare benefits (%)	9.2	28.4	15.2	37.5	14.6	13.2	17.7	25.3
Share of migrants remitting (%)	65.9	42.4	72.2	40.9	65.3	38.6	63.9	31.7
Share of tertiary educated migrants (%)	41.4	23.3	37.1	31.3	49.0	24.4	40.6	29.5
Share of migrants aged 25–34 (%)	36.1	43.1	47.5	59.4	32.0	27.7	46.2	50.8
Average value of permanency indicator (0–1 scale)	0.34	0.46	0.35	0.56	0.36	0.47	0.39	0.52
Average value of circulation indicator (0–1 scale)	0.64	0.47	0.63	0.42	0.63	0.44	0.59	0.40
Sample size	*700*	*700*	*1000*	*1000*	*300*	*1500*	*1513*	*1500*

Source: Own elaboration based on the NBP data.

persons who had arrived directly from Poland decreased in case of the Netherlands and the UK, this decrease was minor. On the contrary, Ireland experienced an increase of the share of migrants coming directly from Poland, which signifies a predominant outflow of the fluid migrants. In Germany, the share of migrants originating directly from Poland also increased, which might be due to an increasing flow of migration from Poland. Contrary to the Slovak case, where a clear reallocation of migrants between receiving countries where labour market conditions varied took place (Kahanec and Kurekova 2014), there is no evidence of mass repeat migration of Polish mobile persons into the considered countries.

The most important change observed is an apparent adaptation of migration strategies. The surveyed migrants, that is, those who stayed,[8] have become much more inclined towards settlement. The shares of migrants with intentions to stay permanently increased significantly, with the magnitude ranging from a twofold (Germany) to fourfold (Ireland) increase. At the same time, the fraction of migrants who declared that no financial incentives in Poland would encourage them to return also increased significantly, meaning additionally that the purely economic motives of migration lost importance. These declarations stand in line with actions, as the shares of migrants who resided abroad without any family members decreased, while the share of migrants who were owners of real estate, or owners of a bank account in the country of destination increased in all cases. The change in the frequency of migration with family members is indeed a novelty and should not be attributed solely to changes in the structure of immigration, since the share of young migrants (aged 25–34) increased during this period.[9]

NBP data indicate a decrease of the share of migrants with tertiary education in favour of secondary vocational education and of very young migrants (aged 18–24) in all countries considered in the study. These changes seem to reflect the situation on the Polish labour market which remains especially difficult in case of young persons with secondary education. Additionally, the fact that over time Polish migration became less selective with respect to human capital can suggest that, contrary to the first post-accession years, in the crisis and post-crisis phase the role of purely 'economic' motives is diminishing, in favour of other factors such as family-related ones. Importantly, the very understanding of a family changes as well. This is clearly visible in the NBP data. Apart from an increase in the share of migrants staying abroad with family members, in all countries considered in 2012 the share of migrants who sent remittances decreased significantly relative to 2009. This signifies that migrants remaining abroad more often with family members have different migrant strategies than before and have loosened ties with their home country because less family members remain in Poland.

As far as participation in the welfare system of the receiving country is concerned, an increase of the share of migrants declaring they receive social benefits can be observed in all countries apart from Germany, where this share is stable. This result is obviously partly due to eligibility constraints, but can also easily explain why migrants, even in view of a worsening situation, prefer to remain abroad rather than return.[10] This observation is clearly consistent with many studies showing a natural tendency to prefer relatively more secure EU destinations despite relatively favourable macroeconomic conditions at home (see Bratsberg, Raaum, and Roed 2014; Iglicka 2009; Krings et al. 2013).

In order to summarise the changes in migration strategies synthetically, two individual indicators – of permanency and circulation – have been calculated. Both indicators have been constructed as the average of responses to sets of questions referring to the length of stay, migration record, return/settlement plans, reservation wage, ownership of real estate at country of destination, registration in the social security system abroad, presence of family at destination, and remitting behaviour. Higher values of the permanency indicator suggest inclination towards settlement; higher values of the circulation indicator suggest inclination towards temporary presence in the country of destination.[11] The results clearly show that the overall trend between 2009 and 2012 is a decrease of the prevalence of circular-like strategies (the average value of the circulation indicator falls from values around 0.60–0.45), and an increase in the inclination towards settlement. The average value of the permanency indicator rises from values around 0.35–0.50. This is true for all countries considered in the NBP survey, although the changes are the most pronounced in Ireland.

It remains an open question, however, to what extent the changes in migrant strategies illustrated by the NBP data are an effect of the crisis, and to what extent they reflect a natural process of settlement. There is reasonable evidence that the strategy of Poles during turbulent times is rather that of 'survival' abroad, perhaps with a reallocation to a different foreign country which is preferred to return. The observed changes in the strategy characteristics are in line with the above-mentioned analysis of Friberg (2012), who has found that in the case of post-accession migration of Poles to Norway, most start out as target-earners, but gradually many of them change their strategies in favour of permanent settlement with families. Other authors pointed to serious dependence of migration strategies on the family situation of Poles also in the British context (Ryan et al. 2009; White 2011).

Nevertheless, the observed effects cannot be attributed solely to the process of gradual settlement of circular migrants. In the NBP study, the share of long-term migrants with single migration episodes increased during the studied period. In the context of a rather stable (or decreasing, as in the case of Ireland) stock, this signifies that the most mobile migrants left, rather than transformed to permanent stayers. Thus, our analysis supports the hypothesis that the economic downturn has led to a polarisation of strategies of migrants: the more mobile, circular migrants left, while those who were less mobile stayed and settled. Therefore, we may say that the effect of the crisis on mobility flows depends greatly on the non-economic dimensions of migrant strategies (translating to different responses).

5. Concluding remarks

The freedom of movement, one of the four fundamental freedoms of the EU, has been seriously tested during the recent economic crisis. On the one hand, the economic downturn has brought 'typical' negative attitudes towards migrants and has amplified activities of right-wing parties highlighting the negative consequences of migration. On the other hand, intra-EU mobility was expected to act as a buffer and to play an important role in the crisis and post-crisis economic adjustments in both countries of origin and destination.

Against this background, this article analysed the impact of changing economic conditions in the sending and receiving countries on migration strategies of Polish migrants.

It provided insight into the role of mobility of Poles in alleviating the effects of the crisis. After analysing two complementary data sources, we claim that the crisis did not lead to significant changes in the stock of Polish migrants in the major destination countries. In fact, the theoretical predictions based on economic theory came true only with respect to short-term or circular migrants. The number of short-term stayers dropped significantly in most destination countries, including those with relatively high shares of seasonal workers, as the Netherlands. In view of the crisis in destination countries, growing uncertainty and pertinent economic disparities between Poland and the EU15, Poles have become less mobile – those who were abroad and fairly settled stayed there, those who were less settled left, and new arrivals became less frequent. This conclusion is of utmost importance as many researchers claim that the ability of migration to alleviate the negative impacts of the crisis are conditional on the flexibility of the flows, particularly on large shares of circular and temporary movements.

On the other hand, an apparent adaptation of migration strategies is also clearly identifiable. Our analysis, in line with other empirical studies, shows that Polish migrants have become much more inclined towards settlement. This change is partially attributable to the economic crisis, given that with respect to economic migrants the labour market acts as an efficient filter: those who have a job tend to stay or settle, those without employment tend to leave. We also pointed to a range of other underlying circumstances, however. These include lifestyle migrations, long-term orientation of Polish migrants, the self-development perspective, or 'Project: ME', and last but not least, the migrants' family situation. The change in the share of persons staying abroad with family members is a novelty in the post-accession migration picture. It is still unknown to what extent this presents an adaptation of migration strategies to the crisis and to what extent it is just a manifestation of a natural process of settlement. In either case, the role of these non-economic factors should not be overlooked, as they change the role migration may play during crisis times.

All in all, the presented findings should not be interpreted as a signal that there are no identifiable adjustment mechanisms in the EU labour market. It is rather that the scale, dynamics, and structure of migration are dependent not only on a broad range of factors including the socio-economic environment such as wage differentials, access to social benefits, and labour market position, but also on migration strategies. Moreover, considering the still relatively unfavourable conditions on the Polish labour market, a tendency to postpone return or to settle abroad should be interpreted in terms of an adjustment mechanism per se.

Notes

1. This is the case of Poland and many receiving countries such as Ireland.
2. These observations should be treated with caution. The 2007 peak levels reflect not only the pre-crisis general trends, but also the effects of the 2007 accession of Bulgaria and Romania, which greatly influenced flows in some countries such as Italy (European Commission 2014; OECD 2014).
3. This data set comprises responses to quarterly surveys with samples covering between 0.2% and 3.3% of the population of a given EU Member State. This approach poses a serious challenge in case of immigration studies. The coverage of the immigrant population varies heavily between countries and is particularly questionable in case of those with relatively limited

numbers of foreigners and also those hosting predominantly short-term or seasonal migrants, who are extremely difficult to capture by means of traditional sampling methods.

4. Polish data show a slightly different picture. According to estimates of the Central Statistical Office, the stock of Polish nationals staying temporarily abroad in EU countries amounted to approximately 750,000 persons in 2004. In 2007 (the peak year) this stock was estimated at around 1.9 million, fell to 1.6 million in 2010, and gradually increased again to 1.8 million in 2013.
5. In net terms; unfortunately, we are not able to analyse the structure of the labour market in terms of flows.
6. The surveys are conducted with Polish citizens aged 16–65, residing abroad at least three months, who migrated for work-related reasons. The sampling methodology assures wide coverage, but not full representativeness of the Polish migrant population (Hołda et al. 2011). Data courtesy of the National Bank of Poland.
7. Hołda et al. (2011) note that although the sample is not representative, the structure with respect to major uncontrolled variables, such as education, resembles that from representative studies conducted in Poland, such as the Polish LFS and Diagnoza Społeczna.
8. There is an obvious selection bias in the data due to the fact that we do not observe those migrants who decided to leave the country. In our analysis, we focus particularly on strategies of those who are still present in destination countries, however.
9. The share of very young migrants decreased.
10. This result is even more striking in view of the fact that the share of migrants registered in the social security systems in the sample has remained stable or even decreased (in the UK) during the studied period.
11. Note that due to the use of different variables, the value of the two indicators for a single migrant need not sum up to 1.

Disclosure statement

No potential conflict of interest was reported by the authors.

Funding

This work was supported by the National Science Centre under grant 'European Welfare Systems at Time of Mobility' [number 2014/14/Z/HS4/00006].

References

Barrett, A., A. Bergin, E. Kelly, and S. McGuinness. 2014. *Ireland's Recession and the Immigrant/Native Earnings Gap*. IZA Discussion Papers No. 8459.

Beets, G., and F. Willekens. 2009. "The Global Economic Crisis and International Migration: An Uncertain Outlook." *Vienna Yearbook of Population Research* 2009: 19–37.

Beine, M., P. Bourgeon, and J. Bricongne. 2013. *Aggregate Fluctuations and International Migration*. CESifo Working Paper, No. 4379.

Benton, M., and M. Petrovic. 2013. *How Free Is Free Movement? Dynamics and Drivers of Mobility Within the European Union*. Brussels: Migration Policy Institute Europe.

Bertoli, S., H. Brücker, and J. Fernández-Huertas Moraga. 2013. *The European Crisis and Migration to Germany: Expectations and the Diversion of Migration Flows*. Discussion Paper Series, Forschungsinstitut zur Zukunft der Arbeit, No. 7170.

Bratsberg, B., O. Raaum, and K. Roed. 2014. *Labour Migrant Adjustments in the Aftermath of the Financial Crisis*. IZA Discussion Papers No. 8291.

Burda, M. 1995. *Migration and the Option Value of Waiting*. CEPR Discussion Papers No. 1229.

Castles, S., and M. Miller. 1993. *The Age of Migration*. London: Macmillan.

Clark, K., and S. Drinkwater. 2008. "The Labour-Market Performance of Recent Migrants." *Oxford Review of Economic Policy* 24 (3): 495–516.

Clark, K., S. Drinkwater, and C. Robinson. 2014. *Migration, Economic Crisis and Adjustment in the UK*. IZA Discussion Papers No. 8410.

Dhéret, C., A. Lazarowicz, F. Nicoli, Y. Pascouau, and F. Zuleeg. 2013. *Making Progress Towards the Completion of the Single European Labour Market*. EPC Issue Paper No. 75. Brussels: European Policy Centre (EPC). www.europe-solidarity.eu.

Drinkwater, S., J. Eade, and M. Garapich. 2009. "Poles Apart? EU Enlargement and the Labour Market Outcomes of Immigrants in the UK." *International Migration* 47: 161–190.

Drinkwater, S., and M. Garapich. 2015. "Migration Strategies of Polish Migrants: Do They Have Any at All?" *Journal of Ethnic and Migration Studies*. doi:10.1080/1369183X.2015.1027180.

Dustmann, Ch., and J.-S. Görlach. 2015. *The Economics of Temporary Migrations*. CESifo Working Paper No. 5188.

Duvell, F. 2009. "The Crisis and Its Possible Impact on Global Migration. Migration and the Global Financial Crisis Virtual Symposium." www.ageofmigration.com.

Eade, J., S. Drinkwater, and M. Garapich. 2007. *Class and Ethnicity: Polish Migrant Workers in London*. End of Award Research Report. Swindon, UK: ESRC.

Engbersen, G., A. Leerkes, I. Grabowska-Lusińska, E. Snel, and J. Burgers. 2013. "On the Differential Attachments of Migrants from Central and Eastern Europe: A Typology of Labour Migration." *Journal of Ethnic and Migration Studies* 39 (6): 959–981.

European Commission. 2014. "Recent Trends in the Geographical Mobility of Workers in the EU." Supplement to the *EU Employment and Social Situation Quarterly Review*, June. www.ec.europa.eu.

Faist, T. 2015. "Transnational Social Spaces." *Ethnic and Racial Studies* 38 (13): 2271–2274.

Faist, T., and E. Ozveren, eds. 2004. *Transnational Social Spaces: Agents, Networks and Institutions*. London: Ashgate.

Favell, A. 2008. "The New Face of East-West Migration in Europe." *Journal of Ethnic and Migration Studies* 34 (5): 701–716.

Fawcett, J. T. 1987. "Networks, Linkages and Migration Systems." *International Migration Review* 23 (3): 671–680.

Fihel, A., A. Janicka, P. Kaczmarczyk, and J. Nestorowicz. 2015. *Free Movement of Workers and Transitional Arrangements: Lessons from the 2004 and 2007 Enlargements*. Brussels: European Commission, DG Employment.

Friberg, J. H. 2012. "The Stages of Migration. From Going Abroad to Settling Down: Post-accession Polish Migrant Workers in Norway." *Journal of Ethnic and Migration Studies* 38 (10): 1589–1605.

Glick Schiller, N., L. Basch, and C. Szanton Blanc. 1992. "Transnationalism: A New Analytic Framework for Understanding Migration." In *Towards a Transnational Perspective on Migration: Race, Class, Ethnicity and Nationalism Reconsidered*, edited by N. Glick Schiller, L. Basch, and C. Szanton Blanc, 1–24. New York: New York Academy of Science.

Grabowska, I., and M. Okólski. 2009. *Emigracja Ostatnia?* Warsaw: Scholar.

Hatton, T. J., and J. Williamson. 2002. *What Fundamentals Drive World Migration?* CEPR Discussion Papers 3559.

Hołda, M., K. Saczuk, P. Strzelecki, and R. Wyszyński. 2011. *Settlers and Guests – Determinants of the Plans of Return Migration from UK and Ireland to Poland in the Period 2007–2009*. National Bank of Poland Working Paper 84.

Holland, D., T. Fic, A. Rincon-Aznar, L. Stokes, and P. Paluchowski. 2011. *Labour Mobility Within the EU – The Impact of Enlargement and the Functioning of the Transitional Arrangements*. Final Report. London: National Institute of Economic and Social Research. www.ec.europa.eu.

Holland, D., and P. Paluchowski. 2013. *Geographical Labour Mobility in the Context of the Crisis*. European Employment Observatory Ad-hoc Request. www.eu-employment-observatory.net.

Iglicka, K. 2009. *Powroty Polaków w okresie kryzysu gospodarczego. W pętli pułapki migracyjnej. Raport z badań*. Raporty i Analizy CSM 1/09.

Isański, J., A. Mleczko, and R. Seredyńska-Abou Eid. 2014. "Polish Contemporary Migration: From Co-igrants to Project ME." *International Migration* 52 (1): 4–21.

Jauer, J., T. Liebig, J. Martin, and P. Puhani. 2014. *Migration as an Adjustment Mechanism in the Crisis? A Comparison of Europe and the United States.* OECD Social, Employment and Migration Working Papers, No. 155. Paris: OECD.

Kaczmarczyk, P. 2013. "Central and Eastern European Migration, Post-World War II to Present." In *The Encyclopedia of Global Human Migration*, edited by E. Ness. New York: Wiley.

Kaczmarczyk, P., and M. Okólski. 2008. "Demographic and Labour-Market Impacts of Migration on Poland." *Oxford Review of Economic Policy* 24 (3): 599–624.

Kahanec, M. 2013. "Labor Mobility in an Enlarged European Union." In *International Handbook on the Economics of Migration*, edited by A. F. Constant and K. F. Zimmermann, 137–152. Cheltenham, UK: Edward Elgar.

Kahanec, M., and L. Kurekova. 2014. *Did Post-Enlargement Labor Mobility Help the EU to Adjust During the Great Recession? The Case of Slovakia.* IZA Discussion Papers No. 8249.

Kahanec, M., M. Pytlikova, and K. F. Zimmermann. 2014. *The Free Movement of Workers in an Enlarged European Union: Institutional Underpinnings of Economic Adjustment.* IZA Discussion Papers No. 8456.

Kahanec, M., and K. F. Zimmermann, eds. 2009. *EU Labor Markets after Post-enlargement Migration.* Bonn: Springer.

Krause, A., U. Rinne, and K. F. Zimmermann. 2014. *How Far Away Is a Single European Labor Market?* IZA Discussion Papers No. 8383.

Krings, T., A. Bobek, E. Moriarty, J. Salamońska, and J. Wickham. 2013. "Polish Migration to Ireland: "Free Movers" in the New European Mobility Space." *Journal of Ethnic and Migration Studies* 39 (1): 87–103.

Lee, E. S. 1966. "A Theory of Migration." *Demography* 3 (1): 47–57.

Martin, P. 2009. "The Recession and Migration Alternative Scenarios." Migration and the Global Financial Crisis Virtual Symposium. www.ageofmigration.com.

Massey, D., J. Arango, G. Hugo, A. Kouaouci, A. Pellegrino, and J. E. Taylor. 1993. "Theories of International Migration: A Review and Appraisal." *Population and Development Review* 19 (3): 431–466.

Moriarty, E., J. Wickham, J. Salomonska, T. Krings, and A. Bobek. 2010. "Putting Work Back in Mobilities: Migrant Careers and Aspirations." Paper presented at the 'New Migrations, New Challenges' Conference, Trinity College Dublin, July.

OECD. 2014. *International Migration Outlook 2014.* Paris: OECD.

Papademetriou, D., M. Sumption, and W. Somerville. 2009. *Migration and the Economic Downturn: What to Expect in the European Union.* Washington, DC: Migration Policy Institute.

Parutis, V. 2014. ""Economic Migrants" or "Middling Transnationals"? East European Migrants' Experiences of Work in the UK." *International Migration* 52 (1): 36–55.

Pries, L., ed., 2001. *New Transnational Social Spaces.* London: Routledge.

Ryan, L., R. Sales, M. Tilki, and B. Siara. 2009. "Family Strategies and Transnational Migration: Recent Polish Migrants in London." *Journal of Ethnic and Migration Studies* 35 (1): 61–77.

Sjaastad, L. A. 1962. "The Costs and Returns of Human Migration." *Journal of Political Economy* 70: 80–93.

Stark, O., and D. E. Bloom. 1985. "The New Economics of Labor Migration." *American Economic Review* 75 (2): 173–178.

Trevena, P., D. McGhee, and S. Heath. 2013. "Location, Location? A Critical Examination of Patterns and Determinants of Internal Mobility among Post-accession Polish Migrants in the UK." *Population, Space and Place* 19: 671–687.

White, A. 2011. *Polish Families and Migration since EU Accession.* Bristol, UK: Policy Press.

Zaiceva, A., and K. F. Zimmermann. 2012. *Returning Home at Times of Trouble? Return Migration of EU Enlargement Migrants during the Crisis.* IZA Discussion Papers No. 7111.

The economic crisis as a driver of cross-border labour mobility? A multi-method perspective on the case of the Central European Region

Laura Wiesböck, Roland Verwiebe, Christoph Reinprecht and Raimund Haindorfer

ABSTRACT

This paper discusses labour mobility from the Czech Republic, Hungary and Slovakia to Austria during the period before and after the economic crisis of 2008/2009. Building up on the TRANSLAB research project, we illustrate various facets of the interregional labour market with a mixed methods approach using regional macro-economic data, national labour market statistics, 20 expert interviews and a longitudinal survey consisting of 1345 cross-border commuters who work in Austria. Empirically we demonstrate that, due to the gradual opening of the Austrian labour market from 2004 to 2011, flows of cross-border commuters have steadily increased. Since 2009 the social composition of cross-border commuters has changed as well. We can observe a growing number of workers seeking employment in Austria who have been most vulnerable during the crisis: the young, the lowly educated and female workers. Moreover, expert interviews show a rising and economically driven demand for employment in Austria.

1. Introduction

Up-to-date empirical studies on post-crisis mobility trends in terms of East–West cross-border commuting remain quite scarce (exceptions include: Bahna 2014; Benton and Petrovic 2013; Galgóczi, Leschke, and Watt 2012). In order to fill this gap, this paper examines recent trends in East–West cross-border commuting in the EU before and after the financial crisis of 2008/2009. Building upon an on-going empirical study of the Central European Region (CENTROPE), the article discusses how the crisis has affected labour mobility flows from the border regions of the Czech Republic, Hungary and Slovakia to Austria. In this Euroregion – an institutionalised platform for cross-border coordination and cooperation – structural imbalances still exist and, according to the European Commission, mobility of labour is a crucial element for reducing regional disparities (Centrope 2012).[1] Cross-border commuting in CENTROPE is framed in multiple ways by on-going societal transformations resulting both from European enlargement processes and the post-socialist restructuring of economic, political and legal institutions. Cross-border commuting can be conceived as a multifaceted process within a rapidly changing environment and under the influence of several major factors.[2] For example, the gradual opening of the Austrian labour market from 2004 (to Malta and Cyprus) until 2011 (to Estonia, Lithuania, Latvia, Poland, the Czech Republic, Slovakia, Slovenia and Hungary) has marked important transitions. Building up on a mixed-method approach, the present paper discusses various key aspects of cross-border commuting in CENTROPE before and after 2009. Thus, we seek to draw a comprehensive picture of the potential relation between the economic crisis and mobility processes. We pursue the following research questions:

(1) How did the crisis affect economic and social inequalities between the subregions of CENTROPE?
(2) How did the crisis affect labour mobility from the border regions of the Czech Republic, Hungary and Slovakia to Austria?
(3) To what extent have the socio-economic composition of cross-border commuters and the mode of their labour market integration changed since 2008/2009?
(4) To what extent has wage mobility among commuters been affected by the crisis in 2008/2009?

In order to answer these questions, we draw upon Eurostat regional macro-economic data (research question 1), national labour market statistics issued by the Austrian Unemployment Service (research question 2), 20 expert interviews (research question 2) and a longitudinal survey comprising 1345 cross-border commuters who work in Austria (research questions 3 and 4). The applied expert survey consists of 20 interviews conducted between 2011 and 2014 with European Employment Services (EURES) employees, business owners and local political leaders in the CENTROPE region. We further analyse a new retrospective longitudinal survey consisting of 1345 commuters from the Czech Republic, Hungary and Slovakia bordering on Austria that was collected in 2012/2013 within the TRANSLAB research project.

This article is structured as follows: in the first part, we provide an overview of the institutionalisation of labour mobility within the EU. We discuss Euroregions in terms of institutionalised cross-border spaces and how they contribute to the regional dimension of European integration. The paper proceeds with an introduction to CENTROPE and the methodological design of a case study to offer an example of this specific context. After illustrating the outcomes of our empirical study, we conclude with an outlook and further important research questions.

2. The crisis and intra-European labour circulation: economic and institutional perspectives

There is a large body of economic literature on migration and mobility dealing with for example the reasons for migration, the directionality and continuity of migrant flows or the utilisation of immigrant labour (Portes 1997). In this paper, we do not adopt one single theoretical model but rather aim to analyse cross-border commuting in times of economic crisis by taking several perspectives into consideration: according to neo-classical theory, migration is driven by geographic differences in labour supply and demand and by the resulting differentials in wages between labour-rich versus capital-rich countries

(Harris and Todaro 1970). While neo-classical economics assumes that people move abroad permanently to maximise lifetime earnings, the new economics of labour migration assumes that they do so temporarily to overcome market deficiencies at home (Constant and Massey 2002). The segmented or dual labour market theory argues that there is a divide between the high-wage primary and low-wage secondary segments in which immigrants are situated (Piore 1979). Here immigration is linked to structural labour market requirements. Workers are attracted through recruitment practices rather than wage offers. World system theory sees migration as a natural consequence of economic globalisation, whereby companies operate across national boundaries (Wallerstein 1974). New approaches involve in-depth studies at a micro-level, for example, by studying differences and similarities between migrants and non-migrants from similar contexts.

When seeking to understand how decisions to migrate are shaped by larger macro-level factors, it is essential to take political structures into account. The EU has been strongly encouraging intra-European mobility through institutional and cultural programmes since the early 1990s. Relevant factors in fostering intra-European movements have included the implementation of the Maastricht Treaty's freedom of movement provisions, recognition of foreign qualifications by the EU member states, the Erasmus and Socrates programmes and the development of a network of European employment offices (Findlay et al. 2006; King and Ruiz-Gelices 2003; Verwiebe et al. 2010). This new mode of migration management corresponds to the flexibility paradigm which has prevailed in the European post-Fordist economies over the past decades (Venturini 2008). It appears to pose a limited integration burden on destination countries while maximising transnational transfers (Triandafyllidou 2013, 4). The main idea behind this process is to generate a 'win–win–win' situation, namely benefits for receiving countries by meeting labour market shortages, for sending countries through guaranteeing remittances for development and for migrants by offering employment and control over the use of their wages (Constant, Nottmeyer, and Zimmermann 2012). The old concept of migration in which individuals leave their country permanently no longer applies to the intra-European context (Favell 2008; Scott 2006; Verwiebe 2008). Rather, an increasing number of people go abroad for short periods of time to find seasonal employment or to commute across national borders on a regular basis (Mau and Büttner 2010). Transnational labour markets and enhanced mobility within these markets are often promoted as the way forward in EU policy to achieve economic integration. A variety of policymakers advocate measures to facilitate the movement of migrants between their homelands and foreign workplaces.[3]

The idea of European economic integration through mobility is also applied on a regional level. The European Commission strongly supports cross-border cooperation initiatives such as Euroregions (Centrope Agency 2012). Euroregions are transnational administrative units that foster collaborations between sub-national authorities in areas such as regional development, transport, local economy, cultural activities or the environment. Although some of these initiatives date back to the 1950s, most of these European cross-border regions were institutionalised in the 1990s. Today there are virtually no local or regional authorities in border areas that in one way or another are not involved in cross-border cooperation initiatives (Perkmann 2003). Euroregions have initiated a new era in international politics as institutional entrepreneurs, as a model of international governance for regional actors contesting the nation-state's monopoly on foreign affairs and international politics (Perkmann 1999, 2002). The establishment of Euroregions is connected with such political visions as a Europe without borders, a new regionalism and a return to shared regional historical and cultural roots (Klatt and Herrmann 2011, 66). The 'integrationist' turn (Klatt and Herrmann 2011) in academic research in this field points to the rise of a new kind of supranational governance in the form of regional transnationalism (Perkmann 2003). Border regions act as pioneers and laboratories of European integration. Thus, they become an important tier in today's system of multilevel government in the EU. Many Euroregions are active agents in the field of cross-border cooperation including enhanced labour mobility (Wiesböck et al. 2015). CENTROPE is a notable example of this development.

3. CENTROPE

CENTROPE is a distinct cultural area and political region consisting of eight federal provinces, regions and counties with a total population of approx. 6.5 million. The largest city in CENTROPE is Vienna, which has a population of 1.8 million and which, along with Bratislava, is one of the two national centres in the region. This is an exceptional situation in that most of the other intra-European border regions are located more peripherally (Figure 1).

Historically the dissolution of the Soviet Union, the EU enlargement and the removal of the last barriers to the free movement of labour have brought about significant changes which, in turn, have led to new forms of interplay between economic, social, political and legal factors (Horvath 2012). Since 1 May 2011, when the final transitional arrangements were lifted at the end of the seven-year transitional period, citizens of the A8 countries have had full access to labour markets across the EU-27.

Commuting within this part of Europe is not a recent phenomenon linked to the creation of the European common market (Terlouw 2012, 354). Formal and informal circularity between the countries have existed for many decades, albeit under specific conditions in the period of state socialism and with a longue history of cross-border mobility which began during the time of the Habsburg Monarchy (Verwiebe et al. 2015, 4). However, CENTROPE is one of many political projects in the EU that foster enhanced

Figure 1. CENTROPE. © Arge centrope. Reproduced by permission of City of Vienna.

mobility to strengthen competitiveness and the regional business location. Mobility of labour is one of the core aims of the CENTROPE Strategy 2013+, emphasising commitment to collaboration that ranges from research and innovation to human capital development, spatial integration and culture and tourism (Centrope Agency 2012). This reflects the differentiation of movement patterns within the EU: from once-in-a-lifetime migration to mobility as a life strategy. This development is also due to the relatively short distances within CENTROPE. For example, someone may easily commute between Bratislava and Vienna, the two most populous metropolitan areas in CENTROPE, within one hour's time.

Regarding the case study methodology, the TRANSLAB project builds on the established methods of 'ethnosurvey' data collection (Massey 1987) and on associated more recent applications for the European setting (Kalter 2011; Wallace and Vincent 2007). From October 2012 to June 2013, the social research department GfK Austria and its Central European partner institutes carried out face-to-face interviews with a total of 1345 commuters to Austria and a reference group consisting of 1334 non-commuters. By commuting, we understand a given individual's repeated and regular (daily, weekly, monthly or seasonal) movement across national borders. The currently employed interviewees (at least 20 hours a week) were age 21–65 and had their primary residence within regions bordering on Austria, for example, South Moravia (Czech Republic), Bratislava and Trnava (Slovakia), and Győr-Moson-Sopron and Vas (Hungary). Considering the lack of appropriate transnational sampling schemes, the best available approximation was done with a subsample of commuters gained via quota sampling, drawing on labour market statistics of the Austrian Public Employment Service.

Additionally we conducted a survey among experts using a semi-structured interview guide. The aim of this step was to deepen the research group's knowledge of the proposed study object. We interviewed a total of 20 experts consisting of EURES employees ($N = 6$), business owners ($N = 7$) as well as local mayors ($N = 6$) and a trade union representative. The expert interviews covered important aspects of the social process of commuting within this special region, such as the structure and development of mobility processes within CENTROPE, including relevant legal and institutional frameworks for cross-border commuting; the role of the EURES agencies, business owners, local political leaders and administrative officials in cross-border commuting; information on companies (size, sector) that hire commuters; possible short- and medium-term consequences (risks and opportunities) of the removal of the remaining barriers to free movement in CENTROPE; and the short- and mid-term economic scenarios for this region. In the following discussion, we focus on the interviews with EURES employees as they, by virtue of their occupational position, have specialist knowledge regarding the specific social contexts surrounding the interregional labour market.

4. The economic context: changes in inequality in sending and receiving regions before, during and after the crisis

Regardless of the political and economic reintegration of the region, CENTROPE is still characterised by relatively high economic and social inequalities. Tables 1 and 2 show that significant differences maintain in terms of household income, regional gross domestic product (GDP) levels, unemployment and poverty.

Table 1. Regional statistics between 2000 and 2011: household income and GDP.

	Household income per capita (PPS)					GDP per capita (PPS)				
	2000	2006	2008	2009	2011	2000	2006	2008	2009	2011
Austria	15,400	18,400	19,200	18,800	19,800	25,100	29,700	31,100	29,500	32,300
Lower Austria	15,600	18,800	19,800	19,300	20,600	20,700	24,200	25,700	24,200	26,600
Vienna	17,300	19,200	19,700	19,200	19,800	34,600	39,300	40,300	38,300	41,300
Burgenland	13,900	17,800	18,700	18,400	19,400	16,600	19,800	20,500	19,900	21,700
Czech Republic	7000	9400	9600	9900	10,200	13,500	18,900	20,200	19,400	20,300
Jihovýchod	6700	9000	9400	9600	9900	12,100	16,800	18,100	17,600	18,400
Slovakia	5500	7800	9500	9500	10,500	9,500	14,900	18,100	17,000	18,900
Bratislavský kraj	8000	12,200	14,400	15,000	16,000	20,700	34,800	41,700	41,600	46,600
Západné Slovensko	5200	7700	9500	9400	10,700	9,000	14,800	17,300	16,000	18,100
Hungary	5600	8000	7900	7900	8600	10,300	14,900	15,900	15,300	16,900
Nyugat-Dunántúl	5800	7500	7900	8200	5600	11,600	15,000	15,500	14,300	17,100

Source: Eurostat (2015); *household income*: balance of primary net income, PPS based on consumption per inhabitant; *GDP*: gross domestic product in PPS per inhabitant.

Table 2. Regional statistics between 2000 and 2011: unemployment and poverty rate.

	Unemployment rate in %					Poverty rate in %				
	2000	2006	2008	2009	2013	2005	2006	2008	2009	2013
Austria	4.7	4.7	3.8	4.8	4.9	12.6	12.6	15.2	14.5	14.4
Lower Austria	4.8	4.0	3.4	4.3	4.5	12.9	12.1	10.9	10.1	12.0
Vienna	7.5	8.8	6.7	7.5	8.4	15.2	17.2	17.0	17.1	23.0
Burgenland	4.8	5.0	3.6	4.6	4.0	11.6	12.4	13.0	11.2	7.0
Czech Republic	8.8	7.1	4.4	6.7	6.7	10.4	9.9	9.0	8.6	9.8
Jihovýchod	7.1	7.1	4.0	6.5	6.8	8.2	8.3	9.0	8.5	6.6
Slovakia	19.1	13.4	9.5	12.0	14.2	13.3	11.6	10.9	11.0	13.0
Bratislavský kraj	7.5	4.6	3.4	4.6	6.4	7.8	7.3	6.9	6.5	8.0
Západné Slovensko	17.6	9.8	6.4	9.9	11.7	13.5	10.4	10.1	10.0	11.5
Hungary	6.6	7.5	7.8	10.0	10.9	13.5	15.9	12.4	12.4	14.3
Nyugat-Dunántúl	4.4	5.7	4.9	8.6	7.8	–	–	–	–	–

Source: Eurostat (2015); *unemployment*: percentage of working age population; *poverty*: at risk of poverty, percentage of population; poverty rate for Hungary only available for NUTS-1 region Dunántúl; poverty rate for Austria in 2013 based on Austrian Statistical Office (Statistik Austria 2015a), not available via Eurostat; poverty rate on NUTS-2 level not available for period before 2005.

Overall, on a national level and in most of the subregions, *household income* (measured by individual consumption levels) has increased since the year 2000, while the income gap between the Austrian subregions and the Czech, Slovakian and Hungarian subregions has decreased markedly during the last decade due to a catching-up process in the Eastern countries (GDP per capita has doubled, for example, in the Slovakian subregions) (see Table 1). Interestingly household income in the Austrian subregions decreased between 2008 and 2009 – the first two years of the economic crisis in Europe – which was not the case in the other subregions of CENTROPE. However, substantial differences between the countries have remained until recently: in 2011, household income in Austria was more than twice as high as that in Hungary, which has the lowest income level followed at close range by Slovakia and the Czech Republic.

We can observe a similar pattern regarding the development of regional GDP per capita in the purchasing power standard (PPS). The GDP in Austrian subregions was two to three times higher than in the other subregions in 2000. A catching-up process has been taking place in the Czech, Slovakian and Hungarian subregions bordering Austria, with decreasing differences in GDP between 2000 and 2011. Moreover, the growth of

GDP per capita decelerated in all subregions of CENTROPE in the years after 2008. The most recent data of 2011 show that the areas in the Czech Republic and Slovakia have a per capita GDP around €18,000 (in PPS), with the exception of the region around Bratislava which has the highest per capita GDP in CENTROPE (€46,600). The Hungarian subregions have a GDP between €14,800 and €17,100. GDP in Austria varies between €21,700 (Burgenland) and €41,300 (Vienna).

The regional *unemployment* rates have changed during the last decade as well. There is a certain extent of catching-up due to improved levels of unemployment in the Czech, Slovakian and Hungarian subregions of CENTROPE. However, since the onset of the economic crisis in 2008, unemployment in those subregions has quickly increased. In the Austrian subregions, a stabilisation (and partially a decline) in unemployment can be ascertained since 2008 on account of successful government stimuli which have avoided large-scale job losses. Interestingly, the *risk of poverty* in relation to the median income level of the national population in Austrian *subregions is higher than in the neighbouring countries.*[4] *Here again, we observe increasing* levels of poverty in all subregions of CENTROPE. With the exception of Vienna, the increase is stronger in the subregions bordering Austria, thus leading to a gradual harmonisation of poverty rates in the entire region.

By and large, since the crisis in 2008, the structures of existing economic and social differences within CENTROPE have changed to some extent: (1) household income/consumption levels as well as GDP per capita have undergone a catching-up process within CENTROPE, which slowed down as of the economic crisis in 2008; (2) since 2008, unemployment has increased much more rapidly in the Czech, Slovakian and Hungarian subregions than in the Austrian subregions; and (3) on the national level, poverty risks in Austria are higher than in the other countries. However, poverty risks in the subregions of CENTROPE have been gradually harmonised since 2008 due to a stronger increase in poverty in the Czech, Slovakian and Hungarian subregions.

5. The scale of commuting: rising flows of and demand for labour post-crisis

How does the crisis affect cross-border commuting? Is there a relationship between the present (gradually decreasing) structural imbalances and the scale of cross-border commuting? Figure 2 provides an answer to these questions using available macro-data.

From 2009 a slight and steady increase in commuters from neighbouring countries has been taking place. This indicates that a reintegration of the region resulted from a gradual opening of the labour market (Commuter Treaty, Professional Employee Regulation 2008, Substitute Workforce Procedure) before the last barriers to free mobility were lifted in May 2011. Correspondingly we would argue that this steady increase in cross-border commuting cannot be solely attributed to the effects of the economic crisis but also has to be seen in the context of the changing legal framework and regional political reintegration.

The graphic provides insight into the dynamics of rising cross-border labour flows from the Czech Republic, Slovakia and Hungary to Austria. However, it is noteworthy that it only illustrates one part of social reality, as the Austrian Labour Market Service (AMS) data solely comprise dependently employed workers. Now, in order to describe the changing patterns and experiences of cross-border commuting during and after the crisis, we refer to the insights gained through expert interviews.

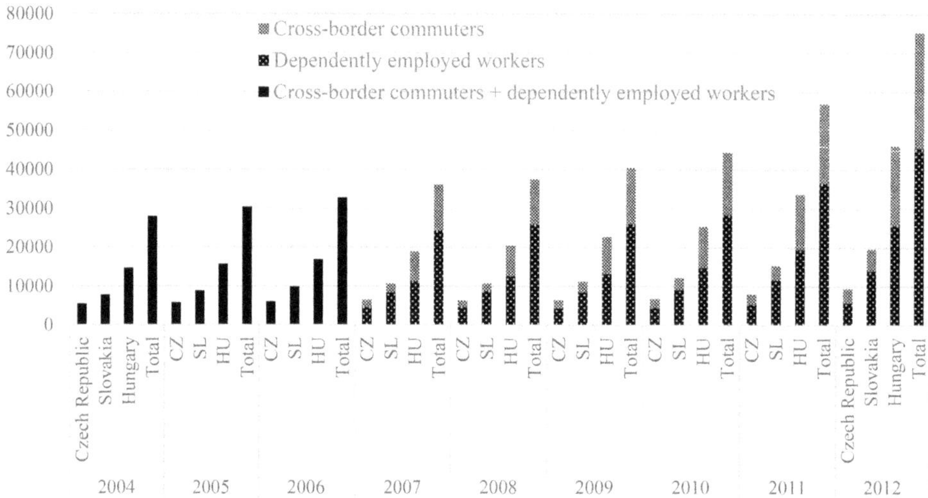

Figure 2. Cross-border commuters and dependently employed workers from Hungary, Slovakia and the Czech Republic on the Austrian labour market (2004–2012).
Source: Austrian Labour Market Service (AMS); own calculations. The data are based on quarterly reports of the Austrian Social Insurance Carrier (HV) which keep records of workers in dependent employment. Marginally employed, self-employed, contractors, foreign-employed are not included. Cross-border commuters: Czech, Hungarian and Slovakian citizens working in Austria with primary residence in their home country. No detailed data available between 2004 and 2006.

According to a EURES employee in *Hungary*, the crisis explicitly initiated movements to find employment across the border for existential economic reasons.

> There are a lot of people who fell into the credit trap. Many people in Hungary borrowed Swiss francs from a bank. A lot of them have pending execution proceedings, their houses have to be auctioned. There was even a case of a woman who had to put her two children into a foster home for the winter season. So there are a lot of hard fates. […] To my opinion, the rising demand [for information on employment in Austria] is clearly related to the financial crisis and the wish to escape from Hungary. One can speak of economic refugees who see their last chance in employment in a foreign country. (EURES Employee, Hungary, June 2012)

This may emphasise the fact that Hungary has been hit particularly hard by the crisis (see Table 2 for the increase in unemployment). Workers from Hungary commuting to Austria are on the rise: in Austria the number of newly registered Hungarians in 2011 (9000) was one and a half times higher than it had been a year earlier, doubling between 2010 and 2012 when it reached 13,000 (Statistik Austria 2015b). The increased demand for jobs for Hungarians is also reflected in the observations of an Austrian EURES employee. Yet according to his experience, there would be a plurality of reasons for recent mobility trends, such as current political developments:

> There are also people who come from Sopron which is only 20 kilometres from here. They have been living there for decades but just recently lost their jobs because of the crisis or the new government in Hungary or because of something else. […]. Hungary is a very, very special case. To some extent the economic development and the labour market situation certainly foster mobility. (EURES Employee, Austria, June 2012)

In this regard, it is important to note that, besides such macro-economic conditions as wage levels and unemployment rates, meso- and micro-factors, including transport infrastructure, urban structure in the border region and family and personal relations, also play an important role in affecting the flow of cross-border commuters. However, economic reasons are considered to be the most relevant drivers of workforce mobility.

Seeking employment in Austria for existential reasons is not only instigated by inhabitants of the border regions. The interviewed Hungarian EURES employee explained that the contemporary crisis has prompted new forms of mobility both across borders and internally:

> A recent phenomenon, for about a year now, has been that a lot of people from Eastern Hungary are moving to Western Hungary because they perceive the border region as a steppingstone to the Austrian labour market. However, most of them are completely unprepared, they leave everything behind and arrive with just a backpack and a map in their hand, they do not collect any information before coming over. Most of them are forced to go back because the labour market in Burgenland is already full. It is no longer possible to find employment there. (EURES Employee, Hungary, June 2012)

Given this example, it becomes clear that commuting involves crucial social and personal costs and may lead to unsuccessful experiences. Besides the local employment situation, social networks and informal knowledge play a central role in defining commuters' labour market outcomes. In these terms, the political and legal vision of intra-European mobility fails to act as a universal remedy and the emerging European labour market is by large structured through social capital.

Overall, the EURES employee in Hungary noticed a rising demand for jobs in Austria; however, there were not enough vacancies in the lower wage labour market segment in the border region of Hungary and Austria. The demand was much higher than actual job prospects:

> There are so many more people who try their luck than actual employments. People are being bounced back. Not everybody will get a job. There are a lot of people who want to work in Austria, but only a few manage to get a job. Nowadays employers can choose from an enormous pool of applicants, so they really can select the best people. I talked to an employer the other day and he said he receives about 400–500 emails for one single job offer. (EURES Employee, Hungary, June 2012)

These observations correspond with the macro-economic situation of Hungary. According to the European Foundation for the Improvement of Living and Working Conditions, the country faced crucial difficulties after the transition from a socialist economy to a market economy in the early 1990s and especially during the financial crisis in 2008. This country has imposed strict austerity measures to meet the expectations of the EU as set out in the Maastricht criteria. Growth incentives have been announced with the aim of ensuring Hungary's compliance with the Europe 2020 objectives (Eurofound 2014). The high demand in labour allows employers to 'be more selective and, in the process, make subsequent worker control, management, and even workplace intensification easier' (Scott 2013, 1093).

In *Slovakia*, a EURES employee not only described the growing interest in finding employment across the borders after the labour market opening in 2011, but also emphasised the increasing extent of job offers and interregional collaboration:

> It is much more work. Previously not so many people were coming here to ask. We also have more vacancies and our co-operation is stronger than it was before. And there are more problems of course because more people are working there and therefore more problems for my side. More and more people are asking me about jobs, accommodation, social security and so on. (EURES Employee, Slovakia, September 2012)

This is also reflected by a study of the European Vacancy Monitor: in 2010 the demand for jobs in Austria increased significantly, especially in wholesale and trade (European Commission 2015). In contrast to Hungary, Slovakia has seen profound economic and social transformation: moving from a centrally planned to a market-driven economy, it became the fastest growing EU economy in the years 2007, 2008 and 2010. This development is comparable to that of the *Czech Republic*: after the declines in export during the economic downturn in 2009, the Czech economy has slowly stabilised (Eurofound 2014).

From an entrepreneurial perspective, the rising demand for work on the interregional job market is largely welcomed. An Austrian businessman, head of a cleaning company in the border region of Lower Austria, Slovakia and Hungary, pointed out that he prefers cross-border commuters over unemployed locals. In his view, mobility due to existential economic reasons is positively connoted as it seemingly manifests in high motivation and work ethic:

> As an Austrian it is not easy to say that, but by now I prefer a Hungarian or a Slovak over an Austrian. That's because they are eager to work. They act from necessity, as back home there are not a lot of opportunities. I call it 'hungry'. They really want to work. […] I notice that the commitment and willingness are higher. You get a more committed and more intelligent worker than in Austria – for the same money. A worker who is able to speak German, who is glad to have a job and who is willing to compromise. (Businessman, Austria, September 2013)

This goes in line with the findings of Waldinger and Lichter (2003, 143) who argued that the employers' approach is to find workers who 'accept the management's wishes with the minimum of bridling' and that 'suitability for subordination will be the crucial, if not determining, consideration'. Summing up, the expert interviews reveal a dynamisation of labour-related movements within CENTROPE, while emphasising a diversification of risks during the last years. Furthermore the interviewees pointed out to the rising demand for jobs, which was partially indicated by the macro-data.

Building up on these insights, the next section discusses the following research question: To what extent has the socio-economic composition of cross-border commuters and the mode of their labour market integration changed after 2009? By reference to our longitudinal data, we discuss the educational levels, industrial sectors, genders and ages of commuters in Austria before and after the economic crisis of 2008/2009.

6. Changing characteristics of commuters: socio-demographic composition and wage mobility before and since the crisis

The present study provides several interesting insights in terms of the social composition of cross-border commuters in CENTROPE before and since the crisis. On average, cross-border commuters after the events of 2008 share the demographic characteristics of workers who proved most vulnerable during the crisis.

(1) Relative youth: 62.1% of the commuters after 2009 are aged between 21 and 35 years compared to 29.8% before 2009. Only 7.7% of the cross-border commuters in CENTROPE are older than 50 after 2009. This is comparable to the study authored by Paci et al. (2010) who pointed out that mobility in a cross-border labour market is a phenomenon marked by younger individuals.
(2) Lower levels of education: The proportion of lower-educated commuters has doubled from 5.4% to 11% after 2009. There has also been a slight increase on the higher end of educational spectrum from 12.9% to 15.3%. The majority of cross-border commuters still have intermediate qualifications.
(3) Women: While before 2009 the ratio of female and male workers was 39.8% to 60.2%, there have been 44.5% female commuters as compared to 55.5% male commuters since then. Recent studies indicate that cross-border commuters are male rather than female (e.g. Drevon and Gerber 2012). However, women who had already been in disadvantaged positions in the labour market prior to the economic crisis are on average disproportionately more affected than men.
(4) Mainly work in service jobs: Work in some areas of the service industries has strongly increased (e.g. trade, gastronomy) after 2009, with labour demand being quite high in these sectors of the Austrian economy. In the health industry, it has decreased but is still much higher than for all other groups of the Austrian labour market. A rather small and declining group found employment in agriculture. The share of cross-border commuters working in manufacturing and construction is decreasing as well over time and is lower than for the other labour groups in Table 3.

Based on the changing socio-economic composition and labour market characteristics of commuters, the following discussion focuses on their careers. To what extent has the wage mobility of cross-border commuters been affected by the events of the financial crisis? In order to discuss this question, Table 4 shows job changes related to upward and downward mobility in CENTROPE before and after 2009. Using the underlying TRANSLAB data, we compare wage mobility patterns among cross-border commuters who work in Austria with the Czech, Hungarian and Slovakian citizens who work on the local labour markets in the respective countries bordering Austria.

Table 4 shows that patterns of upward mobility have clearly changed during the last years. We observe much *more upward mobility* for those who work in Austria and less upward mobility for those who work in the Czech, Hungarian, Slovakian regions bordering Austria *since 2009*. Before the crisis the probability to gain higher wages through job mobility was equally distributed in all subregions of CENTROPE. Interestingly, downward wage mobility can be observed in much lower numbers in the region. However, it has increased for those who got a job in Austria after the crisis. A twofold movement can thus be identified: on the one hand, there is an improvement of opportunities for career advancement for cross-border commuters after the economic crisis and, on the other hand, there is a rise in financial risks of cross-border commuter who started a new job in Austria after 2009.

Using several logistic regression analyses, we finally compare wage upward mobility in the years before and after 2009. Table 5 includes a number of socio-demographic indicators, variables which capture the human capital of cross-border commuters (education/formal training, language command) and their social capital (near and far family

Table 3. Major labour market characteristics of natives, migrants ('foreign-born') and cross-border commuters in Austria before and since the crisis (2012/2013).

	Micro census data Austrian labour market			TRANSLAB data	
	Natives	EU-10	Turkish and ex-Yugoslavs	Cross-border commuters before 2009	Cross-border commuters after 2009
Education					
ISCED 0–2	8.2	5.0	37.6*	5.4*	11.0*
ISCED 3–4	69.9*	66.0*	56.8*	81.6*	73.6*
ISCED 5–6	21.9*	29.0*	5.7*	12.9*	15.3*
Industrial sector					
Agriculture and forestry	5.2*	1.5	0.3*	5.8*	2.2*
Manufacturing and construction	26.2	28.6	40.0*	26.5	22.6
Services	68.6	70.0	59.7*	67.7*	75.2*
Wholesale and retail trade	14.4*	8.9	14.0	7.7*	13.6*
Gastronomy and accommodation	4.4*	11.9	11.4*	15.3*	22.7*
Health service, social work	9.7*	12.6	8.4*	19.3*	15.5*
Other, personal services	40.2*	36.6*	25.9	25.4	23.4
Gender					
Female	44.0	52.0*	40.7	39.8*	44.5*
Male	56.0	48.0*	59.3	60.2*	55.5*
Age					
21–35 years	32.8*	36.3*	34.5*	29.8*	62.1*
36–50 years	44.8*	42.0	49.3*	47.4*	30.2*
51–65 years	22.4*	21.7*	16.2	22.8*	7.7*
***N* (unweighted)**	13,225	280	1053	535	811

Source: Micro Census 2012, Labour Force Survey 2012; TRANSLAB survey 2012/2013; own calculations; data includes workers between 21 and 65 years of age with a main job (minimum 20 hours/week) in Austria; before/since the crisis: job entries until 12/2008 vs. after 01/2009; *statistical differences* of means to the group of cross-border commuters were tested by using Games-Howell *post hoc* tests, taking into account the inhomogeneity of variance and unequal group sizes (*$p < 0.05$).

ties, friendship with Austrians), the relevance of social networks for the job search in Austria, as well as variables covering the labour market sector in which cross-border commuters have found employment.

Empirically, this analysis indicates that some of the 'micro-patterns' of cross-border commuting have changed over the last years whilst others have remained stable:

Table 4. Wage mobility in CENTROPE before and since the crisis.

		Job in Czech Republic, Hungary and Slovakia	Job in Austria	*N*
Wage upward mobility				
Mobility before 2009***	No	71.1	28.9	775
	Yes	51.9	48.1	646
Mobility since 2009***	No	44.9	55.1	713
	Yes	24.2	75.8	553
Total***	No	58.5	41.5	1488
	Yes	39.1	60.9	1199
Wage downward mobility				
Mobility before 2009**	No	61.9	38.1	1387
	Yes	82.4	17.6	34
Mobility since 2009***	No	34.4	65.6	1198
	Yes	61.8	38.2	68
Total***	No	49.1	50.9	2585
	Yes	68.6	31.4	102

Source: TRANSLAB survey 2012/2013; own calculations; data include workers between 21 and 65 years of age with a main job (minimum 20 hours/week) in Austria; before/since the crisis: job entries until 12/2008 vs. after 01/2009; $^{+}p < .1$ $^{*}p < .05$, $^{**}p < .01$, $^{***}p < .001$.

Table 5. Logistic regression for cross-border commuters' wage mobility before and since the crisis (Exp (*B*)).

	Wage upward mobility before 2009	Wage upward mobility since 2009
Women	1.450	1.043
Age	1.040***	1.015^{+}
Without formal training	0.267*	0.166***
University degree	1.225	0.938
Near family ties	0.595***	1.074
Far family ties	1.192	1.064
Friendships with Austrians	1.696*	1.736**
Job search via social network	1.194	1.416^{+}
Gastronomy, hotel management	1.196	0.463**
Health industry and social work	1.063	0.790
Other, personal services	0.772	0.479*

Source: TRANSLAB survey 2012/2013; own calculations; data include workers between 21 and 65 years of age with a main job (minimum 20 hours/week) in Austria; regressions control for the following variables: nationality, region/locality of the job, form of commuting (daily vs. weekly commuting), German language command, previous working experience in Austria, various other branches, size of firm, wage based on collective bargaining, working time in Austria, marriage/familial status; before/since the crisis: job entries until 12/2008 vs. after 01/2009; $^{+}p < .1$ $^{*}p < .05$, $^{**}p < .01$, $^{***}p < .001$; regressions parameters: odds ratios ((Exp(*B*)), a positive effect of the odds ratios is expressed as $e^{\beta} > 1$ and a negative effect as $e^{\beta} < 1$.

(1) Even if the number of female cross-border commuters is on the increase (see Table 3), no significant differences are observed between women and men regarding upward mobility chances.
(2) The effects of age have remained stable over time and indicate that increasing age correlates positively with upward mobility chances.
(3) Cross-border commuters without formal education have much lower and diminishing chances to realise wage upward mobility with a new job on the Austrian labour market (reference group: workers with intermediate qualifications). Interestingly, the regression analyses show no differences in this respect between the workers with intermediate qualifications and university degrees.
(4) Social capital and the use of social networks for job search are partially important to explain the 'micro-patterns' of cross-border commuting in CENTROPE. Although no direct effect of near family and far family ties can be seen on wage upward mobility, the analyses show that friendships with Austrians clearly improve upward mobility chances. Moreover, the use of social network contacts for job searches on the Austrian labour market is also becoming more relevant. The effect on mobility has been significantly positive after the crisis, which was not the case before the year 2009.
(5) Empirically we can also show that since the beginning of 2009, the chance to improve wages through cross-border commuting in such service branches as gastronomy and personal service has decreased. These are branches in which employment for cross-border commuters has increased over the past years (see Table 3) – accompanied, quite interestingly, by diminishing upward mobility chances.

7. Conclusion

The accession of the Central and Eastern European countries to the EU in May 2004 marked a crucial step in the history of European integration. An important consequence was the free movement of capital, goods, services and people to and from Central Europe. CENTROPE is one of many political projects in the EU aimed to foster enhanced mobility in order to strengthen competitiveness among the regional economies. Since its foundation, one of the distinguishing features of the project of European integration has been the overcoming of internal borders. This objective has had remarkable outcomes in the history of cross-border co-operation, resulting in the creation of institutionalised co-operative structures known as Euroregions which receive financial support from the EU. However, given the fear of a massive influx of workers from the new member states with anticipated negative effects on the receiving countries' labour markets, Austria introduced transitional measures to restrict, to varying degrees, the right to work for EU8 citizens for a period of up to seven years (Galgóczi, Leschke, and Watt 2012, 5). The economic crisis has taken place at the time the Austrian labour market opened to workers from neighbouring Eastern European countries. Hence, there are several institutional factors that foster mobility in this region, making it a challenge to picture the effects of the crisis on cross-border labour commuting.

The aim of this paper was to outline changes that have occurred in the aftermath of the crisis in 2008/2009 in terms of (1) economic and social inequalities between the regions of CENTROPE, (2) labour mobility to Austria, (3) the socio-economic composition of cross-border commuters and finally (4) their wage mobility. In order to approximate this social reality, we built upon a mixed-method data base. The macro-data revealed that the financial crisis did not evoke a sharp decline in household income, GDP, unemployment and poverty rate differences in this region while, at the same time, the structural East–West gap in CENTROPE remains to exist. Moreover, there has been an increase in cross-border commuting after 2008 and various events have led to dynamised labour-related mobility in CENTROPE over the past years. Experts currently observe an even higher demand for employment in Austria that cannot be met by the local labour market. 'Pure' economic reasons are considered to be the most relevant drivers of workforce mobility in the post-crisis period. The opening of the borders has acted as a legal window to attempt to escape existential economic problems. All of these factors enable employers in core economies to select commuters from peripheral economies with higher levels of human capital than the locals because of the 'development gap' (Blanchflower, Saleheen, and Shadforth 2007). However, many mobile workers will accept initial downward mobility when moving to core economies, as they expect long-term class advancements (Scott 2013).

On average, most commuters share the demographic characteristics of the workers who have shown to be most vulnerable during the crisis: relative youth, lower and intermediate levels of education, employment in certain branches of the service industry. This was illustrated with descriptive and multivariate statistical analyses. The results suggest that commuter flows appear to be closely linked to the economic, political and social developments prevailing in the regions of origin, economic conditions in the receiving regions as well as the European legal framework, namely access to the full labour market. Overall cross-border commuting can be perceived as a prototypic example of versatile post-modern life concepts, as both multi-local and mobile (Wille 2012). The crisis can be seen as a crucial driver for cross-border mobility by addressing unemployment in the sending region. This is coherent with the policy objects to achieve mobility. At the same time, however, economic and financial crises often lead to a rise in protectionist attitudes.

How do local populations perceive new streams of commuters following the financial crisis? This could and should be the focus of further research in this field.

Notes

1. The establishment and institutionalisation of Euroregions are a core element of the EU Interreg Programme. This initiative aims to stimulate economic and political co-operation between regions in the EU. It is financed under the European Regional Development Fund. The theoretical foundation for these programmes is derived from economists like Mundell (1961), as well as other scholars, who made a substantial claim for the benefits of interregional integration and co-operation as early as in the 1950s and 1960s.
2. Research on cross-border commuting is a relatively new domain within migration studies. This is especially the case for European cross-border commuting (Verwiebe et al. 2015, 1). The EU defines cross-border commuters as people who work in one state while residing in another to which they usually return on a daily basis or at least once a week (Pierini 1997). We also use this definition in the present paper, yet expand this conceptualisation to encompass all types of regular weekly, monthly or seasonal commuting, as is common in current research on cross-border commuters (Houtum and Gielis 2006; Nerb et al. 2009). More than other ideal types of migration – including permanent, temporary or short-term migration – commuting is characterised by regular back and forth movements between regions of destination and origin (White and Ryan 2008, 1472). From the perspective of migration theory, *periodic occupational commuting across borders* can be conceived as a *variant of transnational migration* that results neither in definitely leaving one's region of origin, nor in definitely integrating in a host society, but rather in a precisely *intermediate process* (Fassmann 2003, 438).
3. Of particular note are the freedom of movement for employees and the mutual recognition of educational qualifications, which have been core elements of the European integration process. A decisive breakthrough for intra-European migration came with the Maastricht Treaty. It grants EU citizens freedom of movement and settlement and establishes the legal conditions for the unhindered mobility of EU citizens and the emergence of a transnational European labour market. Under the Maastricht Treaty, EU citizenship grants its holders a status fundamentally different from that of non-EU citizens. On the basis of the Maastricht Treaty, the status of EU citizen includes wide-reaching entitlements to equal treatment in their countries of residence. In addition to establishing the legal conditions for barrier-free migration, the EU has also introduced measures to boost mobility, including exchange programmes such as Erasmus or Socrates, while creating special institutions such as the European Employment Services (EURES) to promote employee mobility (Verwiebe et al. 2010, 276).
4. This difference applies predominantly to the use of national income distributions in defining poverty risks. For example, a clearly lower poverty risk threshold is drawn upon in the Czech Republic, with €4675 for an average household income in 2011 as compared to €13,084 in Austria.

Disclosure statement

No potential conflict of interest was reported by the authors.

References

Bahna, M. 2014. “Slovak Care Workers in Austria: How Important Is the Context of the Sending Country?” *Journal of Contemporary European Studies* 22 (4): 411–426.

Benton, M., and M. Petrovic. 2013. *How Free is Free Movement? Dynamics and Drivers of Mobility within the European Union.* Brussels: Migration Policy Institute Europe.

Blanchflower, D. G., J. Saleheen, and C. Shadforth. 2007. *The Impact of the Recent Migration from Eastern Europe on the UK Economy*. London: Bank of England.

Centrope Agency. 2012. "Centrope Strategy 2013+ Action Plan." Accessed July 7, 2014. http://www.centrope.com/repository/centrope/downloads/centrope_Strategy_Action_Plan_2013_en.pdf.

Constant, A., and D. S. Massey. 2002. "Return Migration by German Guestworkers: Neoclassical versus New Economic Theories." *International Migration* 40 (4): 5–38.

Constant, A. F., O. Nottmeyer, and K. F. Zimmermann. 2012. "The Economics of Circular Migration." IZA Discussion Paper No. 6940.

Drevon, G., and P. Gerber. 2012. "Soziodemographische Profile, die starken Veränderungen unterworfen sind." In *Die Mobilität der in Luxemburg Beschäftigten Grenzgänger*, edited by F. Schmitz, G. Drevon, and P. Gerber, 8–11. Luxembourg: CEPS/INSTEAD.

Eurofound. 2014. "Hungary." Accessed November 11, 2014. http://www.eurofound.europa.eu/countries/Hungary.

European Commission. 2015. "Employment, Social Affairs & Inclusion: Significant Rise in Labour Demand." Accessed February 2, 2015. http://ec.europa.eu/social/main.jsp?langId = en&catId = 89&newsId = 998&furtherNews = yes.

Eurostat. 2015. "Regional Statistics." Accessed February 2, 2015. http://ec.europa.eu/eurostat/data/database.

Fassmann, H. 2003. "Transnationale Mobilität. Konzeption und Fallbeispiel." *SWS-Rundschau* 43 (4): 429–449.

Favell, A. 2008. *Eurostars and Eurocities: Free Movement and Mobility in an Integrating Europe*. Oxford: Blackwell.

Findlay, A., R. King, A. Stam, and E. Ruiz-Gelices. 2006. "Ever Reluctant Europeans. The Changing Geographies of UK Students Studying and Working Abroad." *European Urban and Regional Studies* 13 (4): 291–318.

Galgóczi, B., J. Leschke, and A. Watt. 2012. *EU Labour Migration in Troubled Times. Skills Mismatch, Return and Policy Responses*. Aldershot: Ashgate.

Harris, J. R., and M. P. Todaro. 1970. "Migration, Unemployment and Development: A Two-sector Analysis." *American Economic Review* 60: 126–142.

Horvath, K. 2012. "National Numbers for Transnational Relations? Challenges of Integrating Quantitative Methods into Research on Transnational Labour Market Relations." *Ethnic and Racial Studies* 35 (10): 1741–1757.

Houtum, V. H., and R. Gielis. 2006. "Elastic Migration: The Case of Dutch Short-distance Transmigrants to the Borderlands of Belgium and Germany." *Tijdschrift voor Economische en Sociale Geografie* 97 (2): 191–198.

Kalter, F. 2011. "Social Capital and the Dynamics of Temporary Labour Migration from Poland to Germany." *European Sociological Review* 27 (5): 555–569.

King, R., and E. Ruiz-Gelices. 2003. "International Student Migration and the European Year Abroad." *International Journal of Population Geography* 9 (3): 229–252.

Klatt, M., and H. Herrmann. 2011. "Half Empty or Half Full? Over 30 Years of Regional Cross-Border Cooperation Within the EU: Experiences at the Dutch-German and Danish-German Border." *Journal of Borderlands Studies* 26 (1): 65–87.

Massey, D. S. 1987. "Understanding Mexican Migration to the United States." *American Journal of Sociology* 92 (6): 1372–1403.

Mau, S., and S. Büttner. 2010. "Transnationality." In *Handbook of European Societies. Social Transformations in the 21st Century*, edited by S. Immerfall and G. Therborn, 537–569. Dodrecht: Springer.

Mundell, R. A. 1961. "A Theory of Optimum Currency Areas." *The American Economic Review* 51 (4): 657–665.

Nerb, G., F. Hitzelsberger, A. Woidich, S. Pommer, S. Hemmer, and P. Heczko. 2009. *Scientific Report on the Mobility of Cross-Border Workers within the EU-27/EEA/EFTA Countries – Final Report*. Brussels: European Commission, DG Employment and Social Affairs.

Paci, P., E. R. Tiongson, M. Walewski, and J. Liwinski. 2010. "Internal Labour Mobility in Central Europe and the Baltic Region: Evidence from Labour Force Surveys." In The Labour Market

Impact of the EU Enlargement: A New Regional Geography of Europe?" edited by M. Walewski, F. E. Caroleo and F. Pastore, 197–225. Berlin/Heidelberg: Springer.

Perkmann, M. 1999. "Building Governance Institutions Across European Borders." *Regional Studies* 33 (7): 657–667.

Perkmann, M. 2002. "Euroregions: Institutional Entrepreneurship in the European Union." In *Globalization, Regionalization and Cross-Border Regions*, edited by M. Perkmann and N.-L. Sum, 103–124. Basingstoke: Palgrave Macmillan.

Perkmann, M. 2003. "Cross-Border Regions in Europe. Significance and Drivers of Regional Cross-Border Cooperation." *European Urban & Regional Studies* 10 (2): 153–171.

Pierini, F. 1997. *Frontier Workers in the European Union*. Edited by Pernille Winther. Luxembourg: European Parliament, Directorate-General for Research.

Piore, M. J. 1979. *Birds of Passage: Migrant Labor Industrial Societies*. New York: Cambridge University Press.

Portes, A. 1997. "Immigration Theory for a New Century: Some Problems and Opportunities." *International Migration Review* 31 (4): 799–825.

Scott, S. 2006. "The Social Morphology of Skilled Migration: The Case of the British Middle Class in Paris." *Journal of Ethnic and Migration Studies* 32 (7): 1105–1129.

Scott, S. 2013. "Labour, Migration and the Spatial Fix: Evidence from the UK Food Industry." *Antipode* 45 (5): 1090–1109.

Statistik Austria. 2015a. "Armut und soziale Eingliederung." Accessed December 2, 2015. http://www.statistik.at/web_de/statistiken/soziales/armut_und_soziale_eingliederung/index.html.

Statistik Austria. 2015b. "Migration." Accessed January 2, 2015. http://www.statistik.at/web_en/statistics/population/migration/index.html.

Terlouw, K. 2012. "Border Surfers and Euroregions: Unplanned Cross-Border Behaviour and Planned Territorial Structures of Cross-Border Governance." *Planning Practice & Research* 27 (3): 351–366.

Triandafyllidou, A. 2013. "Circular Migration: Introductory Remarks." In *Circular Migration Between Europe & Its Neighbourhood. Choice or Necessity?* edited by A. Triandafyllidou, 1–22. Oxford: Oxford University Press.

Venturini, A. 2008. *Circular Migration as an Employment Strategy for Mediterranean Countries*. CARIM Analytic and Synthetic Notes: CARIM-AS 2008/39.

Verwiebe, R. 2008. "Migration to Germany. Is a Middle Class Emerging among Intra-European Migrants?" *Migration Letters* 6 (1): 1–19.

Verwiebe, R., S. Mau, N. Seidel, and T. Kathmann. 2010. "Skilled German Migrants and Their Motives for Migration Within Europe." *International Migration and Integration* 11 (3): 273–293.

Verwiebe, R., C. Reinprecht, R. Haindorfer, and L. Wiesböck. 2015. "How to Succeed in a Transnational Labor Market. Job Search and Wages among Hungarian, Slovak and Czech Commuters in Austria." *International Migration Review* 49 (3): 1–36. doi:10.1111/imre.12193.

Waldinger, R., and M. I. Lichter. 2003. *How the Other Half Works. Immigration and the Social Organization of Labor*. Berkeley: University of California Press.

Wallace, C., and K. Vincent. 2007. "Recent Migration from the New European Borderlands." *Review of Sociology of the Hungarian Sociological Association*, 13 (2): 19–37.

Wallerstein, I. 1974. *The Modern World-System I: Capitalist Agriculture and the Origins of the European World-Economy in the Sixteenth Century*. Berkeley: University of California Press.

White, A., and L. Ryan. 2008. "Polish 'Temporary' Migration: The Formation and Significance of Social Networks." *Europe-Asia Studies* 60 (9): 1467–1502.

Wiesböck, L., C. Reinprecht, R. Haindorfer, and R. Verwiebe. 2015. "Cross-Border Commuting and Transformational Dynamics in the Central European Region. What is the Link?" In *An Anthology of Migration and Social Transformation: European Perspectives*, edited by A. Amelina, K. Horvath, and B. Meeus, 187–200. Amsterdam: Amsterdam University Press.

Wille, C. 2012. *Grenzgänger und Räume der Grenze: Raumkonstruktionen in der Großregion SaarLorLux*. Frankfurt/Main: Peter Lang.

Index

Note: **Bold face** page numbers refer to tables & italic page numbers refer to figures. Page numbers followed by "n" refer to endnotes.

INDEX

For Product Safety Concerns and Information please contact our EU representative GPSR@taylorandfrancis.com
Taylor & Francis Verlag GmbH, Kaufingerstraße 24, 80331 München, Germany

www.ingramcontent.com/pod-product-compliance
Ingram Content Group UK Ltd.
Pitfield, Milton Keynes, MK11 3LW, UK
UKHW050753180926
475701UK00007B/1031
* 9 7 8 0 3 6 7 3 2 1 9 2 5 *